Tracy Beach

THE NIGHT OF A THOUSAND HEROES

TRACY BEACH

outskirts
press

The Flood

Dark Clouds hung low among the Lo Fly Range

When broke the storm, Hell's fury seemed unleashed

To wreck and ruin all along the Universe

The lightning played among the giant peaks and crashing thunder smote the mountainside

The awful din of elements at war was echoed from the Canyon depths below

Cloud burst asunder and a deluge came

Twas thus that nature in her maddest mood

Set down the raging waters of the flood

To scourge the fertile valley of the plain

As fair Pueblo man had builded there was crushed and maimed, now prostrate bleeding lies

But not for long, the Spirit that has made this Wonder City of the West
survives and men will build with bigger, broader plans

To meet the wrath of nature unafraid

Walt Drummond

1921

Table of Contents

CHAPTER ONE

A strip of beaded leather and the prophecy

"Goodmorning sir, how may I help you today?" the Concierge asked, as the well-dressed man approached the front desk of the Congress Hotel.

"I'm here to apply for a job." He replied, as a friendly smile quickly spread across his face. "Would you happen to have any openings?"

"No, I'm sorry sir, we don't have anything available as of now, but it is only the end of May and we could easily have a position open up at any time. If you leave me your information, I would be happy to call you when something comes available."

As he handed over a notepad and pencil, the Concierge noticed the man's long, dark hair which casually fell across the side of his jacket. Tied with a wide, decorated piece of leather, his hairstyle easily announced his heritage.

"Excuse me sir, but are you a member of the local Ute Tribe?"

"Oh no sir, I'm Cherokee." The man replied with a smile as he finished writing down his name and contact information. "A medicine man, to be precise. I have also been gifted with the powers of prophecy, which is why I'm hoping to gain employment before August 3rd."

Taken back, the Concierge gave the man a curious look. Being raised around members of the local native tribes, he knew better than to question the man, but he still felt doubt beginning to creep in.

"And what, may I ask, will happen before August 3rd?"

"A big flood is coming soon." The man replied as he turned to look at the Concierge with his piercing dark eyes. "It will be followed by a second big flood." He added, as he dramatically held up his arms. "Lots of water! Ten feet more than the first!"

Now in any other city, this type of talk would be seen as lunacy, but any mention of a flood possibly coming to Pueblo, Colorado always gained a front-row seat.

The area that would one day be known as Pueblo recorded its first flood back in 1855, followed by eight more by 1889. The city itself, which was incorporated in 1870, had tried numerous times to strengthen the banks of the nearby Arkansas River by building levees out of dirt and rocks, but it always turned out to just be a waste of time and money.

On July 26, 1893 the city faced its tenth flood, as the Arkansas River rose to a depth of eight feet and tore apart Pueblo's levees in a blink of an eye. When the waters finally receded, the city chose to rebuild the levees by stacking large boulders along the river banks, which were then covered with sand, rocks and a large amount of confidence that this new creation would finally hold.

Unfortunately, on May 31, 1894, the city's eleventh flood barreled down the Arkansas River and not only tore apart the levees, but flooded the entire city with over three feet of water. As the residents of Pueblo watched the water quickly recede, and mourned the 5 people who lost their lives, the construction crews once again rebuilt the levees.

As large boulders, rocks and gravel were once again piled along the river banks, the city's Engineers smiled at their newest creation and declared the levee's not only impenetrable, but proclaimed that the low lying areas next to the Arkansas River were now safe to inhabit.

Located along either side of the Union Train Depot and encircled by the numerous tracks that projected from it, the shanty communities of Pepper Sauce Bottoms and The Grove quickly sprang to life. As clapboard homes, churches and businesses were constructed in the shadow of the newly constructed levees, the city's Engineers felt confident that they had finally conquered the river.

They were wrong.

CHAPTER TWO

A torrent of water and the bags of wet cement

On the morning of June 2nd, 1921 a dark, ominous cloud began to form over Pueblo, Colorado which eventually consumed the sky. As the approaching storm began to fill the air with the occasional rumble of thunder, a cool wind announced the arrival of rain, which prompted 32-year-old Mayme K. Gray to call her five older children back inside as she began closing the windows to her family's farmhouse.

Located on the west side of the city, the Gray's farm sat along the border of a wide river bed called Dry Creek, named for the lack of moisture it normally contained. During the spring snowmelt that poured down from the mountains near Colorado's towering Pikes Peak, as well as the rain from the summer storms, water would gently flow down the creek which always thrilled the children who loved to play in its cool currents.

Unfortunately, this year's summer storms had been pouring down with a vengeance, causing the creeks dirt embankments to crumble and erode, which brought the edge of Dry Creek closer and closer to the family's farm with each drop of rain. With her children now safely inside the house and one year old Margery playfully bouncing on her hip, Mrs. Gray nervously watched out the window as the water surrounding her home began to puddle, due to the ground being so saturated that it was unable to absorb any more moisture.

As the storm increased and added hail to the mix, 35-year-old Robert Sylvester Gray and his 52-year-old lodger John F. Ferren began moving the larger animals up to higher ground, while 11-year-old Elizabeth Edna and nine-year-old Robert Jr. ran out into the storm to grab the chickens, which they brought into the house.

With the violent storm continuing throughout the day and into the evening, the clock soon chimed the arrival of 7:30 pm, which also marked the final moments of Dry Creek's foothold on its natural channel. As the turbulent water continued to rise and swell, it began to snap apart fencing, sheds, and outbuildings that sat near the edge of the normally quiet creek, while also grabbing hold of any unfortunate animal that stood just a little too close to its torrent.

As the rain and violent swell of Dry Creek continued to chip away at the dirt, rocks, and clay that lined its shores, it began to collapse inward at an alarming rate. Falling into the raging water and adding to the creeks collection of debris, the eroding banks began to lose its grip on more than just the occasional unlucky tree or bush.

It was also losing its hold on the 24th street bridge.

Located a little over a mile upstream from Gray's family farm, the steel train bridge was beginning to heave and sway as it desperately tried to remain on its intended perch. Pummeled by the combined force of rolling rocks, uprooted trees, raging waters, and a disintegrating shoreline, the flood soon proved too much for the almost 250,000-pound bridge, which eventually slid into the waters of Dry Creek around 11 pm.

Satisfied with its destruction, the rain subsided soon after midnight.

Early the next morning, Robert and Mayme Gray awoke to a light rain, as well as the sound of something very heavy pounding against the outside of their home. Pulling back the covers Robert jumped out of bed to investigate, but quickly found himself standing in cold, ankle-deep water, which resulted in him using some very colorful words, as he voiced his instant displeasure.

Startled by her husband's reaction, Mayme glanced over the side of the bed and watched as the water lightly splashed up against the wooden feet of their bedroom furniture, soaking the edges of the blankets in the process. Reluctant to place her own feet into the water, Mayme looked over at her husband Robert and instead listened to him describe what he saw from their bedroom window and it was quite apocalyptic.

The raging waters that dominated Dry Creek had left the Gray's farmhouse surrounded in over three feet of water, which was already beginning to leak into their home. As Robert stared out at the sea of water that had enveloped his farm, he heard the banging sound again and discovered that it was caused by a large tree limb that was floating around their home.

But why were they surrounded by so much water?

When Dry Creek first began to surge, the torrent of water grabbed hold of every piece of debris, tree, or animal that it could find and unknown to Robert and Mayme Gray, the creek then used this collection to build a dam just below the family's farm. With the water now unable to follow its natural course, which would have allowed it to empty into the nearby Arkansas River, it had no choice but to spread out and envelop the Gray's farm.

As Mayme got out of bed and went to wake up her children, Robert woke their farmhand, and together they tried to figure out how to stop more water from entering the house. With everyone busy with their individual tasks, a violent crack of lightning suddenly shot through the sky, announcing the arrival of a catastrophic cloud burst.

Within mere minutes, the heavens opened up and the creek once again began to rage, but the dam below the family's home held firm, which caused the water around the farmhouse to rise at an accelerated rate. As the water rose past the windows, the pressure against the house finally proved too much and the walls began to heave and crack.

Finally creating a weak spot, the quickly flowing torrent began tearing apart their home, just as Mayme finished placing three of her children on top of the kitchen table. As the family's lodger tried his best to hold the table against the wall, which now held nine-year-old Robert Jr., six-year-old Helen, and five-year-old Mildred, Mayme held her one-year-old daughter tightly against her body and prayed. Looking back over at her husband, she watched as Robert struggled to bring three-year-old Marjorie Dale over to the table, while 11-year-old Elizabeth Edna walked closely behind him.

Despite his best intentions, the swiftly flowing water quickly swept little Marjorie off her feet, causing Robert to lose his grip on the already water-logged child. Reaching back for his young daughter,

Robert watched in horror as his oldest daughter Elizabeth reached for her little sister, which resulted in both girls losing their balance and slamming violently into a nearby wall.

Screaming for them to hold onto something, Robert quickly began to wade through the now waist-deep water but was unable to reach them before the current forced his daughters through their homes ruptured kitchen wall and into the raging creek. As his wife screamed for her children, Robert jumped in after them, but was instantly pushed away from his daughters, sending him through a newly made rupture in the dam instead, which eventually deposited him on the shore of the Arkansas River.

But his children were nowhere to be found.

Pulling himself up out of the mud and coughing up water, Robert began calling out for Marjorie and Elizabeth, which quickly attracted bystanders who eagerly offered to help him search for his children. Walking the shoreline Robert soon discovered his daughter's battered bodies, and it was his screams that announced that his children had perished.

"Elizabeth would have been 12!" Robert wailed, as he held the mud-covered bodies of his two daughters tightly against his body. "Her birthday is tomorrow! It's tomorrow!"

As the mud was wiped off the children and their cold bodies loaded into the back of a farm truck, the rumor that two young children had drowned in Dry Creek quickly began to spread around Pueblo, but it only slightly dampened the cities last day of school festivities.

One boy who wasn't going to miss out on any of the end of the year fun was 14 years old Bernard Kelly, who was enjoying his last day of 8th grade. Both he and his classmates found the continuous rain exciting and more of an adventure than a threat, and besides, none of them had ever even heard of Elizabeth or Marjorie Gray.

When the final school bell rang, announcing the beginning of summer break, Bernard eagerly walked out of school with his friends, but as they ran through the rain and began talking about what they wanted to do over the summer, Bernard Kelly found that he had something else on his mind.

He really wanted a new suit.

When school started back up in the fall, Bernard didn't want to begin his freshman year at Central High School wearing his old suit, which consisted of short pants and a jacket, he instead wanted to walk into his new school with long pants like the upperclassmen wore. He had already talked to his parents about it, but they felt that his short pants, which still fit him, would be just fine when school started back up.

As the boys walked away from Saint Patrick's Catholic School and headed down South Union Avenue, they noticed that the street was flooded with about three inches of water. As a vehicle quickly drove past, its wheels forced waves of water high up onto the sidewalks, soaking the boy's shoes, but Bernard and his friends didn't really give the rain much thought, that was until they arrived at the South Union Avenue Bridge that crossed over the train tracks.

Peering over the side, Bernard noticed that the rainstorm was causing a large amount of water to pool along the sides of the tracks and as he watched the switchmen struggle to walk in the thick mud it had created, he wondered how much rain would it take for the tracks to completely disappear underneath the rising water.

If they did, what would happen to the trains?

Up in the bustling city of Denver, Colorado, 114 miles north of Pueblo, the Denver & Rio Grande Train No. 3 had just finished loading up its passengers with plans to arrive at Pueblo's Union Depot at precisely at 7:50 pm. Pulling out of Denver's Union Station at 3:55 pm, the train was right on time with 132 people on board, 109 of which were passengers.

A slight drizzle was noticed by everyone on board, but it didn't cause any concern until almost two hours later when the crew received a request for a weather report from 41-year-old Pueblo Dispatcher Brutus Milton Stearns. The dispatcher was interested in the weather conditions between Palmer Lake and Colorado Springs, which was 67 miles north of Pueblo's Union Depot, as he was hoping the current storm in Pueblo might be letting up soon.

The reply sent back to Pueblo was that the drizzle they had experienced when the train had first pulled out of Denver had gradually turned into a moderately, heavy rain once they arrived at Palmer Lake, but they hadn't noticed any standing water as of yet.

Unfortunately, that changed less than an hour later when the train arrived at the tiny resort town of Kelker, only 40 miles north of Pueblo's Union Depot. The moderately, heavy rainstorm the train had encountered up at Palmer Lake, was nothing compared to the fierce thunderstorm they were traveling through now.

This was definitely not the news the dispatcher in Pueblo wanted to hear.

Despite the storm pounding against the sides of the Denver & Rio Grande No. 3, as it continued towards Pueblo, the staff kept a smile on their faces and focused on keeping their passengers calm.

One passenger was 42-year-old James Hezekiah Clagett, a traveling salesman and Coal inspector for the Syracuse, New York Division of the Solvay Coke and Gas Company. One of his jobs was to inform his potential customers that the Solvay system of heating coal, in their specially designed coke ovens, was more efficient than other methods. The ovens unique design resulted in more coal gas being produced, which would then give the manufacturers more gas to sell to customers for cooking and heating their homes.

But right now he didn't want to talk about Coal.

While sitting in the dining car, enjoying his meal, James instead chose to enlighten his fellow train passengers with stories about how he was a natural born Jinx, due to surviving a few disasters in his lifetime, natural and man-made. While traveling the country on business, he had witnessed a cyclone touch down in Galesburg, Illinois, watched two automobiles collide in New York City, killing both drivers, and in Burlington, Louisiana he had watched the C.B. & Q ice house get struck by lightning and burn to the ground.

Because of this, James explained, he always kept his eyes peeled for any possible scenario that could result in a disaster and then would maintain his distance while warning any passerby's to do the same.

Sitting farther down the train car, enjoying their coffee, were brothers Daniel Creedon, aged 24 and Charles Creedon, aged 22, who had just finished a heartfelt visit to Buena Vista, Colorado, a small mountain town about three hours west of Denver. Their mother Ester, known as Etta, had died when the boys were only two and four years old and after returning home from the War, the brothers decided to visit her grave and pay their respects.

Before their mother's death, the Creedon boy's had lived with their parents in the small mining town of Minturn, Colorado, which was 63 miles north of Buena Vista, but when their mother unexpectedly died, their father decided to have her buried in Buena Vista, as the town was more established. Overcome with grief, the boy's father Michael then gathered up his two young sons and moved to Bingham, Utah, where he soon remarried and started a second family.

Now as adults, the two brothers had returned to Colorado to visit Buena Vista's Mount Olivet Cemetery and had chosen their parent's wedding anniversary date of May 28th to place flowers upon their mother's grave. After spending time with family in Colorado, and listening to their relatives tell them stories about the mother they barely knew, the brothers were now heading back home to Utah.

Not surprisingly, the Creedon brothers were not the only passengers on board who had been involved in the War. Frederick Dallas Cuenin, who was 24, and his wife Lydia, who was 27, were traveling from Boulder, Colorado to visit his parents in the railway town of Salida, which was only 25 miles south of Buena Vista. Their first child was to be born in just a couple of months, as Lydia was already 7 ½ months along, and Frederick wanted to give his wife a small vacation before being tied down with the baby.

Frederick, who went by his middle name of Dallas, had enlisted in a military program called S.A.T.C, also known as The Student Army Training Corps, instead of being drafted straight into military service. The United States War Department had begun this program back in April 1918, in 157 Universities and Colleges around the nation, after fear that these institutions would go bankrupt due to so many college-age young men being sent off to war. To ease the tension, S.A.T.C was implemented, which placed military units on the campuses.

This program allowed young men the ability to not only train to become a soldier, but to attend college as well. Dallas Cuenin enlisted into the new program in August 1918, which sent him to the University of Nebraska, instead of the battlefront. When the War was over, Dallas left Nebraska and headed to Boulder, Colorado to continue his degree in electrical engineering, which is where he met his wife.

And right now, she was his main priority.

With his wife resting comfortably in their sleeper compartment, the couple found themselves serenaded by the driving rain that was beating against the sides of the train car, as the Denver & Rio Grande Train No. 3 continued to barrel down the tracks towards Pueblo's Union Station. Unfortunately for both the passengers and the crew, the dispatcher at Pueblo's Union Depot was hiding a terrible secret from the No. 3, which risked the lives of everyone on board.

The storm was beginning to wash out the tracks.

Less than 20 miles west of Pueblo's Union Depot sat the tiny farming town of Swallows, named after the little bird's that nested in the area. The town consisted of a Grocery store, a School, a Post Office, and a Depot, of which a train had just left at 4:30 pm heading east towards Pueblo.

Unfortunately, this train had been forced to stop six miles short of Pueblo's Union Depot due to what the conductor saw out of the engine's front windows. As the train sat motionless on the tracks, the crew silently watched as a continual stream of dirty brown water, mud, and broken tree branches poured down from a nearby hill and regurgitated itself onto the tracks in front of them.

Donning his rain gear, the conductor exited the train to inspect the tracks, but when he returned he informed his crew that not only did the tracks look unsafe but that he felt they should send the train back to the Swallows Depot to wait out the storm. Then, in an odd twist, the conductor asked for a volunteer to come with him, as he planned on taking the handcart and follow the track's the rest of the way to Pueblo's Union Depot to check their safety.

Confused, the engineer began questioning why the conductor felt that a small two-person hand cart could make it to Pueblo, but not a train, but he was stopped mid-sentence. "I would rather the cart slide into the river, than a train full of people", the conductor replied as he slid on a pair of gloves and straightened his hat. "Now I need you to send a message to both Swallows and Pueblo so they know what's going on and I'll contact you when I get to Union Depot."

As the engineer prepared to throw the train into reverse and head back to Swallows, he watched out the front windows as the conductor and his volunteer crewman set the handcart on the mud covered tracks and headed towards Pueblo.

But Pueblo and Swallows were not the only towns affected by the storm.

A little over 16 miles west of Swallows, sat the town of Florence. Known for its oil fields, coal mines, and apple orchards, the town sat close to the base of Mount Pisgah, which towered 10,400 feet above sea level. The mountain, nestled within other towering peaks, contained both an angry creek called Eight-Mile and a winding mountain road called Phantom Canyon that ran right alongside.

This sinister sounding road, which lead its drivers up to the Gold camps of Victor and Cripple Creek, was originally built for ore wagons and stagecoaches when it was called The Florence free road. Opened for travel on March 22, 1890, the popularity of the roads tight curves and hand cut tunnels caught the attention of Colorado millionaire David H. Moffat, who bought the road in 1893 for his newest railroad.

With tracks quickly laid, the Florence and Cripple Creek Railroad held its maiden voyage on May 11, 1894, but the engineers would soon learn that the train would not be the only thing occupying the tracks.

One night, as the train made a night run up to Cripple Creek, the crew spotted a man walking alongside the tracks wearing a prison uniform. With the inmate's number clearly printed on his back, the engineer jotted it down and made a mental note to call the Penitentiary as soon as the train pulled up to the Cripple Creek Depot.

Contacting the Canon City Territorial Prison, the engineer read off the number he had seen printed across the prisoner's back and was shocked to hear that the number matched an inmate who had recently been executed. Sharing the news with his crew, they quickly christened the area Phantom Canyon.

But Spirits were not the only problem the Florence and Cripple Creek Railroad would be facing.

When the Florence free road had first been built in 1889-1890, it was designed to run right alongside a creek known as Eight-Mile, perhaps to give its travelers something pristine to look at while they traveled, but when the creek got angry it

Phantom Canyon train with Eight-Mile creek running alongside-
Courtesy of the Florence Pioneer Museum and Research center

became more of a poisonous snake following its victims along the side of the road until it found the perfect time to strike.

In July of 1895, a little over a year after the crew of the Florence and Cripple Creek Railroad had their ghostly sighting, a cloud burst high up on towering Mount Pisgah caused a torrent of water to careen down Eight- Mile creek towards Florence, tearing apart trees and bushes as it did. As it built up strength, it set its sights on the railway stop of Adelaide, which was nestled halfway down the mountain and tore apart its Great Elk Hotel, killing six men in the process. Still not satisfied, the angry creek then set its sights on a passenger train that was heading to Florence and decided to chase it down the mountain.

Pushing the train to its limits, the courageous engineer could feel the flood licking the rear axles as he gave his passengers a ride they would never forget. Reaching Florence with his train intact, the engineer soon learned that the flooded creek had not only washed away 12 miles of track but had left another 300 feet of it hanging in mid-air. Not to be deterred, fast acting crews headed straight up Phantom Canyon and had the tracks open for business only 15 days later.

For the next 17 years, Eight-Mile creek remained manageable for the most part, until the afternoon of July 21, 1912, when two church groups got together and chartered a train for a picnic. Chased back into their Pullman cars by a sudden rainstorm, the faithful watched as the water level in the creek quickly began to rise, followed by their train taking off down the mountain at a breakneck speed.

Desperate to reach the trestle, which would allow the train to use the switch back to Canon City, the engineer kept a sharp eye on the rising floodwaters and waited for his chance to switch tracks. Yet, when the engineer saw a wave of water jump over the upcoming trestle, he made the split-second decision to use the switch to Florence instead, saving both his train and all of the passengers.

Unfortunately, the damage to the track and its numerous bridges was estimated to be around $110,000, which prompted the railroad's investors to pull up the tracks and turn the rail bed back into a vehicle road, which was graced by its first automobile on August 30, 1918.

Now, almost three year later, a cluster of black, menacing storm clouds could be seen hanging over Mount Pisgah, drenching the families who lived in Phantom Canyon with non-stop rain and hail. The mountain's residents knew from experience that they needed to watch the storm and hoped that Eight-Mile creek would be able to hold back all of this rain.

It couldn't.

E. C Higgins, known as Woody, stood on the Mesa above his house near Eight-Mile creek and watched as the rain continued to come down, and as he feared, the creek soon began to rise and churn until it finally began to overrun its banks. Exhibiting the anger the creek was known for, a torrent of water began to run wildly down the mountain, tearing out everything in its path and quickly damming up the sharp turns in the narrow creek.

With debris now tangled up along the rocky edges, the surge of water found itself trapped and realized that it needed to run higher and stronger to get down the mountain.

Running to his phone, Woody Higgins called the Florence Police Department and alerted them that a 20 -foot wall of water was barreling down Eight-Mile creek, and heading right towards them. The town of Florence, which was located at the base of Mount Pisgah, had felt the wrath of Eight-Mile creeks temper since the little town was incorporated in 1887 and was very familiar with the destruction it could cause.

Named after the daughter of the town's founder, the city planners had respected the angry creek when they originally platted out its streets and made sure to give Eight-Mile a clear and straight channel to the Arkansas River. Their intention was for the creek to go along its merry way and leave the town alone.

But with news that the creek was once again raging, the residents prayed that the river, which ran along the shores of the town, would be able to contain this new onslaught of water.

With emergency crews on alert and many of the town's residents awaiting its arrival on the nearby hills, the wave of water soon slammed into the Arkansas River with such force that the vibration shook the nearby buildings. With the river's edge dominated by farms and grazing cattle, the debris-filled water quickly engulfed the riverbank, sending a herd of cows into a panic as they ran for higher ground.

Unable to get past the swarm of trees that lined the edge of the river, the raging flood shot up a wave of water in protest as it sharply turned east, forced to follow the natural path of the river. Tearing out any road or bridge in its path, it angrily stormed past the town of Florence and continued towards the nearby town of Portland.

The town that nobody contacted.

Located less than six miles east of Florence and less than 1,000 feet from the edge of the Arkansas River, Portland was one of three factory towns owned by the Ideal Portland Cement Plant. The town and the cement plant both sat at almost the same elevation as the river, which was designed to allow the plant to access the water it needed to function, while giving the residents of Portland a nice river view. The remaining factory towns, Cement and Concrete, had been built high up on the mesa, and the angry river was about to give its residents quite a show.

The Cement plant, which was built in 1899, also contained a steam plant, a private reservoir, two

The town of Portland with the Arkansas River running alongside- Courtesy of the Florence Pioneer Museum and Research center

railroads and a Train Depot, which not only handled fright cars from the Cement plant but passenger trains as well.

Ironically, despite not being aware of the flood barreling towards them from Florence, the residents of Portland had already evacuated their homes for the safety of the cement plants upper floors, due to flood pouring down from a nearby creek called the Hard Scrabble.

Created by snowmelt from the nearby Greenhorn Mountain, which stood at a towering 12,346 feet, the creek was known as a normally calm source of water for the farms that dotted the area, before it quietly emptied into the Arkansas River less than half a mile west of Portland.

But the storm had caused it to rage.

With the Arkansas River already running high, the large amount of water that the Hard Scrabble was pouring into the river gave it the final push it needed to raise itself up and over the deck of Portland's train bridge and flood the tracks.

With the steel bridge now finding itself submerged, storm debris quickly began jamming itself up against the steel structure and like an angry Beaver, began damming up the river. With nowhere to go, the mud infused flood water quickly overpowered the river banks and began to spread itself out like a

Portland train bridge with the Cement plant in the background-Authors personal collection

virus, consuming the town of Portland, as well as its Art Deco street lamps.

Thankfully, the strong block walls of the Ideal Portland Cement Plant were still holding strong, as the floodwaters rose up to the building's first-floor windows, harassing the employees and their families who were trapped inside. Despite the refugee's best efforts to keep the inside of the building dry, the water was still quietly seeping in around the massive steel doors and creeping towards the plant's lower level, which held very valuable machinery.

Maybe building a Cement plant only 700 feet from a large water source, wasn't the best idea.

Due to the quickly rising water, Portland's train dispatcher found himself trapped inside the towns Depot, which was located directly across the street from the Cement plant. Built upon a raised concrete platform, the dispatcher stared out the windows of the Depot and watched as one massive wave after another dynamited over the top of the nearby steel train bridge.

Quickly getting on the phone, the dispatcher contacted Florence, as well as some of the nearby Depots and alerted them that not only was the Arkansas River flooding but that Portland was now underwater. Satisfied that his information had been delivered, the dispatcher began preparing to abandon the Depot for the high and dry upper floors of the Cement plant, but his plans quickly changed after he received a spine chilling call regarding a passenger train heading to Portland.

From the Swallows Depot.

In reverse.

Originally headed to Pueblo's Union Depot, the train had stopped six miles short due to the tracks being covered in a cascade of muddy sludge, which was pouring down from the nearby stream beds. The train's conductor had ordered his remaining crew to throw the train into reverse and head the 14 miles back to the Swallows Depot, while he took a handcart to Pueblo to check the tracks, but by the time the train had arrived in Swallows, their Depot was already taking on water. Making a split-second decision, the Engineer decided to keep the train in reverse and take it another 16 miles west to the Portland Depot, which, unknown to him, was also underwater.

A lot of water.

With the news that a passenger train was headed his way, the Portland dispatcher quickly slid on his raincoat and buttoned it up tight, before glancing back out the windows. The Depot, which was perched upon an almost three-foot tall slab hadn't yet taken on much water, but he knew that once he opened the door that would all change.

After moving his paperwork up onto a high bookshelf, he grabbed the doorknob and quickly pulled the door open, which allowed the flood water to pour into the little building. Rushing out onto the platform, the dispatcher found that the rapidly moving water was fighting his attempt to close the door and lock it, but with a little extra effort he managed to succeed with only a minimal amount of water covering the floor.

Placing his keys back into his pocket, he carefully walked over to the edge of the Depots flooded platform and stared down at the submerged tracks, which were sitting under at least four feet of water.

But that passenger train was still coming.

The average height of a standard Pullman Train car, wheels to roof, was around 13 feet, which meant that even if the train arrived at the Depot at just that moment, it would be almost half submerged in the flood water, that is if the waves didn't push it off the tracks first.

Knowing that he needed to check on the steel train bridge, the dispatcher waded over to the edge of the Depots platform and holding onto the handrail, carefully stepped down into the waist deep water. After giving his body a few seconds to adjust to its frigid temperature, he looked towards the bridge, which was less than 750 feet away from the Depot and saw an amazing sight.

Through the pounding rain, the dispatcher could see what appeared to be hundreds of men swarming around the steel bridge pulling at tree branches, lumber, and debris that had been jammed underneath it by the strong current. As the dispatcher struggling to wade through the ever rising water, he finally reached a group of men near the base of the bridge that appeared to be in charge and told them something he knew they didn't want to hear.

Portland employees- Courtesy of the Florence Pioneer Museum and Research center

"Hey! Hey! There's a train coming! A train!" the dispatcher screamed, as he desperately tried to have his voice heard over the roar of the floodwater, as it pounded against the side of the bridge. "A passenger train is coming! It's coming and we need the tracks cleared!"

Glancing over to the bridge and then back over at the dispatcher, a look of panic covered the man's face, as another tidal wave slammed into the side of the steel train bridge, raining torrents of water down onto its debris covered tracks. Leaving the terrified man where he stood, the dispatcher continued wading through the water and screamed his request to every man he saw until his urgency was finally acted upon.

With a large group of men now at his beck and call, the dispatcher was able to direct the cleanup of the tracks, but as he joined the men in tossing tree branches and debris off the east side of the bridge, a deep, rumbling sound was heard coming from the direction of Florence.

And it sounded like rolling thunder.

Looking towards the sound, the men noticed that an enormous wall of water was coming down the Arkansas River at almost three times its natural height, which quickly collided with the torrent that was still pouring down from nearby Hard Scrabble creek, resulting in an impact that sounded like a continual blast of dynamite. As the swells combined, they shot up into the air like the geyser of Yellowstone's old faithful, before crashing back down to earth and rejoining the already engorged river.

Bracing themselves for the inevitable impact, the men on the bridge quickly squatted down behind its steel frame, lowered their heads, and held on. Within seconds, the torrent slammed into the bridge, which gave a violent shudder, but luckily held tight.

The flood from Eight-Mile creek had just arrived.

With the river refusing to give up its attack on the bridge, the men finally had to admit their defeat and quickly headed to the north side of the bridge, so they could head up onto the cliffs and high ground. Once free of the river, the continual rain assisted the men in washing off the thick layers of mud and foliage that the floodwaters had just baptized them with.

As a crack of thunder echoed through the sky, announcing a new deluge of rain, a strange beeping sound was heard in the distance. Fearful that it was the incoming train, the men quickly ran back over to the bridge and fought the continual pounding waves to throw debris off the tracks, that is, until one man made a startling discovery.

Slapping his fellow workers on the back and attempting to shout over the sound of the storm, the man pointed to the west, about a half-mile away, and alerted everyone to a line of lights in the distance, which appeared to be coming towards them. Glancing up and wiping the rain from their eyes, the men realized that the sound was coming from a line of vehicles with their headlights ablaze, honking their horns in greeting.

It was the residents of Florence.

When the flood from Eight-Mile had been called into the Florence Police station, by a man who lived up on Phantom Canyon, the word had gone out for anyone willing to assist people that might be stranded in the rising water. As a large group of men was gathered up, some were informed that the dispatcher at the Portland Depot had reported that their town was flooding. Gathering up tools and vehicles, 100 men broke off from the group and quickly headed the five miles east to Portland.

One of the men arriving from the town of Florence to help- Courtesy of the Florence Pioneer Museum and Research center

Unfortunately, getting there wasn't going to be easy. Many of the roads the Florence group encountered had been washed out, which forced them to build numerous makeshift bridges to reach the flooded town, but now that they finally had Portland in their sights, the men discovered that they still had one more bridge to build and it was over the washed out Hard Scrabble creek.

And a little help would really be appreciated.

Lowering themselves into the deep water that waited for them over the side of the compromised steel train bridge and swimming towards the stranded Florence vehicles, a group of Portland men gathered random logs and floated them towards the waiting vehicles. As they neared the washed out bridge caused by the rage of Hard Scrabble creek, the Portland men began constructing a makeshift walking bridge as the Florence men did the same, meeting in the middle within the hour.

Now with 100 extra men to help clear the debris trapped around the Portland Bridge, the blockage was soon pulled loose, causing a torrent of water to begin following under the bridge, instead of just over it.

As shouts of victory quickly filled the air, the men began to focus their energy on clearing the debris off the train tracks, which is when they heard the sound.

It was like a repetitive, urgent whistle.

And it was getting louder.

Looking downriver the men witnessed an almost 20- foot wall of water coming up the tracks, as the train's engine desperately pushed its Pullman cars against the floodwater, creating a magnificent fountain as it did. With most of the men watching the unusual phenomenon, a handful of others quickly scanned the tracks for any last piece of debris, before calling out for everyone to clear the bridge.

Watching the results of their collective efforts pay off, the exhausted men silently watched as the backward train, led by one of its Pullman passenger cars, followed the submerged track up to the carefully cleared off bridge, continuing its festival of water as it did. The train, which was barely visible through the colossal spray, quickly crossed the steel bridge before following the tracks back down, where it slid into the deep water with a monumental splash.

But once it did, it couldn't stay on the track.

Bobbing up out of the water like a cork , but still coupled together, the Pullman cars quickly floated up and began to rock and sway in the almost six foot deep water, with only the weight of the steam locomotive staying firmly planted on the submerged tracks. Still in reverse, the engine managed to deliver its Pullman's to the Depot, despite them jumping around like towels on a clothes line.

Finally allowed to rest, the overworked engine gave off a large puff of steam in celebration of a job well done.

Ironically, the same flood waters that threatened the survival of everyone on board the Pullmans turned out to also be its saving grace, as the waves from the flooded river were pushing everything towards the Depot instead of away from it. Now tangled amongst trees, and debris, the flood waters continued to slam the Pullman cars against the Depots concrete platform, over and over as its glorious fountain of water quickly fell back to earth,

Screaming for help, the dispatcher climbed down from the bridge and re-entered the water in order to swim over to the compromised train. Glancing behind him for just a second, he couldn't help but smile, as scores of overworked men jumped into the water after him, all determined to see their quest through to the end.

Despite all of the struggles and tension the incoming train had caused him and the people of Portland, the worst thing that could happen to the passengers now was wet clothes and soggy luggage and from the way, the Pullman cars were bouncing around in the current, possibly a few bruises and broken bones as well.

Finally reaching the steps that would lead him up to the Depots raised platform, and pulling himself up onto it, he was relieved to be in water that was now less than waist deep. As he shook river silt and sticks from his raincoat and straightened his hat, the dispatcher got his first good look at the terrified faces of the passengers.

As he watched thick layers of mud and debris slid off the train cars, he questioned the severity of the situation. The light weight of the Pullmans was still causing them to not only float above the tracks but also allowing the flood waters to continue slamming them into the platform with each wave. This threatened the safety of not only the passengers, but anyone who tried to save them.

As the men from the bridge finally arrived on the Depots platform, an impromptu meeting was called and after discussing all of their options, only one solution was agreed upon by all.

They had to flood the Pullman's.

Grabbing the attention of the Porters trapped inside and motioning for them to pull open the Pullman's exterior doors, the passengers inside quickly realized what was about to happen and began to panic. During their entire quest to reach safety, the inside of the Pullman cars had remained dry, but now that they had arrived at the Portland Depot, the realization that the cars would flood once the doors were opened terrified them.

Instructing the passengers to hold onto something, the Porters gave the doors a few strong tugs, which caused the mud infused river water to pour into the Pullman car's. Attempting to keep order, the Porters barked at everyone to calm down until the weight of the water finished settling the Pullmans back onto the tracks, before they tried to disembark.

With the Pullmans now partly stabilized, but still rocking, the passengers were helped onto the Depot's platform, but were shocked to find that they were not allowed to enter the Depot itself. As they were lead towards the stairs, the passengers were informed that they now had to walk down the steps and swim across the street to the towering Cement plant.

The Portland Cement plant and train Depot- Courtesy of the Florence Pioneer Museum and Research center

With many of the passengers refusing and choosing to instead stand on the platform and argue, the rest were helped down the flooded steps and into the body numbing water, as the men from both Portland and Florence created a human chain to help them cross safely. As the compliant passengers began entering the Ideal Portland Cement plant and climbed the steps up onto the second floor, the defiant passengers finally gave in and reluctantly entered the frigid water for the safety of the cement plant as well.

Shivering from the cold and exhausted from their unexpected swim, the train passengers soon realized that their complaints were minor, compared to what the residents of Portland were going through. As they made their way up to the second floor and stood in their now cold, waterlogged clothes, the passengers found themselves faced with the families whose livelihoods had been dependent on the now flooded cement plant.

But Hardscrabble and Eight-Mile were not the only creeks that this summer storm was flooding.

Up in the Wet Mountain Range, which overlooked both Florence and Portland, sat a small farming town called Siloam. The Wet Mountains were so named due to the extreme amount of snow they accumulated during the winter, which would melt in the spring, and run down the numerous creeks where it would water the fertile farmland that covered the mountains.

The town had been built alongside the normally quiet and tranquil Red Creek, but today the peaceful waterway had turned into an angry beast, which left many of the town's residents wondering about the destruction the water would cause once it reached the bottom of the mountain and poured into the Arkansas River.

As the town's people watched the storm intensify, one man knew he had to report it. Grabbing his phone around 6 pm and asking the Operator to connect him with the Florence Police Department, the man was shocked to discover that not only was Hardscrabble Creek and Eight-Mile also raging, but the swollen Arkansas River was wreaking havoc in Portland.

Fearing that the City of Pueblo hadn't yet been alerted about the incoming flood, the man then asked the operator to connect him to the Pueblo Police Department, which luckily took the man's information quite seriously.

After ending the call, the officer quickly put a call into The Pueblo Water Works and asked to speak to 60-year-old John Nittinger, who was the Water Engineer. Informing him of a possible flood coming down the Arkansas River from the Portland area, John was asked to begin blowing the fire whistle, which was mounted on the outside wall of the Water Works building.

The residents of Pueblo understood that two blasts meant there was a fire, while one blast meant that the danger had passed, but the last time a continuous blast was heard was on November 11, 1918, to mark the end of the World War.

John Nittinger, seated and wearing a hat
- Courtesy of The Pueblo County Historical Society

Whenever the fire whistle was blown, people knew to call the Water Works building and ask about the location of the fire, but today Mr. Nittinger was informing callers that he was not blowing the whistle for a fire, but for an approaching flood coming down the Arkansas River, which immediately put quite a strain on the Telephone operators.

Mrs. Joseph E. Prior was the Chief operator that night at The Mountain States Phone Company when the steam siren on the side of the Water Works building began emitting its chilling wail. Making a call herself to the Water Works, Mrs. Prior was shocked to hear that the siren was in regards to an approaching flood.

As church bells began adding their warnings to the ear-piercing sounds of the siren, Mrs. Prior informed all her girls on duty to call every home in the low lying areas and urge them to seek higher ground immediately. Unfortunately, instead of being filled with fear or concern, many of the residents they contacted were instead irritated about being disturbed, explaining to the operators that they had just sat down to dinner and had no desire to leave their homes.

But one man who was taking the approaching flood quite seriously was Union Depot Dispatcher Brutus Stearns.

At 6:30 pm Dispatcher Stearns received an emergency phone call from the Swallows Depot, which immediately sent a chill down his spine. In a frantic tone, the dispatcher from Swallows explained that not only were their tracks sitting under four feet of water but a 40-foot section of it had just slid into the Arkansas River.

Which made Dispatcher Stearns question the safety of the last train still due to arrive at the Union Depot.

Continuing to push through the driving rain, The Denver & Rio Grande train No. 3

Collapsed tracks near Swallows- Courtesy of The Pueblo County Historical Society

continued towards Pueblo, with the conductor making notes of the high water he encountered, which was within three feet of the tracks. Conductor Calvin Groves informed his crew that he hadn't seen so much standing water since the Pueblo flood of 1894, but even then, the water had never gotten this high.

Arriving at Pueblo's Union Depot at 7:50 pm, the conductor and his crew began exiting their train's locomotive, as crewmen arrived to uncouple it from the Pullmans and take it to the roundhouse. As another bolt of lightning streaked across the waterlogged sky, Conductor Groves watched as his passengers began popping open their umbrellas in preparation for their mad dash into the Depot.

With the crew continuing to assist the passengers, Conductor Groves buckled up his jacket and headed inside the Depot himself, as he needed to register his train's arrival before heading into the restaurant for a quick bite to eat. As the sounds of sirens and church bells filled the air, Conductor Groves headed upstairs to the Telegraph office, located up on the second floor, where he was informed of an unexpected layover.

"Conductor Groves, you and your crew are released from duty until further notice and we ask that you please inform your passengers that the stop will be eight to ten hours", Dispatcher Brutus Stearns announced, as he handed the message over to the Conductor. "We have received reports that a flood is coming down the Arkansas River and for everyone's safety, we are stopping all train travel."

"Sir, if you don't mind me asking. Shouldn't we get the trains out of the yard before the flood arrives?" Conductor Groves asked, as he held the message in his hands. "The train yard is already saturated and this rain doesn't look like it's about to stop any time soon."

With a shake of his head, Dispatcher Stearns pointed back to the message Conductor Groves was still holding in his hands. "Please advise your passengers of the delay."

As the Conductor walked out of the office, the Dispatcher and the Telegraph operator exchanged a concerned look. They were both aware that this storm had not only washed out the tracks at Swallows but at 7 pm the approach to the Missouri Pacific bridge had also washed out, resulting in them detouring the Manifest Freight Train No. 62 over to a connection near the stock yards.

Arriving back on the train platform, Conductor Groves entered one of his Pullman cars and asked a Porter to get him an updated passenger list. Quickly glancing through all the names, it appeared that out of all of the passengers who had been aboard his train, 26 had already disembarked, while 83 were still on board awaiting the next leg of their journey.

Looking up from the list, the conductor silently watched as marble-sized hail began to beat against his train's windows, resulting in nervous whispers echoing among the remaining passengers. Focusing his eyes through the water soaked glass, Conductor Calvin Groves could barely make out the shape of the Missouri Pacific No.14, which was parked right alongside the Denver & Rio Grande No. 3, as the sound of the steam siren again broke through the storm.

He had to get his train out of here.

CHAPTER 3

The double-edged knife and the flying trees

Thirty-year-old Harry K. Inman had just left work when the fire whistle first began to blow. He knew that the high pitched whistle could mean a lot of things, but the rain that was violently beating against his truck's windshield was giving him a bad feeling. With a pit beginning to form in his stomach, he quickly turned his truck around and headed back to work.

Harry was the Superintendent of Pueblo's Street's and Sewer Department, located at 125 South Santa Fe Avenue, but he also helped care for the city's horses. Before he had left work, Harry made sure that they were all back inside their stables, but something about this storm just didn't feel right.

Pulling up to the City Corral, at 417 West 1st Street, Harry hopped out of his truck and went inside to look for John Lathim who had worked as the Corral's caretaker for as long as Harry could remember, but as he looked around, he realized that John was nowhere to be found. Heading upstairs, where John had a bunk room, he found it deathly quiet, with the only noise being that of the rain upon the roof and the horses that were directly under his feet.

The city had 12 horses that normally spent their days delivering ice and milk, but right now they were restless. Heading back downstairs, Harry could see that the storm was causing the yard to pool with standing water and he knew it was only a matter of time before the water reached the corral. As the siren continued to blow, he headed over to the phone and called the Water Works, which resulted in news that he didn't want to hear.

With a regrettable sigh, Harry Inman immediately called his 24-year-old wife Mary and told her the bad news. He reassured her that she and the children, three-year-old Roy and one-year-old Robert, would be perfectly safe from the approaching flood as their house, at 108 West 18th Street, was well over 17 blocks north of the engorged Arkansas River, but with John Lathim missing, Harry would have to stay and care for the horses.

Reassuring her that he would be fine and would just be putting his Army training to good use, Harry blew her a kiss into the phone's receiver before ending the call. As he hung up, a flash of lightning caught his eye, directing his gaze towards the corral's waterlogged windows. He just wished that John was there to help him with the horses, but he understood why he wasn't.

Back on April 11th, at just around 8:50 pm, 60-year-old John Lathim had been robbed right outside of the corral by a pair of young Mexicans who stabbed him for his wallet and the $30 that it contained. With

City Hall only a few blocks away, John managed to walk over to the building where he was evaluated by Health Officer Jim Burns and when the Police arrived, John surprised them all by handing over the 7 inch long, double edged knife he had been stabbed with.

He informed the officers that he had just come out of the stable doors when the first man ran up to him and began stabbing him repeatedly in the chest, while the second man reached into his back pocket and grabbed his wallet. As John fought the men off he grabbed their knife in the process, which caused the cowards, which he described as short, stout, and young to take off running towards Greenwood Street, where they disappeared into the shadows.

As Doctor Burn's helped John remove his canvas work jacket and Jersey sweater to inspect his wounds, he discovered injuries to his left arm, as well as a small wound over his left breast, but nothing life-threatening. As the Doctor inspected the heavy jacket, he informed John that its sturdy fabric had prevented the knife from going into his heart and had saved his life.

With the police unable to find his attackers, the young thieves continued their crime spree by breaking into a home on Greenwood, just minutes after their attack on John, where they made off with $40, clothing, and jewelry. Not satisfied, the thieves then attacked a woman who was crossing a nearby bridge after work and had stolen her purse. With the criminals never brought to justice, John blamed himself for not stopping them and it changed him.

John had continued to live and work at the City Corral, but with the fire whistle screaming from the top of the city's Water Works building, Harry Inman feared that the noise and all the commotion outside may have spooked him, but he still wished John would come back and help him with the horses.

But you can only wish for so much.

Walking out of the office and into the main corral, Harry watched as the water from the flooded yard began to pour over the threshold and creep towards the stalls, and he knew it was only a matter of time before the corral began to flood. Buttoning his coat uptight, Harry walked over to the building's main doors and opened up the left side, which put him face to face with not only a pounding rainstorm but incredible displays of lighting, which repeatedly lit up the sky.

Heading over to the closest stales, Harry grabbed the led ropes of the first two horses and began walking the hesitant animals out into the storm. Despite the water being only a few inches deep, the speeding vehicles, which raced by without a care, were causing waves to splash up onto the legs of the already terrified animals and it took all Harry had to keep them moving.

Four blocks to the east of the corral was a hill called Tenderfoot, which he hoped would be high enough to keep the horses out of the expected flood, as it was the tallest point he could think of within walking distance. Two by two, Harry moved the horses up to the top of the hill and tied them to trees, before going back to the corral for the next pair. Each time he led the next set of horses out into the rain, he would spot groups of thrill-seekers not only playing in the rising water but running towards the nearby bridges to see the flooded Arkansas River.

Finally, with all 12 horses safely tied up to nearby trees, Harry headed back down the hill for his Holt Caterpillar Tractor, which was parked next to the corral. As he jumped into the seat and brought the engine to life, he glanced over at his work truck and wondered if he should grab that one first. Confident that he had time to retrieve both of them, he quickly drove his tractor up the hill and parked it next to his horses, before heading back to the corral to grab his truck.

Unfortunately, as he walked back towards the corral he noticed how deep the water was getting. Despite keeping to the sidewalks, Harry found that the water was beginning to lap over onto his shoes, even when a passing vehicle wasn't splashing him from the flooded street.

He also noticed that most of the vehicles that passed by, weren't driving away from the flooded river, but towards it.

Some of those thrill-seekers, who chose to ignore the warning wails of the Water Works siren, were 14-year old Bernard Kelly and two of his school friends, as well as his 19-year-old sister Eileen and her boyfriend.

Bernard Kelly Senior Year book photo-
Courtesy of The PCCLD Special Collections

Eileen Kelly Senior Year book photo-
Courtesy of The PCCLD Special Collections

The Kelly family lived high up on the Bluffs, which overlooked the Union Depot train yards, but the group decided that a little adventure was just what they needed. Heading over to the South Union Avenue Bridge, which crossed over the train tracks, the group fought the rain as they walked the remaining three blocks to the now raging Arkansas River and the North Union Avenue Bridge that crossed over it.

When they arrived, the group discovered that the bridge was barely visible as every square inch was covered in excited sightseers, who cheered and sang as waves of river water splashed high up into the air and rained down over its captive audience. Unable to get onto the bridge itself, Bernard and his friends began walking down the side of the levee towards the Main Street Bridge, which was only a block away, when they noticed that not only was the Arkansas River running very high, but it was also giving off a terrible odor.

Similar to the smell Bernard had noticed inside of the Gym at his school, the river water was giving off a dank, sort of sour smell, like a combination of plants, tree's and living creatures all dissolved together in silty water and then cooked for a long time. As they continued to walk, a tree would occasionally be tossed high up into the air by the strong river current, causing the foul smelling water to spray down onto their group, but luckily the continual downpour of rain was there to wash it off.

Arriving at the Main Street Bridge, and also finding it full of sightseers, the group began looking around for a spot with a better view of the river. Sporting a satisfied smile, Bernard discovered a few freight cars sitting stranded on a nearby track and motioned to his friends to climb up on top.

Impressed by her little brother's discovery, Eileen and her boyfriend quickly followed him up onto the freight car for their bird's eye view of the angry river. As the fire siren continued to scream out its warnings, a kind of holiday spirit took over the ever growing crowd, with people dancing and cheering as the water continued to rise.

The scene before them was undoubtingly dramatic. Tree branches, lumber, pieces of wooden structures, and the bodies of animals were being whipped around in the constantly rising water, which soon began to splash over the top of the levees. Aware of the dangers, Police officers tried to break up the crowd and pleaded with them to seek higher ground, but the officers quickly realized that their demands were falling onto deaf ears.

They just hoped that their fellow officers were having better luck convincing the people living in the low lying areas to evacuate for higher ground.

But hoping doesn't make it happen.

Reporting to the Police station in droves, volunteers from all walks of life quickly began filling the lobby, and asking Officer John Sinclair, the 54-year-old Night Captain, how they could be of service. Fireman, Elks Lodge members, Railway men, Steelworkers, Veterans, and even Boy Scout Troop No. 6, pledged their assistance and patiently awaited further instructions.

"I want you to all break into groups and evacuate everyone that you can from the low lying neighborhoods of Pepper Sauce Bottoms and the Grove, as well as any homes bordering the levees. We are also opening up the Courthouse on West 10th Street as a shelter, so you can send people up there." Captain Sinclair explained as he pointed towards the north. "Now, keep in mind, not only will you be trying to convince people to leave their homes, but both neighborhoods were hit pretty hard with an outbreak of Diphtheria awhile back, so be careful."

As concerned whispers began taking over the group, the Captain offered his volunteers a quick lesson on how Diphtheria spreads, which is mainly contracted by infected people not covering their mouths when they coughed or sneezed. As the volunteers began to discuss this new piece of information, the Captain thought of one more item he thought he should mention.

"Oh, and one more thing. A lot of the people in these areas are immigrants and most of them don't speak English, so good luck."

With the volunteers beginning to head out, Boy Scout Troop No. 6 stayed behind, as Doctor Edwin Cary, the 36-year-old Scout Master wished to offer an idea for Captain John Sinclair to consider, which proved to the Captain that Scouts really are prepared.

"Sir, if we could get together a collection of rain gear, lanterns, and flashlights, my Scouts could form a human chain of light starting at the Main Street Bridge all the way to the Court House steps, in case the power goes out." Scout Master Cary suggested as he pointed over to the large group of boys dressed in their proper Scout attire. "I have more than enough Scouts to not only cover the entire 11 blocks, but to aide in the evacuations as well."

Pleased with his suggestion, the requested supplies were quickly gathered up and loaded into 29-year-old Assistant Scout Master George White's truck, while Scout Master Cary took a handful of Scouts with him to the low lying areas, so they could begin assisting with the evacuations.

As the last volunteer left the Police Station and walked out into the storm, Captain John Sinclair, who preferred to be called Jack, watched as another bolt of lightning once again streaked across the blackened sky.

Jack Sinclair had moved to Pueblo in 1891, from Dodge City, Kansas, and had arrived just in time to experience the 1894 flood, but today, as he looked out the rain streaked windows of the Police Station, he didn't remember it ever being this bad.

Back in 1887, when he still lived in Dodge City, Jack had joined a Vaudevillian Musical group called The Dodge City Cowboys, which consisted of 25 men dressed in broad hats, woolen shirts, leather leggings, spurs, and a belt containing a six-chambered ivory handled revolver. They sang songs, told jokes, shared stories, did tricks with their pistols, and even did impersonations. The high light of his career was on March 4, 1889, when the group was invited to perform at the inauguration party for President Benjamin Harrison.

On tour with his famous Cowboys in 1891, the group played a few shows in Pueblo, which is when Jack Sinclair fell in love with the city and decided to stay. He continued to tour with his group until he joined the Pueblo Police Department in 1906, but continued to play for the crowds at the local Theaters, but he feared this storm was going to wash away the city he had grown to love.

He just hoped that people would evacuate before it was too late.

But you can only wish for so much.

With a pickup truck full of eager, but nervous Boy Scouts, who ranged from 14 to 19 years old, Assistant Scout Master George White drove to the edge of the Grove and instructed the boys to fan out and knock on as many doors as possible.

Almost instantly the Scouts had doors slammed in their faces, were yelled at in a language they didn't understand, or were faced with a family who had a sick loved one that they insisted was too ill to be moved. As the Scouts continued to point out not only the rising water but the ear piercing wail of the Water Works siren, they only succeeded in getting a handful of people to evacuate, as most believed that the levees would hold back the river.

But the city never built a levee to hold back Fountain Creek.

Pushing his car through the pouring rain, 31-year-old Raymond C. Chapman was frantically trying to reach Pueblo, even as the road continued to wash out in front of him. In his passenger seat sat a very nervous traveling salesman who had hitched a ride with him back in Colorado Springs and Raymond was getting worried that he had put both of their lives at risk.

As Raymond continued to push his vehicle through the storm, he would occasionally glance over at the thick, angry waves of water that were erupting out of Fountain Creek, which ran right alongside the road and flinched each time he was forced to drive over the debris the creek was hurtling onto the road in front of him.

Fountain Creek originated in a town called Woodland Park, which was a little over 60 miles north of Pueblo and flowed past Colorado Springs until it merged with the Arkansas River near Pueblo's Union Depot. Following the same poor design that placed Phantom Canyon's road right alongside the banks of

Eight-Mile creek near Florence, the main road from Colorado Springs to Pueblo was also built right along the banks of the now swollen and very angry Fountain Creek.

Which like Eight-Mile creek, had a dark history.

Originally called "La Fontaine Qui Bouille", which is French for "The Fountain that boils", it was named by French explorers who discovered the creek and felt that it bubbled like a fountain, but on June 10, 1864, it did a lot more than bubble.

Created by the seasonal snow melt from Mount Herman, which sits at an elevation of 9,063 feet, the creek followed it natural course for around 17 miles until it reached the small mining town of Colorado City, which was the first settlement to be constructed in the shadow of Pikes Peak. Founded in 1859, when the area was still considered part of the Kansas Territory, the little town held over 300 cabins in 1864, but that all changed when the calendar flipped over to June 10th.

Due to a combination of snowmelt and a few days of torrential rain, Fountain Creek began to billow and surge, until it built up enough power to pounce upon the little town with a 30-foot swell of water, killing several people.

On July 26, 1885, as well as on August 1, 1886, Fountain Creek surged again, this time combining with Shook's Run and Cheyenne Creek to wipe out not only homes and livestock but railroad bridges, all while devastating the nearby town of Colorado Springs.

And now, on June 3, 1921, Fountain Creek decided that it was a great day for history to repeat itself.

Which was causing Raymond Chapman to have a really bad day.

While fighting a never ending rainstorm, Raymond had to keep one eye on the road, as well as one eye on Fountain Creek, and after a few terrifying hours, he had never been so happy to see Pueblo. Pulling up to the Vail Hotel on North Union Avenue, where his passenger had rented a room, he heard what sounded like a siren. Getting out of his car, to see what was going on, he overheard people talking about a flood.

Following the crowd, Raymond was shocked to see that the water from the Arkansas River was already level with the underside of the North Union Avenue Bridge. As people cheered the arrival of each debris infused wave of foul smelling flood water, as it slammed against the side of the steel bridge, Raymond felt an icy chill run down his spine.

Quickly glancing back over at the Vail Hotel, which sat only a stone's throw away from the compromised bridge, Raymond ran over to the building, and walked into the lobby where he found his passenger still waiting to get his room key. In a pleading tone, he begged his passenger to come with him to the Congress Hotel, which was located on higher ground, but he adamantly refused.

With a defeated tone, Raymond wished the man good luck as he headed back to his car, which is when he noticed an unnerving sight. The trolley cars, which normally traveled up and down Union Avenue, were evacuating the area and carrying with them very few passengers, as most of the crowd was too spellbound to leave.

As he glanced back towards the bridge, Raymond could see that the floodwaters were beginning to flow over the levee and leach out onto the street, which only seemed to excite the crowd even more. Not caught in the rivers spell himself, he quickly jumped into his car and headed for higher ground.

Which was what 14-year old Bernard Kelly and his friends were also about to do.

From atop the boxcar he was perched on, Bernard began hearing a high pitched whistle, which he soon realized was coming from a group of frantic Police officers who were ordering everyone away from the river. Seeing the boys up on the boxcars, an officer motioned for them to come down, as he pointed to the river. "The levees are breaking! You need to come down from there and get to higher ground!"

Ignoring the officer, Bernard turned his attention back to the show the river was putting on and watched as another tree hurtled through the rising water with the speed of a freight train and smash into the side of the bridge, before flying high up into the air and landing back into the turbulent water on the other side. Seeing that a second tree was following the same path, Bernard joined the crowd in their anticipation of another joyous splash, but this time the tree refused to re-enter the river and instead landed onto the waterlogged street instead, causing the formally cheerful crowd to scatter.

Curious why the tree didn't stay on its original course, Bernard wiped the rain from his eyes and turned his attention back to the rebellious piece of timber, which is when he noticed that the river had finally jumped the levee. Glancing back towards the bridge, he quickly realized that a mountain of debris had become jammed underneath it, which was causing the foul-smelling river water to overflow its banks.

As a bolt of lightning once again shot across the rain drenched sky, a new group of sightseers approached the crowd and began screaming that the levees around Victoria Avenue, which was only two blocks away, had just collapsed.

The city was flooding.

Climbing down from the boxcar with her boyfriend, Eileen motioned for Bernard and his friends to quickly follow her, as she needed to get her group back up onto the Bluffs. Glancing around at the ruptured levees, and knowing that they had to get back onto South Union Avenue, which was one block over, she grabbed her brother's hand and told his friends to follow them.

Squeezing between the former party goers and dodging flying debris, Eileen pulled her charges across the now flooded Main Street Bridge, and headed down Main street, all while keeping her eyes out for the East D street intersection, which would take them back over to South Union Avenue. She knew that once there they would only have to walk two more blocks to the South Union Avenue Bridge, which crossed over the train tracks, but Eileen never thought in a million years that she would have to dodge flying manhole covers to do it.

With the river water quickly pouring out into the streets, it began leaching into every opening that it could find, which included the already swollen sewers. As they began to overflow, the manhole covers danced and bounced, until the river water built up so much pressure that it popped the cast iron covers into the air like they were bottle tops.

As the streets continued to flood, Eileen struggled to pull her troop past hundreds of former thrill seekers in order to reach the South Union Avenue Bridge, which was the Holy Grail for everyone caught downtown. Unfortunately, mixed within the frantic crowd were numerous vehicles, which unceremoniously were baptizing people with the sour smelling flood water as they quickly drove by.

One of those drivers was 38-year-old Joseph William Birrer, who had brought not only his 35-year-old wife Elizabeth and three children to watch the excitement at the South Union Avenue Bridge, but his 16-year-old Niece Elsie as well. When Joseph had first heard about all the excitement down at the Arkansas River, he quickly gathered up his family so they could share in the excitement that was overtaking downtown, but he soon discovered that he had actually put them all in terrible danger.

As the floodwaters began to crash over the disintegrating levees and panic began to spread amongst the formally excited crowd, Joseph began screaming for his children as he grabbed his wife by the hand and began scanning the area. Hearing the urgency in his voice, the kids quickly ran through the frenzied crowd and were soon ushered into the back seat of their family's automobile, as people begged and pulled at them for a ride.

Wiping the rain from his eyes, Joseph quickly joined his family inside their vehicle but when he glanced in his rearview mirror, he

Elsie and Ruth Birrer and their families car-Courtesy of Floyd Birrer Jr.

noticed that his kids looked terrified. With guilt welling up inside him, he took a calming breath before he started his automobile, put it in gear, and began heading towards the bridge.

Trying his best not to hit any of the people who insisted on running down the center of the flooded street, Joseph began thinking about not only his wife and niece but his 18-year-old daughter Ruth and his twin 15-year old son's Lloyd and Floyd. His boys were considered his family's miracle children and right now he was mentally slapping himself for putting them at risk.

The boys were the sole survivors of a surprise set of quadruplets, with poor Floyd being born with not only an enlarged heart but a cleft palate, which was sewn up soon after birth. His son had fought so hard to get where he was, yet now, because of Joseph's own childish desire to show his children a flooded levee, his son might not live long enough to earn that Boy Scout Eagle badge which he had been working so hard on.

Keeping a close eye on the rising water and a tight grip on the steering wheel, Joseph was relieved to discover that the family's car sat up just high enough that it easily drove down the flooded street and up and over the South Union Avenue Bridge, but not everyone was so lucky.

Harry K. Inman, the Superintendent of the Pueblo City Street's and Sewer Department had, unfortunately, found himself stranded on West First Street, frantically trying to get his trucks water-logged engine to turn over. He considered trying to push it the four blocks up to Tenderfoot Hill, where he had already taken his Holt Caterpillar tractor and 12 frantic horses, but he found that he just didn't have the strength.

As the water continued to rise up around him, he wondered if he might still have time to get his tractor and use it to tow his truck up the hill, but then he realized that he would then be risking the loss of not only his work truck, but the tractor as well. Grudgingly leaning back in the driver's seat, Harry watched as swarms of frantic people ran past his staled truck and listened to them scream each time a flash of lightning lit up the sky.

With a loud sigh of utter annoyance, Harry buttoned up his jacket and tried to mentally prepare himself to not only abandon his work truck but face the sudden hailstorm that had just begun to beat against the windshield. Leaving the headlights on to light the way not only for himself but for the people running past him, Harry walked the four blocks up Tenderfoot Hill one last time.

CHAPTER 4

Protesting cattle and the
bravest sister in the world

"Keep moving, and stay on the sidewalk!" Eileen Kelly screamed over the roar of the storm, as she continued to pull her little brother Bernard and his friends down South Union Avenue. She knew that the streets were too dangerous to walk on after watching the steel covers of the manholes pop off, due to the floodwaters overfilling the sewers and she had already watched several people on the street just simply vanish underneath the rising water.

But just when she thought this night couldn't get any worse, the street lights began to flicker.

Fearing that the rising water was beginning to short circuit the nearby power station, the once joyous flood watchers quickly realized that soon their only source of light would be from the occasional automobile headlights or bursts of lightning, which made a few people question if they should even continue walking down the street at all. One of these men was 26 years old Charles Raymond Lewis who looked down at the almost knee-deep water he was standing in and realized that it would be best if he stopped trudging through the water and got inside the nearest building instead.

Charles, who preferred to go by his middle name of Raymond had been having dinner with his 28-year-old cousin Bertie Monroe Lewis, who preferred to be called Bert, when the fire whistle first began to scream from the side of the Water Works building. Curious what all the fuss was about, the two men noticed a crowd walking down South Union Avenue and when they followed them, the two men discovered that not only was the Arkansas River flooding, but the raging water was battering the steel bridge that crossed it.

The party atmosphere they witnessed was extremely appealing to Raymond, who had already been planning for a night on the town anyway, but his cousin Bert decided that he wasn't really in the mood to play in the rain and just wanted to head over to their rooming house and get out of his wet clothes. Seeing that the trolleys were still running, Bert climbed aboard but Raymond decided to stay at the river for just a little while longer, as he had overheard a police officer say that the levees were going to break and he wanted to watch the streets flood.

With a tip of his hat, Bert wished his cousin luck and watched as only a few more people joined him on his trolley ride. As he looked out of the windows he noticed that quite a few trolleys were beginning to fill the streets, and they all appeared to be heading north, away from the North Union Avenue Bridge, and the flooded river.

Leaning over and questioning the Trolley driver, Bert discovered that the Trolleys were normally housed in a parking garage attached to the Power Company's main building, but now that the building was in danger of flooding, the Trolleys were heading for higher ground.

The Arkansas Valley Railway, Light and Power Company sat along the banks of the Arkansas River, at 101 South Victoria Avenue, which was only one block from the now compromised North Union Avenue

Watching the street flood on 3rd and North Main Street

Bridge. The Power Company used its proximity to the river to create its much needed cooling ponds, but now with the levees in danger of breaking, the building might flood and with it, the Trolley's parking garage.

As the last Trolley made its escape to higher ground, the levees soon began to heave and crack, giving the eager party goers the finale that they had been waiting for. With large chunks of rock and cement sliding into the angry river, the putrid smelling flood water was finally free from its confinement, and quickly began claiming the city as its own. Pouring into coal shoots, basement stairways, gutters, sidewalk grates, and squirreling itself down alleys, the water laid claim to everything it touched.

Including the Power Station.

With the lights continuing to flicker, Raymond Lewis realized that he was running out of time. With no way to reach the rooming house, where he was sure his cousin Bert was watching this waterlogged circus from his dry and warm accommodations, Raymond began looking for a way to get out of the flood's path. Noticing a man enter a three-story tall brick building along South Union Avenue, Raymond quickly trudged through the deep water and followed him inside.

Finally out of the pouring rain, Raymond lifted his head and discovered that the building he had just entered, at 130 South Union Avenue, was actually a rooming house. Located only one block south of the North Union Avenue Bridge, and already flooded with ankle deep water, Raymond quickly sloshed over to the front desk, pulled out his wallet, and asked for a room up on the third floor.

With his room key safely in his jacket pocket, Raymond waded back through the flooded lobby and sat down on a nearby couch, which faced the building's large front windows, as he wanted to watch the floodwaters chase people down the street. Drenched to the bone and finding the slow flicker of the dying street lights hypnotizing, Raymond soon laid claim to the entire couch and closed his eyes.

While he drifted off, the fire whistle on the outside of the Water Works building gave out one last shriek, followed by a sad, desperate squeal as the street lights flickered away, leaving the entire city in total darkness. As the rain continued to pummel the thrill seekers, a sudden streak of lightning shot across the sky, causing a sinister reflection not only in the deep water that surrounded everyone but in the front display windows of every store on South Union Avenue as well.

As people began to panic, Bernard's sister Eileen stopped leading her troop down the sidewalk and pushed them tightly against a nearby building, fearful that they would be knocked into the rising water, which is when she noticed a soft glow breaking through the darkness. Wiping her rain soaked hair out of her eyes, she quickly realized that the glow was coming from around the Union Depot, which meant that they were getting close to the bridge.

Using the next bolt of lightning as her guide, Eileen was finally able to discover where the crowd had congregated and, seeing her chance, grabbed Bernard by the arm and began leading her group towards the light, which soon revealed the outline of the South Union Avenue Bridge. As her troop began walking up out of the floodwaters and onto the center of the bridge, Eileen realized that the glow wasn't coming from the Depot itself, but instead from the headlights and illuminated interiors of passenger trains that were still sitting in the train yard.

Suddenly, like the blast of a canon, a violent crack of thunder shook the bridge, which was immediately followed by a fresh deluge of rain, treating Eileen and her troop like ants caught in a waterfall. Once again grabbing her little brother, she started to run across the bridge but was caught off guard by something the glowing light wanted to show her.

Looking over the side of the bridge, she could make out not only the shapes of three trains sitting on the tracks but figures of men frantically wading through mud and barking orders that were muffled out by the storm. As the next bolt of lightning lit up the sky, her glance was shifted over to the edge of South Union Avenue, where Eileen noticed a wave of thick, muddy water pouring down into the train yard.

They needed to get those trains out of here.

And nobody could agree more than Conductor Calvin Groves.

Conductor Groves, of the Denver & Rio Grande No. 3 had been standing inside the second floor dispatcher's office in Union Depot with 44-year-old Robert Theodore Boxwell, who was the Conductor of the Missouri Pacific No. 14, and 41-year-old Elijah Alvert Bruner, the Conductor of the Manifest Freight train No.62, when the lights inside the office had first begun to flicker.

As the conductors grabbed their flashlights, in anticipation of the room growing dark, their concerns about the storm were interrupted by the Telegraph Operator, who began reading aloud an incoming message. As the room quieted, he informed the men that the levee at the West Fourth Street Viaduct, near the State Mental Hospital had just collapsed, which meant that very soon the others would follow suit and the city would surely flood.

As the men began discussing their options, the lights in the room once again flickered and then began to dim. With a stern expression, Conductor Groves looked over at Dispatcher Stearns and demanded that he allow the Denver & Rio Grande No. 3 to leave the train yard for higher ground. As the two men began to argue, the lights in the room quickly flared up with an unusual brightness, before going out completely and leaving the room cloaked in total darkness.

Which is when they heard the screams.

Clicking on their flashlights, the men ran out into the hallways and noticed a group of waterlogged people coming up the stairs to the second floor, which promoted the Depot staff to run and gather towels and hot coffee. Sitting down on a nearby bench, a few of the people began talking about the levee at the North Union Avenue Bridge collapsing and trapping them in the rising water. Grabbing the

Dispatcher by the shoulder, Conductor Groves spun him around and demanding that he make the call.

Running back to his office, Dispatcher Stearns quickly contacted the Yard Master and soon learned that the track the Missouri Pacific was on was clear and that the train would be able to leave the station if the conductor chose to do so, but unfortunately, the Manifest No. 62 was blocking the Denver & Rio Grande from leaving. The No. 62, which was pulling 46 cars of freight had its engine and a few of his lead cars parked across a switch, but the Dispatcher assured Conductor Groves that with a little nudging from the engine, its cars could be bumped back away from the blocked switch without much trouble.

With all the men in agreement, instructions were immediately given to the Switch Foreman, 33-year-old David Moses Wilson, to take a few of his men over to the roundhouse and bring engine No. 605 around to the Denver & Rio Grande No. 3 for coupling, as it had been removed when the No. 3 had first arrived.

Joining Foreman Wilson on his trip up to the Roundhouse, was 53-year old Engineer Madison Champness Coffey, 34-year-old Fireman Ira Imri Hupp, 41-year-old Conductor Joseph Nathaniel Miller and 31-year-old Fireman Ernest Patterson Alexander, who had been instructed to retrieve engine No. 632, and use it to move some of the coal cars up to higher ground.

Pleased to hear that Foremen Wilson was heading to the roundhouse to retrieve the engine for the Denver & Rio Grande No. 3 , Conductor Calvin Groves buttoned up his coat, grabbed his flashlight, and followed the other two Conductors down the dark staircase and out to their waiting trains.

Satisfied that he had handled the flood news professionally, Dispatcher Brutus Stearns was surprised to hear a knock on his office door, as well as hearing the voice of a man asking if he could please speak to him. Illuminated by the light of his oil lamp, Dispatcher Stearns opened his door and discovered two men who appeared to be soaked to the bone, with one of them wishing to tell him a rather peculiar story.

After introducing himself as the Conductor of a train that had been due to arrive in Pueblo hours before, he explained that because of excessive water, mud, and debris covering the tracks, he had sent his train back to the Swallows Depot, while he continued on to Pueblo using only a handcart, as he felt it was his duty to check the safety of the tracks so he could report on their condition.

Studying the shivering men, who were obviously numb from the cold, Dispatcher Stearns politely listened to the Conductor's report, before thanking him and his crewman for their dedication and concern for the safety of his passengers, and then sending them off to find warm clothes and a hot meal. He didn't have the heart to inform them that the Swallows Depot had called in the report almost two hours earlier, informing the Dispatcher that the two men were on their way.

As the men left the office and headed back downstairs, Dispatcher Stearns noticed that they had left rather large puddles of water on his office carpet, which caused him to question if the first floor of the Depot was taking on water. Heading downstairs, the Dispatcher soon discovered that indeed it was, and its arrival had resulted in a ballet of organized chaos.

Amidst the raised voices, Union Depot employees were quickly stacking items on top of tables and bar tops, while the express and baggage men were loading packages, traveling bags, and trunks onto trucks parked outside. As the Dispatcher continued to walk through the ankle deep water and into the main waiting room, he reassured everyone that the water wouldn't rise more than it did during the flood of 1894, which only reached a depth of 12 inches, but thanked everyone for their combined efforts.

As Dispatcher Stearns headed back upstairs to his dry, second-floor office, Conductor Elijah Bruner of

The Manifest No. 62, was busy using his train's engine to bump his train cars away from the blocked switch, which would not only allow the Denver & Rio Grande No. 3 to be coupled with its inbound engine, but also give Conductor Bruner a chance to get his own train out of the yard before the water got to deep.

Dispatcher Brutus Stearns might not have thought the storm and rising water was a big deal, but one man who did was 43-year-old James Hezekiah Clagett.

James Clagett was a passenger on the Denver & Rio Grande No.3 and had seen enough disasters in his life that he knew when to run for the hills. During his travels as a Coal Inspector and salesman for The Solvay Coke Company, he had seen car accidents, Cyclones, and lightning strikes, which is why he was removing his baggage from the train's sleeper compartment and heading for higher ground.

When the passengers of train No. 3 were first told that they would be having a possible 10-hour delay, due to the storm, James had left the train to stretch his legs and take a look at the flooded river. Walking just a couple of blocks up to the North Union Avenue Bridge and squeezing past the party goers, he saw that not only was the water less than six inches from the top of the levee but that a dam, made up of debris, had clogged itself underneath the steel bridge.

Quickly heading back to Union Depot, James Clagett re-entered The Denver & Rio Grande train, grabbed his suitcases, and began warning the other passengers about the possibility of a flood. As they laughed off his prophecy, James reminded them of the Eden train crash of August 7, 1904, which sent over 100 people to their deaths when the Missouri Pacific Flyer No. 11 was washed away in a flash flood near Fountain Creek.

The Eden train crash- Courtesy of The Pueblo County Historical Society

The train stop at Eden, which was less than five miles north of Pueblo's Union Depot, had been experiencing a deluge of rain that night but despite the warnings, the Conductor still chose to cross the bridge over the swollen creek. As the wooden train bridge began to collapse, the locomotive and first three train cars were pulled into the raging water. Fortunately, the airline cable between the third and fourth Pullman cars snapped from the weight, which immediately triggered the brakes and kept the remaining three Pullman cars safely on the tracks.

And James Clagett had a terrible feeling that the Denver & Rio Grande No. 3 was going to suffer the same fate.

Pointing off into the distance, James informed his fellow train passengers that when the No. 3 train finally pulled away from Union Depot, the track it would take ran right alongside Fountain Creek, and since the Arkansas River was flooding, it meant that Fountain Creek was also flooding. After traveling through all 10 train cars and begging people to head for higher ground, he was disappointed to discover that only two women agreed to gather up their belongings and follow him up onto the Bluffs.

And it wasn't a minute too soon.

With the Manifest No. 62 now clear of the switch, the Denver & Rio Grande No. 3 was quickly coupled up to engine No. 605 and with Dispatcher Brutus Stearns announcing that the train was cleared to leave the station, the last call was made for passengers to board. With large puffs of smoke rising out of the stack, and a celebratory blow of the train whistle, Engineer David Wilson began moving the train down the waterlogged track, just as a majestic bolt of lightning once again lit up the sky.

As The Denver & Rio Grande No. 3 headed out of the train yard and towards the Santa Fe Bridge, Conductor Elijah Bruner of the Manifest watched it pass and could see through the windows that its passengers appeared to be celebrating, as they danced and laughed inside their heated Pullman cars.

Conductor Bruner understood why the No. 3 was chosen to leave ahead of him, but it didn't ease his mind. The Denver & Rio Grande No. 3 was coupled to only 10 cars, where his train was coupled to 46, but while the passengers of the No. 3 were sitting high and dry inside their heated coaches, Conductor Bruner's own passengers were getting drenched.

Of the cars the Manifest Freight train No. 62 was pulling, seven of those were full of cattle, which had been loudly mooing their protests for hours. The gapped wooden slats of the cars originally meant for ventilation, had been allowing heavy rain and hail to pummel the animals inside, which made him wonder how many of them would actually survive this trip.

As the Denver & Rio Grande train No. 3 began to fade from sight, a yardman climbed aboard The Manifest and informed Conductor Bruner that he would be following the same tracks as the Missouri Pacific, instead of the No. 3. With an uncaring shrug of his shoulders, the Conductor gave out a celebratory blow of his whistle just as the man exited his train, allowing him to begin pushing his engine through the debris infused water that now covered the tracks and head towards the Santa Fe Bridge.

Unfortunately, after only traveling the length of a few city blocks Conductor Bruner caught sight of a red signal lantern swinging wildly ahead of him, which caused him to stop his train just within sight of the Missouri No. 14. As the rain continued to pound against his train, he watched as the red lantern jumped down into the now waist deep water, waded towards the No. 62 and climbed aboard, all while attached to the hand of a frantic crewman.

"The Santa Fe Bridge in unpassable! You have to back up!" The crewman yelled as the pounding rain tried its best to silence the man's message. "The No. 14 and the No. 3 are going to try and switch over to the Missouri Pacific transfer track, but you have to back up!"

"If I'm only blocking the No. 14, then why isn't the No.3 already using it?" Conductor Bruner yelled back, as he could see that the train was still sitting on the adjacent track.

"The switch is blocked with storm debris!" the crewman responded, as he got ready to disembark the Manifest. "We have a crew trying to free it now, but I still need you to back up!"

Agreeing to follow the man's request, Conductor Bruner watched as the crewman and his lantern jumped down into the rising water and headed back out into the storm, but just as the Conductor began setting things in motion, he heard what sounded like another train whistle. Turning towards the sound, Conductor Bruner noticed that a single engine had just pulled up to the Denver & Rio Grande train No. 3, from a side track, and stopped.

Knowing that this engine's arrival couldn't be a good sign, Conductor Bruner slid on his coat and grabbed his flashlight, before he jumped down into the waist deep water himself. Entering the engine of the Denver & Rio Grande No. 3, Conductor Bruner found himself standing next to not only Conductor Groves of the No. 3 and Conductor Boxwell from the No. 14, but 53-year old Switch Foreman Winslow Watts Deaton.

"If you can't get that switch cleared, you will have to cross the bridge! You can't come back to the Depot!" Foremen Deaton informed the men, as he tried to talk over the roar of the storm.

"We can't cross the bridge!" Conductor Calvin Groves explained, as he pointed towards the angry cascade of water catapulting over the steel frame of the Santa Fe train bridge. "Hell, we don't even know if the entire bridge is even still even there!"

"Let me try to get the Missouri over the bridge, while your men keep trying to unblock the switch." Foreman Deaton suggested as he shook some more rain off his coat. "You just can't take any of these trains back to the Depot, you just can't!"

With a nervous nod of agreement, Conductor Boxwell led Foreman Deaton over to the Missouri No. 14, while Conductor Bruner headed back to the Manifest No. 62, to wait for further instructions.

But the train yards were not the only area's around Pueblo that were flooding

Luckily, a Boy Scout is always prepared.

Stationed at the bottom steps of the Pueblo County Courthouse, located at 215 West 10th Street, a storm drenched Boy Scout held a lantern up as high as he could, while repeatedly yelling for people to seek shelter inside the building. As he tried to put on a brave face and not flinch every time a bolt of lightning streaked across the sky, he continued to remind himself that what he was doing was saving lives. The rest of his fellow Scouts were stationed at every street corner from the Courthouse to the Main Street Bridge, which created a seven block long chain illuminated by lanterns and flashlights.

With a single Scout standing alone on the corner of each block, the boys wrapped one arm around the closest street sign, while using their free hand to hold their lantern's high, all while screaming for people to follow the lights. As the floodwater continued to rise, the Scouts closest to the Main Street Bridge gradually had to abandon their posts, which is what the hundreds of volunteers in Pepper Sauce Bottoms and the Grove were about to do.

With the water now over waist deep, the volunteers in the low lying squatter towns were becoming so desperate that they were now resorting to breaking down doors and dragging people out of their homes, as so many of the residents were simply refusing to head for higher ground. One group of volunteers, after dragging a woman from her flooded home, watched in shock as she managed to not only wiggle free from their grasp, but dive underneath the water, and hide in her houses crawl space.

Wiping the water from their eyes once more, the volunteers were just about to give up when they heard what sounded like a child screaming.

Followed by a shotgun blast.

In a panic, the men began to quickly wade towards the repeating blasts, but the screaming fell silent by the time they reached the house. Kicking open the front door, and cautiously shining their flashlights inside the flooded home, the men saw furniture and children's toys floating around in the deep, icy water, as well as the blood soaked body of a man who appeared to be holding a gun.

Checking the man for life, and not finding any, the volunteers suddenly realized that they recognized him. Earlier in the evening, they had attempted to evacuate an Austrian man and his family but the man had refused to leave, saying that he had just paid a year's rent and that nothing would make him abandon his home.

As the volunteers continued to shine their flashlights around in the ever rising water, they began calling out for the man's wife and children, which is when one of the volunteers felt something touch his leg. Jumping back a little, he looked down to see what looked like a doll floating around under the water. Grabbing at the assumed toy and lifting it partially out of the water, the man was shocked to see the face of a child, frozen in fear, as its body leaked blood into the water.

Quickly pulling up the child and placing it onto a nearby kitchen table, the volunteers checked for life but found that none remained. Continuing to check the house, they soon discovered the bodies of the man's wife and two more children, which they carefully laid on top of the table before leaving and closing the door behind them.

CHAPTER 5

Waterlogged shoes and a box full of chickens

"Mama! Mama! Wake up, we have to go!" Jacob Blatnick yelled at his 49-year-old mother Mary, as his sisters began putting on their shoes. At 27 years old, Jacob was the oldest of the four kids and after his father died in 1908, he had become the man of the house at the ripe old age of 15.

Jacob, who worked at the Steel mill as a fireman, was shocked to find that not only had his family refused to evacuate their home in the Grove, at 903 East B Street but that his mother was sound asleep upstairs. As he ran up to his mother's room to wake her, his 15-year-old sister Stephanie followed close behind, explaining to him that they thought the evacuation orders were just rumors.

"A few of the neighbors stopped by and said that the river was flooding and that we needed to evacuate, but Mama said we would be fine because we were next to the Bluffs," Stephanie explained, as Jacob woke up their mother. "We did bring things up from the basement and set them on the porch, but only because of all the rain."

"It's true that the Bluffs near our house can keep us safe, but when there is this much rain, they begin acting more like a dam," Jacob explained to his sister, as he helped their mother gather up a few things before heading downstairs. "That's why the water is rising so quickly. Think of the Grove as a big bathtub, but with no drain to pull, which is why we need to get up onto the Bluffs!"

As his family quickly slid on their jackets, Jacob thought that he heard something chirping. Looking around for the source of the sound, he finally shined his flashlight towards his sister Stephanie, who was holding a wooden box in her hands. "We had 10 chicks hatch last night." She added with a smile, as she opened up the peeping box. Glancing inside, Jacob could see a collection of fuzzy yellow puffballs attempting to hide underneath a very confused looking mother Hen.

With a slight laugh at the sight of his little sister's chosen item to save, Jacob finished draping his mother and sisters, 24-year-old Anna, 21-year-old Kerstina, and 15-year-old Stephanie, as well as her box of chickens, with blankets before taking them out into the storm. Stepping onto their home's front porch, Jacob's family got their first good look at the waist deep water that had filled the Grove, while reminding them that they needed to hold their blankets up high and to keep moving.

As a flash of lightning danced above their heads, Jacob was thankful that not only was his family's home only a block from the Bluffs but that the Bluffs also held a section of Railroad track which ran across the top. Helping his family up out of the water and onto the track, Jacob began shining his flashlight down both sides, which is when he spotted a set of old cattle cars. Grabbing his mother's hand, Jacob led his family down to the cars, where he tugged at each door until he found one that easily slid open.

After helping his family inside, he handed his mother the chickens, blankets and flashlights while apologizing for the roof of the cattle car only having a few boards, as his sisters were already searching for the driest spots. Before sliding the door closed, he informed his mom that he was heading back into the Grove to search for more people, as he had a feeling that it wasn't just his own family that had refused to heed the warnings.

All Jacob Blatnick wanted to do was save as many people as he could.

But Engineer Madison Coffey just wanted to save his crew.

While the conductors of the Denver & Rio Grande No. 3, and the Manifest No. 62 sat in their trains waiting to see if Switch Foreman Winslow Deaton would be able to get the Missouri No. 14 across the flooded Santa Fe Bridge, Engineer Coffey was busy trying to find a safe place to park engine No. 632, so it wouldn't capsize in the rising water.

During all the chaos involved in getting the Denver & Rio Grande No. 3 coupled up to engine No. 605, 53-year-old Engineer Madison Coffey, and his three-man crew had joined Foreman Wilson up to the Roundhouse, as they also had an engine to retrieve. Where Foreman Wilson had been instructed to bring out engine No.605, Engineer Coffey had been instructed to retrieve engine No. 632, and use it to move some of the coal cars up to the higher ground.

When Engineer Coffey and his firemen Ira Hupp and Ernest Alexander, along with his Conductor Joseph Miller had first arrived at the roundhouse, the standing water on the tracks was only about ankle deep but was much deeper along the sides, where it had already begun to pool.

After taking engine No. 632 out of the Roundhouse, the men were able to move the first set of coal cars over to a new track, but when Engineer Madison Coffey headed the engine over to retrieve the next set of coal cars, his men discovered that they were unable to couple them, as the water in the yard was too deep.

Defeated, Engineer Coffey and his men waded back through the now knee deep water, climbed back aboard the engine, and decided to have a serious discussion about the storm. As another bolt of lightning lit up the sky, Engineer Coffey and his men began debating about not just the coal cars, but about which set of tracks they thought would give them the best chance of keeping their engine upright in case the water continued to rise.

Deciding on an area almost 600 yards away from the Roundhouse, Engineer Coffey maneuvered the Engine through the mud infused water, with the train's cattle catcher creating a magnificent fountain as it headed down the track. The area the men had decided on was located near the western rim of the Grove, where the tracks and railroad ties were deeply embedded in concrete, instead of sand, which they hoped would prove to be more stable.

Arriving at their final destination and watching the water continue to rise around the engine, the men began to wonder if the Denver & Rio Grande No. 3 and the Missouri Pacific No. 14 had made it safely over the Santa Fe Bridge, and out of this nasty storm.

But they hadn't.

As colossal waves of water continued to batter the steel train bridge, the Denver & Rio Grande No. 3 found itself still parked at the blocked Missouri Transfer Switch, with its headlamp illuminating not only the constant downpour of rain outside but the piles of storm debris that the crew was frantically trying to clear from the blocked switch.

Sitting next to the No.3, on a parallel track, was the Missouri No. 14, whose headlamp was illuminating the torrent of flood water that was catapulting over the Santa Fe Bridge. With the transfer switch still not clear, Engineer Asa Harris, of the No. 14, found himself still arguing with Switch Foreman Winslow Deaton, who insisted on taking the No. 14 over the compromised Bridge.

"It isn't safe! Even if the bridge is still standing, which nobody knows if it even is, those waves could flip over all the Pullmans, and take the engine with it!" Engineer Harris explained as he pointed out the front window of the parked train. "We have to back up and go back to the Depot!"

"We can't go back to the Depot!" Switch Foreman Deaton reminded the Engineer, as he pointed towards the back of the train. "Did you forget that there is a Freight train parked behind you? Do you have any idea how long it would take the Manifest to push its 46 cars back to the Depot! We have all run out of time! We have to try to cross the bridge!"

As an angry silence filled the engine, Engineer Harris looked over at Conductor Robert Boxwell and asked him to make the call. With a glance back out of the engines front window and with a heavy sigh, he agreed to cross the bridge.

With the Missouri getting ready to make its attempt, Conductor Calvin Groves of the Denver & Rio Grande train No. 3 and his Engineer David Wilson finally accepted defeat, and gave up on clearing the blocked switch. With the water still rising and the rain refusing to stop, the men watched with waited breath to see if the Missouri could cross the flooded Santa Fe Bridge and bring an end to this nightmare

It couldn't.

As Conductor Groves held his head down in defeat, he noticed that the lights inside his engine were beginning to flicker. Raising his head, he looked around and was able to catch the last beam of light escape his head lamps before his engine went dark. As the storm continued to wail outside, Conductor Groves leaned out of his engine compartment and was unable to see any light coming from his Pullmans, or anywhere else.

As screams quickly filled the Pullman cars, Porters began lighting lanterns and tried their best to calm everyone down. As some began to pray, it was revealed that the floodwaters had short-circuited the train's batteries, which were located underneath the cars. As expected, when the Missouri No. 14 limped back off the bridge and once again found itself parked next to the No. 3, it was also no longer illuminated.

With both trains lacking interior lights, as well as headlamps, the only light to be seen from either was from the Porters, who were carrying lanterns from car to car. With nothing to do but wait, the passengers began to question what might be happening outside their stalled trains and what the rest of Pueblo must be dealing with.

One person who was dealing with the flood, but not enjoying it at all, was a battered and bruised 25-year-old woman named Helen Welch.

Helen was working at the Colonial Theatre, at 218 North Union Avenue, when the fire siren first began to scream out its warning. Her uncles, 40-year-old William Henry Foster, and his brother, 37-year-old Ira Clyde Foster had the Theatre built only ten years earlier, after purchasing a prime, downtown plot near the North Union Avenue Bridge and it was their pride and joy.

To be closer to work, Helen and her family had rented apartments only a block away, which were located inside the Labor Union Temple building. This beautiful four-story tall building housed Whitton's Undertaking Company and The Sutton Mercantile Company on the first floor, while renting out apartments and meeting rooms on the upper three. It also sported 3 ½ foot thick sandstone walls, making it one of the most formidable structures in the city, which paired well with the newly built Memorial hall, which was less than two blocks away.

When the fire sirens first began to wail, The Colonial Theatre was full of patrons, but Helen didn't really pay it any mind, as rainstorms were always good for business. Eager to get out of the weather, people would happily buy a ticket to a show, if it meant a few hours of dry and warm entertainment. After selling the last tickets for that night's show, Helen told her uncles that she was going to head over to the Temple building and check on her aunts, but would be back as soon as she could.

Turning to look out the front windows of the Theatre, Helen noticed people dancing and playing in the waterlogged streets, as she began slipping on her jacket. Heading out into the storm, she was surprised to discover that the water was splashing up over her ankles, causing her to struggle a bit just to keep her balance, as she was wearing her favorite pair of T-strapped leather shoes.

As she continued to walk down the sidewalk, she started to hear an odd banging noise coming from the street. Looking around for the source of the noise, she finally noticed that the manhole covers were jumping and banging against the iron rim of the manhole, like an angry pot threatening to boil over. As she curiously watched the manhole covers pop and dance, she suddenly realized that it was caused by the storm drains being so full of rain water that the pressure of the water was pushing up against the covers.

She just hoped that the lids didn't float away, as it would give someone a terrible fright if they accidentally fell into an open manhole.

Finally arriving at the Temple building, and shaking the rain from her jacket, Helen slid off her shoes and headed upstairs to check on her two aunt's, Blanche and Irene. After explaining to them that their husbands were fine and just finishing up at the Theatre, Helen headed back downstairs, confident that her two 33-year-old aunts could handle being in their apartments alone for just a little while longer.

Sliding her waterlogged shoes back on and reluctantly walking out the front door of the Temple building, Helen was suddenly faced with not only knee deep water but a street comprised of utter chaos. The rain-filled sky, once a joy to so many people, now echoed with the shriek of high pitched police whistles, as officers ordered the once festive party-goers off the North Union Avenue Bridge, while directing them to seek higher ground.

As Helen stood on the sidewalk, she watched as people attempted to run through the deep water and fall, only to get back up and fall once more. She heard people screaming over the sound of the fire whistle, while desperate drivers repeatedly honked their horns in an attempt to clear the frantic crowd off the bridge, so they could have room to drive out of this soggy madhouse.

But Helen needed to get back to the Theatre.

Carefully wading through the rising water, Helen finally reached the safety of the Theatre but discovered that the flood had already begun to claim it. With the lobby taking on water, she noticed that her uncles had already laid their prized $350 Electric Piano on top of a wooden table, in an attempt to keep it dry, as well as their collection of coin operated candy dispensers that were always filled with such wonderful treats.

Finding her Uncles William and Ira up near the stage, Helen began describing to them what she had just walked through just to get to the Theatre and felt that the thick stone walls of their apartment building would be the safest place for them to be. Following their niece into the Theatre's lobby to see the rising water for themselves, the two men stood in shocked silence as they watched the chaos unfold in front of their own eyes.

It was time to go.

Grabbing their jackets, and turning off the lights, the trio took one more look at the inside of their beloved Theatre before heading outside into the storm, locking the door behind them as they left. Stepping out onto the sidewalk, Helen and her uncles instantly found themselves standing in such rapidly flowing water, that they had to brace themselves against the buildings as they walked towards their apartment.

Unfortunately, once they reached the intersection the trio suddenly realized that they were facing a major problem. With the swiftly flowing current racing down the flooded streets and with no buildings to hold onto for support, the deep water threatened to wash them away before they could ever reach the sidewalk on the other side.

Deciding to lock arms and step off the sidewalk together, the group carefully placed their feet down, but the strong current took advantage of the instability of Helen's heeled leather shoes and quickly washed her off her feet. As the swiftly flowing floodwaters pushing her out into the middle of the busy street, her uncles began to inch themselves towards her just as Helen managed to stand back up, only to get knocked off her feet a second time.

Hearing the sound of a car horn, Helen looked up just as a vehicle sped by, splashing a fountain of water over both her and the frantic crowd that continued to rush past. Finally finding her footing, Helen was able to stand once more, and take a few wobbly steps, before suddenly vanishing underneath the water.

Shocked, her uncles watched as the floodwaters quickly popped Helen back out of the uncovered manhole and dropped her back onto the flooded street with a victorious splash. Coughing and spitting out water, Helen managed to sit back up, only to be caught in a swiftly flowing current that launched her against a nearby building, located at the corner of Union Avenue and Richmond Street.

Wading over to their niece, who was once again struggling to stand, William and Ira managed to grab hold of her arms, and together they carefully lifted her up out of the rising water. As Helen raised her left hand, to brush the hair out of her face, they noticed all the blood.

Not knowing how badly she was hurt, William and Ira kept Helen pressed up against the buildings as they walked her the remaining half a block to the Temple Building, where they struggled to pull the door open against the rising water. Finally inside, and closing the door behind them, they carefully helped Helen up to their 3rd-floor apartment.

Seeing Helen's bloody, and waterlogged clothes immediately sent Helen's aunt's into a panic, as she was quickly helped into the bathroom to be cleaned up. Intending on keeping their nieces dignity intact, Blanche and Irene chased their husbands out, before carefully removing Helen's blood stained clothes.

While cleaning their nieces wounds, they not only discovered that Helen's right wrist was possibly broken and that she had torn open her left hand, but her entire left side was covered in a grisly collection of bloody skin tears and quickly forming bruises.

But she would live.

As would the employees at the Telephone Company

Located only a block south of the Power Company, at 112 West D Street, the three story tall brick building which held the Mountain States Telephone Company was a tornado of organized chaos. Sitting at their stations and sending out as many distress calls as they could, the Telephone girls were pulling plugs faster than they ever had before, because this time, lives depended on it.

When the fire siren on the side of the Waters Works building first began to scream out its warnings, and the people of Pueblo learned that it was due to a flood and not a fire, the Phone girls found themselves overwhelmed with distress calls. Josephine D. Pryor, the 47-year-old Day Chief Operator, Margaret Williams, the 35-year-old Night Chief Operator, and Byron Ernest Thady, the 20-year-old Night Wire Chief quickly found themselves not only in charge of the day shift operators but the night shift as well.

Byron Thady- Authors personal collection

Every hand on deck.

At 7:30 pm and with the flood warnings in full swing, the three story Mountain States Telephone Company building contained 39 telephone operators, two Chief Operators, one Wire Chief, and 12-year-old Helen G. Engle, who promised to stay quiet while her sister worked. Helen's sister, 30-year-old Adalina C Engle, who went by the name Lena, had been in charge of her youngest sibling when the fire siren first sounded out its alarm, and with no time to take her home, she brought Helen to work with her.

As the water began to rise and the flood began to overtake downtown, the calls went from people being interested in why the fire siren was going off, to shrieks and people pleading for help. The calls upset so many of the girls that some began to panic, which is when Byron Thady would take the headset and try to speak some words of encouragement to the caller.

Which is when a few of the girls began questioning Byron Thady's wet pant legs.

Drenched to his knees, but not wishing to scare the girls any further, Byron simply returned their inquiries with a polite smile, before heading back down to the flooded first floor to retrieve more boxes of records and whatever phone equipment he could safely carry back up the stairs. Unknown to anyone but himself, a large tree branch had broken out one of the first-floor windows, causing a constant flow of mud infused water to pour into the building.

Bringing up yet another box to the second floor, and stacking it against a side wall, Byron was thankful that it was the Telephone Company's policy to blacken out all of the first and second-floor windows. Originally done to prevent sunlight from shining onto the switchboards, tonight it had the added effect of helping to keep the girls more focused, as it prevented them from looking out into the storm.

That was, until the lights began to flicker.

Aware that the rising water was most certainly short circuiting The Arkansas Valley Railway, Light and Power Company, Byron quickly headed back downstairs and started up the Phone Companies emergency generator, so that the Telephone girls wouldn't realize that the power was going out. Intending to appear as though nothing was amiss, Byron grabbed yet another box of phone equipment from the flooded first floor and climbed the stairs up to the second floor where he added the box to his ever growing pile, before locating Mrs. Pryor, the Day Chief operator.

"I've started the generator, but I'm not sure how long it will keep the lights on, so you might as well send the girls up to the third floor", Byron suggested, as he prepared to head back downstairs for more boxes. "I don't know how high this water is going to get."

As Mrs. Pryor began sending the girls up to the third floor, some of them began raiding the cafeteria, while others grabbed the break room's hand-wound Victrola record player, as well as all the records, so they could keep themselves entertained.

Seeing that the telephone girls were calmly walking up the stairs, Byron headed back down to the flooded first floor where he noticed that the lights were already beginning to wane. Wading to the flooded engine room, which held the generator, Byron frantically began looking around the room for a flashlight or a lantern before the lights went out.

Not finding either, Byron looked around the engine room for something he could make a lantern with, as he was quickly running out of options. Spotting an oil can, as well as an old work shirt, he grabbed them and quickly set them onto a nearby workbench. After tearing the shirt into a long strip, Byron unscrewed the top of the oil can, sat it down on the bench, and using a nearby screwdriver and hammer, poked a decent size hole into its top.

Setting the top aside, he then grabbed the ripped up shirt and shoved it into the oil-filled can until the fabric was thoroughly saturated, before pulling one end of it up out of the can. Grabbing the can's top, he threaded the oil soaked shirt through the newly formed hole and screwed the lid tightly back onto the can.

And with one strike of a match, Byron's homemade oil lamp was complete.

Shoving the extra matches into his shirt pocket, Byron Thady waded out of the engine room, set the lamp on a nearby shelf, and grabbed another piece of phone equipment, which he carried up the stairs to the now dark second floor.

With almost everything Byron deemed important now sitting high and dry, Byron Thady headed back down the stairs one final time, this time to retrieve the Cable records, the most important of all the companies' documents. The records, which were inside a set of binders, not only contained the names, addresses, and phone numbers of every single one of The Mountain States Telephone Company's Pueblo customers but also all the codes and points where the phone lines connected to the company's main distribution frame.

Byron Thady had left the Cable records for last, as he knew that the binders were inside one of the first floor offices, and since that door had remained shut, Byron was pretty confident that the room had remained at least partially dry.

Arriving back on the first floor, Byron quickly noticed that yet another first floor window had been knocked out and the water was now almost up to his waist and rising fast. Grabbing his oil lamp, Byron waded over to the coveted office, sat his homemade oil lamp onto a nearby cabinet, and tried to pull open the office door, but it barely gave an inch.

With an annoyed sigh, Byron realized that the pressure of the water inside the flooded building was pushing itself against the door, holding it shut. Letting go of the doorknob, he began wading through the room looking for something to pry the door open with.

Pushing aside floating furniture, and random debris, Byron finally spotted a sturdy piece of wood that had washed into the building, which he quickly grabbed and floated over towards the office door. With one foot braced against the door frame, Byron succeeded in inching the door open just enough that he could slide the end of the wooden board inside, which he then used to pry the door open.

Lifting the board a few feet above the rising water and jamming it between the edge of the door and the frame, Byron Thady quickly grabbed his oil lamp, ducked underneath the board, and slid into the office. As the floodwaters eagerly poured into the once dry room, Byron waded over to the fireproof cabinet, unhooked the latch, and began grabbing the binders, which is when he noticed that the water level around him had stopped rising.

Looking back towards the office door, he was disgusted to see that it was once again shut.

With no need to hurry, and beyond exhausted, Byron put the binders back inside the cabinet and decided to take a break. Wading over to the desk, he sat down on its top and listened as the rain and hail pounded against the windows, while a rumble of thunder shook the sky. As he focused on the sound, he thought he could hear people screaming, but with the windows of the office darkened, he could really only speculate about what was actually going on outside.

Which is when he heard the crash.

Grabbing his oil lamp and turning it towards the noise, he noticed that a large tree branch had poked a hole in the office's window. As the water began seeping in, the gnarled end of the branch began rocking back in forth inside the fractured glass like a ship caught in a storm.

In a panic, Byron waded over to the cabinet, grabbed the cable records, and headed back over to the office door. Setting them and the oil lamp down on a nearby shelf, he managed to turn the doorknob just as the tree branch finished breaking through the window.

CHAPTER 6

The blood soaked hero and a warehouse full of lanterns

With the never ending storm still pounding against the parked trains, many of the passengers inside the Missouri No. 14 and the Denver & Rio Grande No. 3 had already crawled into their sleeping compartments and gone to bed, while Conductor Elijah Bruner of the Manifest No. 62 was defying orders and heading back to Union Depot.

Despite Switch Foreman Deaton insisting that the conductors couldn't return their trains to the Depot, due to the high water, Conductor Bruner felt that he had no other option. Where the other two trains had the privilege of keeping their passengers warm and dry inside their Pullman cars, the passengers being hauled by the Manifest were in danger of drowning.

Of all of his freight cars, seven of them were full of cattle and he couldn't,

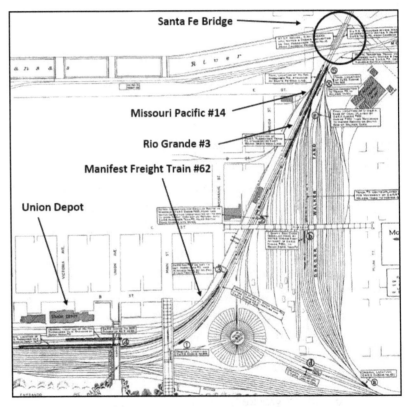

Train yard map showing the location of the three trains, the Santa Fe bridge and the Union Depot when the first flood hit- Courtesy of The Pueblo County Historical Society

with a good conscience, allow them to drown without at least trying to save them. If he could just get his train back to Union Depot he could unload them onto the passengers loading platform and give them a fighting chance.

After all, they were just cows, not timber wolves.

Deciding not to follow the Manifest back to the Depot and instead choosing to wait out the storm at the foot of the Santa Fe Bridge, the crews inside the two passenger trains focused instead on keeping people calm, which was not an easy task. As the water outside the trains continued to rise, the Pullman cars began to rock and sway with the current which caused both the No. 3 and the No. 14 to continually bump into each other, as they were sitting only a few feet apart on parallel tracks.

As the clocks chimed the 10 pm hour, three waiters from the Denver & Rio Grande Train No. 3 began to notice that their dining car was beginning to take on water. Walking across the damp carpet, 31-year old Robert John Lewis cracked open the car's vestibule door to see how the storm was doing and heard what sounded like muffled screaming. Looking towards the Missouri No. 14, Robert noticed that the interior gas lamps inside their Pullman cars were no longer illuminated, which he found odd, as the Porter's inside the Rio Grande No. 3 had simply lowered their lights so their passengers could sleep, instead of extinguishing them.

Clicking his flashlight to life and shining its beam towards the Missouri, Robert felt his stomach drop, just as a bolt of lightning helped confirm the scene that was playing out in front of him. Laying on their sides and swaying in the strong current was a collection of the Missouri's Pullman cars with dozens of passengers swarming across the overturned coaches and it appeared as if they were heading towards the engine.

Riding the car's like a cowboy on a bucking bronco, and guided by the faint glow of a lantern, a small group of passengers managed to reach the engine compartment of the No. 14 and attempted to climb inside. Expecting to find the engine compartment dry, the passengers were shocked to find that not only was Engineer Asa Harris and his crew standing in waist deep water, but the compartment wasn't big enough to accommodate all of the passengers.

With panic setting in and the passengers struggling to find a place to stand, the lever that opened the engines firebox was accidentally stepped on, allowing floodwater to pour onto the burning coals, which resulted in an unexpected blast of steam filling the cabin. Fleeing the engine, and scrambling back towards its attached coal car, Engineer Asa Harris joined the frantic crowd, with 37-year-old passenger Frank Dillon Spicer right behind him.

As the two men continued to follow the passengers past the coal car and back down the overturned Pullman's, Engineer Harris looked over at the Denver & Rio Grande No. 3 and noticed that not only were all of its car's still upright, but three men were standing on the outside vestibule of the dining car.

Attracting the attention of the men, Engineer Harris leaned his body off of the side of the overturned Pullman, and with a gap of only about a foot, he grabbed for the outside handrail of the dining car, but in doing so his feet slipped, and he disappeared in the debris filled water. In a panic, Robert Lewis and his 32-year-old co-workers Earl David Houston and Maxwell Hughlett knelt down and grabbed at the Engineer, pulling him up onto the dining car's platform.

Looking back over at Frank Spicer and motioning for him to reach for Robert's hand, the Pullman cars from the Missouri No. 14 suddenly began to twist and groan as the train's waterlogged engine suddenly capsized, which quickly threw Frank Spicer into the water, along with almost 30 other passengers. Desperate to help, the waiters from the No. 3 attempted to pull the passengers aboard, with Robert Lewis even attempting to jump into the water to save a little girl, but the strong current proved too much for them and the passengers slid right out of the waiter's hands.

As Frank Spicer was washed downstream, he was able to grab hold of a large piece of wood, which he clung to for only a short time, as a large log soon knocked it out of his arms. As Frank frantically tried to keep his head above water, he suddenly felt a sharp nudge on his back, which to his surprise turned out to be the remains of a large, framed house. Eagerly climbing on, Frank accepted his ride and waited to see where it would take him.

With a collection of the Missouri's passengers now floating towards an unknown fate, the waiters from the Denver & Rio Grande No. 3 helped Engineer Asa Harris stand up and lead him into one of their train's first class Pullman cars, which was coupled in front of the Dining car. Motioning for a Porter to fetch Engineer Harris a warm blanket, so he could get out of his wet clothes, the three waiters headed back through their dining car and into the second to last Pullman car to check on the passengers and were disheartened to see that it was also taking on water.

After a quick meeting with the Porters from both the second to last Pullman and the end Pullman, it was agreed that all of the passengers should be moved up to the first class Pullman car that Engineer Harris was now sitting in, as it wasn't yet taking on water. As the Porters began waking up the sleeping passengers, the waiters began moving them through the dining car and towards the first class car, in order to ease the congestion of so many passengers moving through the train at once.

Surprisingly, as Robert Lewis continued to help wake up the passengers, he discovered 76-year-old Margaret Fitzpatrick calmly singing a Hymn while knitting in her seat, and appearing to ignore everything that was going on around her.

"Mam, I am here to escort you and the other passengers to the first class Pullman, where it might be more secure," Robert informed the elderly woman as she continued knitting, never even dropping a stitch. "Mam? Mam? Excuse me, but you are in great danger and I need to get you and the other passengers to the next Pullman car, for your own safety."

Finishing her next stitch, Mrs. Fitzpatrick stopped singing and looked up at Robert with a smile. "Young man, If the Lord wants me to go in this way, it will be his will. I'll be staying right here."

Confused, Robert Lewis left the woman and continued to the next set of passengers, with one of them being 57-year-old Dayton J. Kramer, who was a jeweler from Salida, Colorado. Curious why he was woken up, he sleepily pulled back the curtains of his sleeping compartment to see passengers wading in water that appeared to be several inches deep. Closing the curtain so he could get dressed, Dayton overheard one of the Porters inform the crew of a situation that caused Dayton to quickly slip on his clothes.

"The end Pullman car has over turned and all my people are drowned!" the Porter informed his co-workers, as he pointed back towards the last train car. "I did all I could to save them, but it was no use!"

Shocked, Dayton Kramer quickly slipped on his shoes as he listened to the frantic Porter repeat his experience to anyone who would listen, which included 24-year-old Dallas Cuenin, also of Salida, who was helping his pregnant wife Lydia down the aisle. With his military training taking over, Dallas glanced back towards the location of the submerged train car and asked a Porter if he could please escort his wife to the First class Pullman, as he would join her as soon as possible.

Dallas Cuenin-Authors
personal collection

Against his wife Lydia's objections, Dallas gave her a quick kiss before quickly walking towards the back door of the Pullman car, but unfortunately, he wouldn't get very far.

The sound of the storm was changing

For hours Conductor Calvin Groves of the Denver & Rio Grande No. 3 had been listening to the rain beat against the sides of his engine, while the water that surrounded him continually splashed mud and debris up against his train, but now there was a new sound.

And it was getting closer.

With the train's batteries short-circuited, and no power available to light up his engines headlamp, Conductor Calvin Groves leaned out of the side of his locomotive and hung his small oil lamp into the storm. As he struggled to focus his eyes, he finally noticed a dark, shadowy mass in the distance coming towards his train, filling the air with the growl of continual thunder.

Quickly pulling himself back inside the engine, Conductor Groves immediately grabbed the lever for the steam whistle and let it scream out it's warning, just as the 10 foot wall of water smashed into his train. With a violent shudder, the engine held firm, as its attached Pullman cars quickly lifted up off the tracks and rode the torrent of water like a kite at the end of a string. Still coupled to the train's engine, the Pullman cars swayed and flipped, violently tossing around its occupants like toys, as debris began smashing out the windows.

As the flood continued its attack on both the Denver & Rio Grande No. 3 and the Missouri Pacific No. 14, it rocketed down the already submerged train yard, where it set its sights on its next victim.

Hearing an unfamiliar rumble outside of his train, Conductor Bruner of the Manifest No. 62 shone his flashlight out into the storm, which caught sight of something dark and foreboding heading right towards him. Curious what it could be, he tried to grab the attention of one of his crew to take a look, but by then it was too late.

"Hold onto something!" Conductor Elijah Bruner screamed, as the wall of water slammed into the engine, causing it to rock violently from side to side. As Conductor Bruner and his crew began to pray, the engine and its freight cars quickly capsized, leaving his crew and seven cars full of cattle to the mercy of the storm.

As the cars tumbled and rolled underneath the turbulent water, the cattle cars broke open, releasing almost 200 terrified bovine's into the mess. Able to ride the current and swim for quite a few miles in normal flowing water, the animals that survived the initial impact began searching for higher ground, but quickly found themselves disoriented in the violent storm.

With the floodwaters now overflowing with cattle, and the air filled with the sounds of their terror, Conductor Bruner and his crew held onto the submerged engine as they waited for another lightning strike to illuminate their surroundings. As the desired flash finally revealed the scene playing out in front of them, the men discovered that they were rather close to the South Main Street Bridge, but now they would have to find a way to get over to it.

Counting on the lighting once more, Conductor Bruner and his crew jumped onto a nearby pile of debris, intending to ride it over to the bridge, but only the engineer managed to reach their destination. As the man grabbed hold of the bridge's steel skeleton and struggled to pull himself up out of the turbulent floodwater, he was shocked to discover that although he was now safe, he was alone.

And so was Dallas Cuenin.

Choosing to stay inside the second to last Pullman car of the Denver & Rio Grande Train No. 3, in order to rescue the trapped passengers in the final train car, Dallas felt the horrific impact of the flood as it slammed into the train. Pummeled by suitcases, dishes, bedding and a collection of unidentifiable objects, Dallas sought refuge inside of a sleeper compartment until he felt the Pullman car right itself enough that it was now only rocking from side to side in the rough water.

Stepping back out into the aisle, Dallas was relieved to see that the wall mounted oil lamps were still giving off their warm glow, which allowed him to focus his eyes on the current situation. One of the first things he noticed was that a few of the Pullman car's windows had been knocked out, which was allowing water to pour inside each time it rocked in the current, which reassured him that the Pullman was floating on top of the water instead of underneath it.

But he knew that could soon change.

Glancing back towards the exterior door that would grant him access to the last Pullman and the trapped passengers, Dallas discovered that the door was blocked by many of the items he had been pummeled with earlier. As his Pullman continued to bob and sway in the water, Dallas knew he needed to find another way to the final Pullman, and his car's knocked out windows gave him the exit he was looking for.

Quickly climbing out of the window and onto the top of the Pullman car, Dallas was suddenly faced with not only pounding rain but an onslaught of debris, tree branches, and flaming pieces of lumber that threatened to push him into the water. With the Pullman's oil lamps still shining brightly and giving him the light he needed, Dallas crawled over the car until he reached the rear, which is when he felt his heart skip a beat.

Where was the Pullman?

Where was the God Dam Pullman!

As he held onto the car, he quickly realized that its back end was dramatically tilted downward, which was blocking his view of its exterior vestibule. As a flash of lightning illuminated the sky and reflected onto the water, Dallas noticed that the area that should contain the final Pullman was simply comprised of floating lumber and debris.

Curious, he lowering himself down onto the submerged vestibule and holding onto the metal rail for stability, he took a deep breath and dove under the water. Swimming down a few feet, he was not only able to find the coupler, but discovered that it was still attached to something. Kicking his legs around, he hit something solid.

Coming up out of the water, he quickly swam over to the questionable debris pile, pulled himself up on top and found it to be unexpectedly sturdy. As he began tossing the lumber and debris away, Dallas began noticing a faint glow under the water, which faded in and out as the current above it bucked and churned.

The Pullman's interior oil lamps!

Quickly tossing off the rest of the debris, Dallas felt the Pullman car begin to resurface under his feet, but only enough to expose the top of the windows. Lowering himself over the side, he began knocking on the glass which caused the glow from inside the Pullman to flicker, which could only mean that someone had to be causing a shadow.

Laying his hand onto the glass and motioned for whoever might still be alive to move out of the way, Dallas lowered himself into the water, grabbed hold of the Pullman's exterior trim and began pounding on the glass with the heel of his boot until he felt it begin to give.

Relieved that he was making progress and fueled by his heartbreaking choice to leave his pregnant wife in the hands of a Porter he barely knew, Dallas continued pounding on the glass until he felt it break.

If he could save at least one person, then his sacrifice would be worth it.

But he didn't find just one survivor.

He found 20.

Quickly sliding into the submerged coach, Dallas noticed that the inside of the Pullman had stayed partially dry, but now that he had busted out a window, water was pouring in, so he had to work fast.

"Excuse me! Excuse me! Can I have your attention please?" Dallas asked in a raised, firm tone, as he projected his voice over the screams of the confused passengers.

"The trains were all hit by a flood and your car, as you already know, is underwater. I need you to climb out of this window and pull yourselves up onto the top of the Pullman." Dallas explained, as he pointed to the murky waterfall that was now filling the train car. "There is also a terrible storm outside, so when you get out, you need to hold onto something! Now, let's go!"

Noticing a few Porters in the mix, he instructed them to go out of the window first, so they could pull the passengers up once they had exited the Pullman, which they eagerly agreed to. With their help and the added fear of the rapidly rising water inside the train car, Dallas found that the passengers were very willing to evacuate.

Until he encountered an unexpected problem.

A very big problem.

Stuck in the Pullman cars window was an English woman who easily weighed 200 lbs., if not more and if they couldn't get her through the busted out window, she was going to drown. With her husband and nine children pushing from underneath, and the Porters pulling at her from outside the train car, the hefty woman finally popped loose from her confinement, which is when the passengers began noticing all of the blood.

As Dallas began helping the next passenger through the window, he didn't understand the concerned looks he was receiving, until he looked down at his arm. Sliced open by the glass of the busted out Pullman window, he had been unknowingly wiping blood into his hair, as he brushed it back out of his face, which gave Dallas the appearance that he was bleeding from his mouth and ears.

With an unconcerned shrug, and a reassuring smile, Dallas helped the last passenger out the submerged Pullman and not a moment too soon, as the floodwaters had just reached the last of the wall mounted oil lamps. Back outside and facing the storm once again, Dallas began counting the passengers and realized that two of them were missing.

"Hey! Didn't you say there was 20 people in that car?" Dallas yelled over at one of the Porters, as he struggled to keep his balance on top of the swaying Pullman. "I only counted 18!"

"Yes, sir!" the Porter screamed back at him, as another bolt of lightning pierced the sky. "I counted them myself after the Pullman sank!"

Not giving it a second thought, Dallas headed back over to the busted out window but was immediately stopped by a few of the people he had already saved. As the men tried to keep him from re-entering the Pullman, saying it was for his own safety, Dallas found that he had to shove the ungrateful men off of him before he was able to plunge back into the now pitch black train car to search for the two missing passengers.

Once inside, Dallas began calling out for the stragglers, which is when he heard what sounded like someone praying. Calling for them to come towards his voice, but not hearing a response, he waded through the now chest deep water until he located Mrs. Maria Rossi and her companion.

Talking to them softly and taking them by the hands, Dallas managed to get the women out through the window, before sitting then down on top of the sunken Pullman. Knowing that he needed to get all of these passengers out of the storm, Dallas walked over to the Porters and instructed them to not only lead the passengers off the Pullman, but help them cross over to the top of the next car.

"These Pullman's are unstable!' Dallas screamed, as he pointed towards a faint light in the distance. "See that light? That's where we are headed!"

Helping the passengers over to the next Pullman, and then onto the dining car, Dallas kept an eye out for his wife Lydia or any passengers besides the ones he had just freed and was growing concerned that perhaps his group were the only survivors.

When Dallas had left his pregnant wife in the hands of the Pullman Porter, she had joined a group that consisted of Dining car waiters Robert Lewis, Maxwell Hughlett, and Earl Houston, as well as passengers Dayton Kramer, who really regretted not tying his shoes before the flood struck the train, 43-year-old Colorado Springs Sheriff Frank Nicholas DuCray and 70-year-old Sarah J Wellwood.

Walking through the Pullman, the group of about 25 people had managed to make it into the dining car right before the flood slammed into the train, which not only caused the Dining car to tilt violently but resulted in Dayton Kramer losing one of his shoes.

Reaching around in the darkness for his missing footwear, Dayton found himself surrounded by heart wrenching screams, which heightened each time the partially submerged Dining car rocked in the turbulent water. Holding onto the sides for stability, the passengers immediately noticed that the walls were wet, which meant that water was starting to come inside the train car.

Prayers that overpowered any that you would ever hear inside of a church chapel began echoing throughout the dining car, as the passengers begged the Lord to save them, and forgive them for any sins that might have resulted in this torment. In one corner of the Dining car was a 19-year-old colored woman named Rosie Farrar, who was traveling alone from Chicago, but she wasn't calling out for

Sheriff Frank Ducray-
authors personal collection

the Lord, but instead for her absent father. Seeing that she needed comfort, Sheriff DuCray squeezed past the other passengers and attempted to calm her down.

"Sweetheart, I know all this is very scary, but we are all in this together", the Sheriff explained to not only her, but anyone else within earshot, which included 24-year-old Daniel Creedon, and his 22-year-old brother Charles. The brothers, who were traveling back to Bingham, Utah after visiting their mother Ester's grave in Buena Vista, has already informed the other passengers that after surviving the War, they had no intention of dying inside of a flooded train car.

With most of the Denver & Rio Grande's Pullman's floating well above the tracks, they were still colliding with the mostly sunken Pullman's of the Missouri No. 14 which had caused the windows of the No. 3 to shatter.

Attempting to evade the onslaught of water that was now pouring in through the broken windows, the passengers trapped inside the No. 3's Dining car began scrambling to find something to hold onto, but unfortunately, only the tables were bolted down. As the Denver & Rio Grande once again collided with the Missouri Pacific, the resulting impact caused chairs, serving carts and an endless collection of dishes, glasses, and cutlery to tumble around the flooded aisles, knocking almost a dozen passengers lose from their hold inside the now compromised Dining car.

As the passengers struggled to steady themselves, the car tilted once more, causing a wave of water to not only pour in through the shattered windows, but push some of the passengers out the other side, with 19-year-old Rosie Farrar being the first to go.

Reaching out to grab her, Sheriff Frank DuCray missed her by only a hair, before turning around and frantically trying to grab at one of the Creedon boys, but once again he was too late. As the brothers were washed out into the storm, Daniel was immediately crushed

Daniel Creeden-authors
personal collection

between the outside walls of the Denver & Rio Grande Dining car and one of the Missouri Pullmans, with the impact quickly extinguishing his young life.

Watching his brother die, Charles could be heard screaming for him as the angry floodwaters quickly washed him down stream, along with over a dozen other passengers.

Desperate to save the people that remained, Sheriff DuCray screamed through the darkness for everyone to hold on to something, as the dining car finally floated away from the Missouri Pacific far enough that it could partially right itself. Wading over to one of the busted out windows and looking out into the storm, the Sheriff turned back towards the passengers and gave them news he knew they didn't want to hear.

"Look, if we stay in here, we are all going to die, but if we leave the Dining car we also might die" Sheriff DuCray explained as he wiped the water out of his eyes. "But at least we will do it on our own terms."

"Unfortunately, we all just saw what happened to poor Daniel, so we know that we can't leave through the windows, so I think its best that we head outside through the Dining car's exterior door." The Sheriff explained as he pointed toward the front of the car. "Now, be aware that when I open that door the car's going to fill up real quick, so I need you to all hold onto something until the water stabilizes."

In silent agreement, the passengers watched as Sheriff DuCray waded over to the end of the Dining car and attempted to open the exterior door. As he struggled, a few of the men joined him and together they managed to get it open, which caused a new onslaught of water to pour into the train car.

As some of the passengers began to scream, the Sheriff reminded them to just hold on until the water equalized, at which point the Sheriff swam out the door, and onto the exterior vestibule, where he was able to use its railings to pull himself up onto the roof of the Dining car. After a quick look around from his new vantage point, he leaned back over the side and offered his hand.

Finally free of the Dining car, and huddled together on its roof, the passengers were finally able to see the destruction that the flood had caused. As they shivered in the pouring rain, the survivors noticed that numerous buildings around them were on fire, which gave off just enough light for them to realize that quite a number of them were wearing nothing more than nightclothes.

As Sheriff DuCray began checking on the passengers, he thought he had heard someone screaming out in pain. Heading towards the sound, he saw a visibly pregnant young lady cradling an elderly woman's foot. "I think her ankle might be broken." Lydia Cuenin explained to the Sheriff, as the woman next to her offered a scarf to wrap around the injury.

With 70-year-old Sarah Wellwood wincing at his touch, all Sheriff DuCray could do was sit down and try to keep her from sliding off the roof of the Dining car, as a few of the passengers already had. As he sat next to Sarah and Lydia, they watched as a few of the passengers attempted to jump onto piles of floating debris, only to be struck by the still rocking Missouri Pacific No. 14 and disappear under the water.

Surprisingly, most of the Denver & Rio Grande No. 3 train cars had stayed coupled together, possibly due to some being completely submerged and acting like anchors for the rest. Due to this stability, a debris field had begun to form between the No.3 and the nearby Nuckolls packing plant, which sat along the edge of The Grove.

As the debris continued to accumulate, the Denver & Rio Grande No. 3 passengers were unaware that a second debris pile was also forming between the Missouri Pacific No.14 and the former Schlitz Brewing Company's warehouse, which sat on the opposite side of the flooded tracks on Oneida Street.

With framed houses, lumber, furniture, and automobiles continuing to pile up, the passengers from both trains began giving the debris piles a serious look, especially the pile that was quickly constructing itself between the No. 14 and the former Schlitz Warehouse. On any other day, the train would be over 200 feet away from the Warehouse, but with the tracks now submerged under 10 feet of water, the Missouri Pacific was now swaying and churning only a few feet from the stone buildings back door.

Inside the second floor of the Schlitz Warehouse was the building's owner, 70-year-old German immigrant Henry C. Borndruck and his 53-year-old wife Edna who not only helped her husband run an insurance business out of the building but they lived there as well. Henry had originally run the Schlitz Brewing Company out of the building, but after Prohibition took effect on January 1, 1916, he had been filling his days with finding people great deals on insurance instead.

When the water first began to rise, Henry and Edna had moved up onto the second floor, which is when they first noticed that the storm had stranded three trains on the tracks near their building. After watching the Manifest Freight Train No. 62 throw itself into reverse and head back to Union Depot, the couple waited for the other two remaining trains to follow its lead, but instead were forced to watch as the flood pounced upon them and then tried it's hardest to tear them apart.

Now after hours of watching the turbulent waters smash the two remaining passenger trains into each other, Henry realized that the Missouri Pacific No. 14 was sitting very close to the second floor windows of his warehouse, he just wasn't sure how to safely get the passengers into the building, but he knew he had to try.

Hanging a lantern out of the window to attract the passenger's, Henry began screaming over the roar of the storm, as he waved for them to come towards his building. Eager to get out of the rain, a few did take him up on his offer and after carefully crossing the debris field, were able to crawl in through the buildings second floor windows , which gave hope to the remaining passengers.

But nobody needed hope more than 32-year-old Ruby Ellis.

Trapped inside one of the Missouri Pacific Pullman cars and frantically trying to keep her nine-year-old daughter Mildred Mary above water, the Wichita, Kansas mother was thankful that she wasn't alone in her struggle. Despite being surrounded by the screams and desperate prayers of the other passengers, Rudy knew that a full train car was more likely to attract the attention of a rescue party than one that held only a few people.

With the Pullman laying over on its side, Ruby found that she not only had to stand on the curtain rods of the cars sleeping compartments in order to reach the air pocket inside the train car, but with her daughter Mildred not tall enough, she also had to put her daughter up on her hip so she could breathe.

"What should I do mother?" Mildred asked as she continued to shiver in the icy floodwater.

"Keep your chin up and pray baby," Ruby responded, as she adjusted her daughter on her hip once more. "Just pray."

As little Mildred began to repeat "Jesus I trust you, Jesus I trust you", the submerged train car was struck by an unseen object, which caused it to roll and spin in the strong current, finally coming to rest at an upward angle. Seeing her chance, Ruby Ellis pulled her child towards the higher end of the train car, where she discovered not only a broken out window, but fresh air.

And a pair of hands.

Motioning for her to back away from the window, her unseen savior began kicking out the frame in order to make room for Ruby and her daughter to escape their waterlogged prison. After being helped up onto the top of the tilted train car and regaining her bearings, Rudy was shocked to discover that she was now expected to take her daughter across a large, swaying mountain of debris.

Looking across the floating collection of logs, furniture, and lumber, Ruby watched as other passengers were being helped in through a nearby building's window, while an older woman held up a lantern to guide the way. Holding tightly to her daughter's hand and giving out a silent prayer, Ruby carefully began climbing over the debris field and into the building.

Crowded with water soaked train passengers, Rudy noticed that many of them were wearing nothing but their nightclothes, as they all gathered around the room's sole fireplace in an attempt to ward off their chill. Chosing instead to walk her daughter Mildred over to another of the building's windows, Ruby was shocked to see the true condition of the Missouri Pacific No. 14, as its cars twisted and flipped in the deep water.

Due to the light from a nearby burning building, Ruby and the other survivors could make out the image of the passengers from the Denver & Rio Grande No. 3 crawling over their own mountain of storm debris in order to enter the Nuckolls packing plant, which was almost directly across the flooded tracks from the Schlitz Brewing Company's warehouse.

But not everyone from the No. 3 had that luxury.

Jammed inside a partially submerged Denver & Rio Grande First class Pullman car, which was also referred to as Tourist Sleeper No. 1618, were around 40 passengers and one train Engineer that had all come to the realization that they were going to have to help themselves if they wanted to survive. As the water continued to pour in through the cars busted out windows, the captives discussed their situation, and agreed they if they didn't do something fast, they were all going to drown.

Before the flood had struck the trains, Missouri Pacific Engineer Asa Harris had been pulled into the Dining car of the No. 3 after a large group of passengers had swarmed his train's engine, causing it to fill with water and capsize. Origianlly moved into the First-class Pullman in order to warm up after his unexpected swim, he now found himself once again standing in icy flood water.

The First Class Pullman Engineer Harris was in, the No. 1618, was coupled between the No. 3's Dining car and another First-class Pullman, which was also referred to as Tourist Sleeper No. 1638, and after a vote with the other passengers, it was felt that moving up into the No. 1638 car was their safest choice. With the Porters double-checking that everyone was in agreement and reminding them that once the exterior door was opened, their car could possibly sink, the deed was done.

As the water began filling the train car, the Porters quickly found themselves battling a surge of water that was running harder and faster than they expected, making it almost impossible for them to reach the cars exterior vestibule. Seeing that time was quickly running out, a few of the men pushed past the Porters, grabbed hold of the exterior hand rail of the vestibule and using it as a guide, grabbed each of the railings spindles in turn and blindly pulled themselves through the rushing water until they located the exterior door of the No. 1638 and pushed it open.

But they were not welcome.

As the men attempted to enter, they were instantly treated as unwanted guests, as they immediately found themselves fighting with the car's Porters who tried to force them back out and re-close the door. With the formally dry First-class Pullman quickly taking on water, the passengers from the compromised First-class Pullman began forcing themselves inside, which resulted in the car becoming unstable and tilting over to one side.

Admitting defeat, the Porters began grabbing the last of the unwelcomed passengers and pulled them in before quickly closing the exterior door, but the damage had been done. With the unwanted house guests now doubling the cars maximum capacity, and bringing with them a large amount of flood water and debris, the First-class Pullman was only able to remain upright for a few more seconds before flipping completely over onto its side.

With over 40 people now crammed into a Pullman meant for 20, the passengers all struggled to stand on the once dry seats, as they held onto the curtain rods of the sleeping compartments for support. Standing in cold, waist-deep water, the situation was made all the dire as the light from the interior mounted oil lamps had been quickly estinqished by the sloshing flood water.

Now trapped inside of a pitch-black, partially submerged train car, 19-year-old Eleanor Demfer and her friend 20-year-old Dorothy Lustkandl from Saint Louis, Missouri who had been en route to San Francisco for vacation, were really regretting leaving their original First-class Pullman.

As they stood in the inky darkness, with the water splashing above their waists, Eleanor noticed a dim light shining through the windows and what appeared to be a large building with lanterns moving around inside. Caught off guard, due to her distraction, Eleanor was almost knocked off her perch as a large pile of debris suddenly smashed into the sides of their foundering Pullman, knocking out several more windows as it did.

With the water now eagerly racing throughout the inside of the train car, it began to use its icy claws to pull at the passengers in an attempt to force them out of the busted windows, tearing at their clothes as it did. As Eleanor struggled to keep both her and her friend Dorothy's head above the rising water, she suddenly heard the scream of a young woman over the roar of the storm and she sounded terrified.

"My baby! For God's sake, will someone save my baby?"

Looking towards the back of the Pullman, Eleanor could see the faint form of a woman standing on the back of a seat, holding onto a curtain rod with one hand and a small bundle in the other. "My strength is failing me, please someone grab my baby!"

After checking that her friend Dorothy was still able to keep her head above the water, Eleanor allowed herself to let go of the curtain rod and swim through the center of the submerged Pullman towards the frantic woman. Taking the baby, Eleanor held the child above her head as she maneuvered herself back through the flooded train car, where she rejoined her friend.

Holding the baby up over her shoulders with one hand and the curtain rod in the other, Eleanor found that she now had to encourage Dorothy to keep hanging onto the curtain rod, as her strength was also failing.

"They will come for us, just hold on. I'm sure they will come for us."

Staring out the windows, Eleanor watched as the light of the lanterns she had seen earlier appeared to be coming closer to the Pullman. Encouraging the other passengers to scream for help, confident that the lights were coming for them, Eleanor was relieved to see a new face suddenly appear in the frame of one of the Pullmans missing windows.

"Is everyone all right?" Dallas Cuenin asked, as he shone a flashlight into the Pullman train car. "We are here to get you out, so hold on just a little while longer."

As relief filled her body, Eleanor let go of the curtain rod, paddled over to Dallas, and handed him the baby. "It's Mama is in the back of the train car."

As Eleanor and Dorothy were helped out of the Pullman and escorted across the tops of the submerged train cars, Dallas Cuenin and a small army of other surviving passengers helped this new carload cross the debris field over to the Nuckolls packing plant, which gave him the chance to scan all the passengers for his wife Lydia. Unknown to Dallas, his wife and many of the other passengers from the dining car were already inside the Nuckolls packing plant, including Waiters Robert Lewis, Maxwell Hughlett, and Earl Houston, as well as Sheriff Frank Ducray and 70-year-old Sarah Wellwood, who was being made comfortable as she nursed her broken ankle.

As Dallas continued to inspect the inside of the train car , as well as the churning waters around it for more flood victims, he met Dayton Kramer who was still looking for his lost shoe or at least one he could wear before he attempted to climb over the mountain of debris to the Nuckolls Plant. As Dallas began helping Dayton look for a shoe, they began hearing a lot of noise coming from the plant, as people hung out of the windows and began frantically pointing towards the direction of the Santa Fe train bridge.

While struggling to hear what everyone was yelling about, Dallas and Dayton noticed that the water around the trains was starting to rise, causing the debris field to twist and turn as the current began changing course. Glancing back over at the Nuckolls packing plant, and trying his best to hear them, Dallas suddenly realized what they were saying.

There was a second flood coming.

CHAPTER 7

Man's best friend and a frantic game of fire hockey

Situated farther down the tracks, and close to Union Depot's Roundhouse were Engineer Madison Coffey and his men in engine No. 632, who had also been pummeled by the flood water, but like the Denver & Rio Grande No. 3, their engine had remained on the tracks, but they were not sure for how long.

From inside their flooded engine compartment, the men shone their flashlights into the inky blackness and watched as the coal cars they had previously moved to a secure location tumbled past them, while mountains of debris fought for the top spots in the raging water.

Climbing out onto the engine's coal car for a better view, the men sat and watched as driftwood, automobiles, and furniture blazed past them, with some of the debris violently smashing into the side of their engine, threatening to push it over.

Which is when they heard the dog.

Shining their flashlights out into the turbulent water, the men finally spotted a large dog clinging to a pile of debris, yelping and crying as he held on for dear life. Desperate to save the animal, Conductor Joseph Miller quickly lowered himself off the side of the coal car, and called out for the scared animal to swim towards him, which it did. Heading towards the sound of his voice, the waterlogged dog eventually got close enough for the Conductor to grab its collar and give it a tug.

Quickly realizing that the dog was too big for Conductor Miller to pull up by himself, Firemen Huff and Alexander lowered themselves into the water and began pushing the dog up from underneath, while Engineer Coffey grabbed handfuls of fur and pulled. After a stressful few minutes, the dog finally plopped itself up onto the coal car, where he immediately thanked his rescuers by shaking water all over them.

"Hey, this is one of those Newfoundland's!" Engineer Madison Coffey announced with a laugh, as the men began to pet the 150-pound dog. "No wonder he was so dammed heavy!"

Newfoundland dog
- authors personal collection

As men continued to coo over the wet animal, a pile of lumber suddenly slammed into the side of their train's engine, causing the dog to temporarily lose his footing, slide across the wet metal of the coal car, and land in the engines flooded cabin with a nerve wracking splash. Quickly scooting across the coal car and peering inside, the men were relieved to find that the dog had already pulled itself up onto a raised bench, where it once again began to shake the water off his fur.

Shining their lights back into the flood water, the men not only spotted the large pile of lumber that had just bumped into them, but noticed that it was also beginning to pile up against the side of their engine. Fearful that the debris might eventually push them over, Engineer Coffey began looking around for a means of escape, which is when he spotted a bright light shining through the storm.

About 300 feet away from their compromised engine stood the towering Colorado Bedding Company, which was giving off a welcoming glow on its upper floors. Looking for the safest way over to the building, Engineer Madison Coffey informed his men that they should use the piles of debris as a type of bridge and make a run for it.

But the dog couldn't come.

As the men looked towards the building and the debris field they would have to cross just to get over to it, they feared that their new mascot wouldn't be able to make it. Even though the engine was now beginning to lean, it was still holding strong against the floodwaters and would at least give the dog a fighting chance.

Shining their flashlights back towards the building and looking for things they could grab onto, Engineer Coffey and his men finally noticed a Telegraph pole sticking out of the water, about 40 feet away from the engine and it was in a direct line with the Bedding Company. Giving the dog one last pat, and reminding him to stay, the four men carefully began walking over the piles of debris, until they reached the Telegraph pole.

Holding onto the pole's wooden crossbeams, the men began shining their flashlights into the windows of the building, all while screaming for help over the sounds of the angry floodwaters. Luckily a light soon shone down on them, quickly followed by a rope being thrown from the second floor of the building. With Telegraph wires in one hand and the rope in the other, the men carefully inched themselves toward the three-story-tall brick building, where a man named Earl Slackett pulled them in through a window.

After a round of grateful handshakes and introductions, Engineer Coffey and his men were taken up to the third floor, where they discovered not only a fire burning inside of a metal barrel but a pot of hot coffee sitting off to the side. Excusing themselves from their gracious host for just a moment, Engineer Coffey and his crew headed over to the windows and shone their flashlights back towards the engine, but their beams were not strong enough to illuminate the image they desperately wanted to see.

Suddenly, a bolt of lightning shot across the sky, reflecting light onto the still rising floodwaters, revealing to the men the figure of a large animal sitting partially inside the cab of their engine and being a very good boy.

But not everyone was so relieved.

Trapped inside one of the Telephone Company's first floor offices was a Night Wire Chief named Byron Thady and the Angel of death was tapping him on the shoulder. He had fought against the floodwaters to enter this particular office, so he could retrieve his company's vital Cable records, but now he was trapped inside.

The battle he was fighting didn't just involve the rising water that was inside the office, but the rising water that was outside the office door as well, as the combined pressure against the door was keeping him from opening it. As he climbed back up on top of the desk, holding his homemade oil lamp with one hand, and the binders that contained the Cable records in the other, he realized that he simply had to be patient.

Byron understood that his best chance of escaping the flooded office was to wait until the water reached above the door, so the pressure could equalize, but with the rooms low ceilings, he could drown if his theory was wrong.

Finally, after what seemed like an eternity, Byron watched as the door finally disappeared underneath the rising floodwaters, which is when reality suddenly set in. The standard height of an office door is almost 7 feet tall, which was still around 6 inches taller than Byron, and the entire time he had been waiting, he had been standing on top of a desk, which had allowed him to hold his homemade oil lamp up out of the water.

Byron Thady escaping the flooded first floor with the cable records
-Authors personal collection

To reach the office door, Byron would not only have to get off the desk but swim over to the door, which would extinguish his lamp, throwing the entire room into complete darkness. But as Byron glanced around the flooded office, he realized that the water inside the room was still rising, which meant that soon the water would be up to the ceiling, and he had run out of options.

With a tight grasp on the binders, Byron Thady let go of his oil lamp and watched as his only source of light quickly sank into the water, before he pushed off from the desk and began swimming towards the direction of the office door. Feeling around in the now pitch-black room, Byron located the top edge of the door frame, took a few deep breaths, and dove down into the water, using the frame as his guide in his quest to find the doorknob.

Following the frame of the door with his free hand, Byron blindly grabbed hold of the doorknob, turned it, and gave the door a push, relieved that it easily allowed his exit.

Popping back up inside the control room and glad to finally be free of the office, Byron Thady wiped the hair out of his eyes, while he looked around and realized that he could see a shimmer of light shining through the buildings broken windows. Curious, he swam over to them and noticed that an odd, flickering light was reflecting off the water, which seemed rather strange to him, as the electricity had been out for hours.

With a shrug of his shoulders, he thanked his good fortune and used the mysterious light to guide his way back over towards the staircase, and up to the second floor, where he found a very worried Mrs. Pryor. With an exhausted smile, Byron Thady pointed out the binders before following her up to the third floor, where he laid the waterlogged binders on a nearby table, praying that they were salvageable.

While Mrs. Pryor quickly opened up the binders, popped out the pages, and directed some of the Phone girls to layout the Cable records so they could dry, Byron walked over to the windows and once again saw the mysterious light.

Byron Thady didn't know where the light was coming from.

But the Boy Scouts did.

The Lumberyard was on fire.

The King Investment and Lumber Company, which filled an entire city block between West 6th and 7th, and Elizabeth Street was not only submerged under 11 feet of water but was engulfed in flames.

When the flood had originally begun submerging downtown, 59-year-old George E. King, and his 18-year-old son Francis E. King, as well as his 38-year-old Yard Superintendent William K. Tappen and 21-year-old Nephew Harvey Granville Burtis had driven over to the lumber yard, which they found submerged under 3 feet of water.

Immediately entering the office building, the men began moving records and equipment up to the second floor, completely unaware that a train car full of Quicklime, which had just been delivered that afternoon, had already caught fire inside one of the Lumber Yards outbuildings.

Quicklime, also known as Calcium Oxide has many uses, such as being used in the manufacture of Cement and glass, removing impurities from steel and Iron, and even eliminating the odor of decomposition when burying the dead. Unfortunately, the Calcium in the compound is highly reactive with water, which will cause the Calcium to quickly heat up, thus igniting anything nearby.

Such as a lumber yard full of wood.

With the Lumberyard encompassing most of a city block, it took Mr. King quite a while to realize that the mill was on fire until he saw the flames breaking through the roof of the out building, which in turn ignited the building that contained Mr. King, his son, and his two employees. Trapped up on the second floor, which itself was now already flooded with over a foot of water, the men found themselves quickly running out of options.

But luckily for them, a Boy Scout is always prepared.

For the last 5 hours, the Boy Scouts from Troop No. 6 had been stationed on every street corner, from the Main Street Bridge to the Pueblo Court House where they had been directing flood victims to safety, when they began hearing that a nearby Lumber Yard was on fire. Passing the message along, a Scout ran into the Courthouse and informed 36-year-old Scout Master, Dr. Edwin Rucaldo Cary, that there were men trapped inside.

Not knowing how many people were stranded, Scout Master Cary quickly gathered up his Assistant Scout Master's George W. White and Charles Hopkins, both 29 years old, as well as his own 11-year-old son Robert, and drove his truck the 5 blocks up to The Mineral Palace Park, so they could grab a couple of rowboats.

Built in 1891 and filling 27 acres, The Mineral Palace Park was the pride of Pueblo. Containing Lake Clara, named after Clara Latshaw who helped the City acquire the land, it also held a boathouse, a bandstand, Botanical Gardens, a

Exterior of The Mineral Palace
- Courtesy of the PCCLD Special Collections

Zoo, and even a Merry-go-round, but it was the boats Scout Master Cary was after.

Finding that he wasn't the only one interested in assisting the stranded, the Scouts were only able to obtain two rowboats which they secured to their truck, before driving back to the edge of the flood. Arriving at the corner of 7th and Main Street, the Scouts parked their truck, unloaded the boats, and pushed them off into the water.

With flashlights in hand, the first rowboat held both Assistant Scout Masters White and Hopkins, while the second held Scout Master Cary and his son Robert, but unfortunately, only one boat would make it to the Lumber Yard. With the current stronger than expected, the Scout Masters struggled to row their boats the four blocks needed to reach the Lumber Yard, with 11-year-old Robert Cary falling overboard only minutes after entering the flooded street.

Due to the darkness of the storm and fighting not only constant rain but the raging current, the Assistant Scout Masters inside the first rowboat was unaware of the second boats true fate. Reaching the Lumberyard, Scout Masters White and Hopkins found it engulfed in flames which gave them the light they needed to locate Mr. King and his men, who they found hanging onto a section of fencing outside the Lumber Yard.

Frantically screaming for help while struggling to keep their heads above water, the terrified men were relieved to see that their saviors had finally arrived, unaware that two rowboats had originally attempted to reach them, not just one. While Assistant Scout Masters White and Hopkins were busy loading George King and his son into the rowboat, intending to take them back to the truck, they were unaware that Scout Master Cary was being tumbled and tossed underneath the raging floodwaters, while his son sat safely inside their rowboat, shaken but alive.

As the Assistant Scout leaders approached the edge of the floodwaters at 7th and Main Street, they were relieved to see that a group of men were patiently waiting to escort Mr. King and his son Francis to the Courthouse. After helping the exhausted men into their waiting chariot, Assistant Scout Masters White and Hopkins headed back out towards the Lumber Yard to rescue the two remaining employees, praying that they were not too late.

Dodging piles of debris, upturned streetcars, and floating automobiles, the Assistant Scout Masters finally arrived back at the Lumber Yard to help William Tappen and his 21-year-old Nephew Harvey Burtis into the rowboat, which is when they noticed a bigger problem. With the height of the flood water now topping the fence that surrounded the lumber yard, large piles of burning wood and debris, originally ignited by the newly arrived shipment of Quicklime, were now breaking free of their confinement and easily gliding over the fence , where they were quickly snatched up by the violent torrent and washed down the street.

Witnessing the disaster unfold in front of them, the 4 men helplessly watched as each flaming pile of lumber crashed into nearby buildings, hesitating just long enough to set them ablaze, before igniting the next building in its path. With no way to stop it, the Assistant Scout Masters took the men back to 7th and Main Street, where they began informing people of the bad news.

Unfortunately, the information would have to be delivered by word of mouth, as not only were the Telephones out of order but so were the Telegraphs.

Hours earlier, at 9:10 pm to be exact, 40-year-old Associated Press Operator Howard Coriour Hayden discovered that his Telegraph sounder had ceased giving forth its familiar clicks of dots and dashes, preventing him from sending out the night report for the Pueblo Chieftain Newspaper.

The Pueblo Chieftain's office was located on South Union Avenue, near the Vail Hotel, but Howard Hayden was not about to let a little flood stop him from doing his job. Sliding the stories into his satchel and buttoning up his coat, Howard Hayden ran out into the flooded streets but with no trolley cars available, began wading towards the Western Union Telegraph office, but was quickly stopped by armed guards.

Instructed to keep people off of the flooded streets, the men asked him where he was headed, to which he replied 415 North Main Street, on a very urgent matter. Shaking their heads and pointing him towards higher ground, the guards explained that he would need to walk two blocks over to Santa Fe Avenue in order to get out of the rising water and that he needed to avoid downtown altogether.

With a smile and a tip of his hat, Howard headed over to the designated street, but then realized that he could still access the Western Union Telegraph office as Santa Fe Avenue not only intersected with 4th street, but North Main Street was only one street over. Not wanting to be stopped again, or possibly arrested, Howard Hayden began looking around every corner and avoiding every person he saw, until he finally reached the Western Union Office a little after Midnight.

Seeing a lantern glowing in the upstairs window, Howard Hayden continued trudging through the now chest-deep water until he reached the front door of the building. After struggling to open the door, he finally heading upstairs where he met 37-year-old Night wire Chief Emory Albert Mitchell.

Emory Mitchell had originally been ordered to abandon his Telegraph station and head to higher ground just a little before Midnight, but chose instead to continue sending out messages until his clicker stopped producing the familiar dashes and dots. Looking out into the storm, Emory was pretty confident that all the floating debris he could see outside his windows had knocked his Telegraph wires loose, but he knew he couldn't reconnect the lines by himself.

But as luck would have it, a soak and wet reporter had just entered his second floor office.

Emory Mitchell, on far right
-Authors personal collection

With Howard Hayden willing and eager to lend Emory Mitchell a hand, the two men gathered all the materials they would need to reconnect the wires, placed them inside boxes, and headed down into the buildings flooded first floor. Placing the boxes upon their shoulders, the two men waded out of the building and into the storm, in search of Telegraph poles.

Shining his flashlight through the rain, Emory Mitchell located his first pole, climbed to the top, and checked the connections, before climbing down and going to the next one. His goal was to connect the Telegraph line from his building to The Mineral Palace Park, which was over 10 blocks away, and set up a communication center inside the Palace itself, which he prayed was above the flood line.

The world-famous Colorado Mineral Palace, which held the world's largest collection of minerals and gems, had been designed to resemble an elegant Egyptian Palace. Containing 16 foot high statues, a 72-foot tall domed ceiling, wonderfully painted murals, and a grotto constructed of stalactites and stalagmites, the building was quite a sight to see.

But right now Emory Mitchell didn't care about the buildings beauty, he just hoping that it was out of the flood zone.

Arriving at The Mineral Palace after 1:00 am, and pleased to find that the building was sitting high and dry, Emory and Howard quickly began setting up a line of communication, and at 1:30 am, their urgent but brief message was finally delivered to not only the Associated Press, and the Governor of Colorado, but all of the small neighboring towns that lay east of Pueblo along the Arkansas River, as they were next in line to feel the floods wrath.

Interior of The Mineral Palace
- Courtesy of The Pueblo County Historical Society

"Conditions here very bad. Rescue work going on. Send everyone you can. Hundreds in danger"

Then the clicker once again stopped producing its familiar dashes and dots.

Sitting back in his chair, and looking over at Howard Hayden, Night wire Chief Emory Mitchell prayed that their messages had been received and that help would soon arrive. As the two men began talking about how they could try to re-wire the Telegraph lines again, an explosion was heard in the distance and it sounded like it came from near Union Depot.

Ignited by a pile of flaming lumber, the Florman Paint Companies factory had gone up in flames, which had resulted in explosion after explosion of its numerous oils, paints, and varnishes. The factory, which was located at the corner of the Santa Fe tracks and Central Main Street, had received a special mention for its creative float design only 21 days earlier during Pueblo's Industrial Parade and now the entire factory was threatening to burn down the city that had gifted them with that honor.

During the cities May 13th parade, thousands of people filled Main Street and watched as the Rood Candy Company won for Most Artistically decorated automobile, while the Lithia Bottling Company had won for Best Decorated float, but now less than a month later, the Parade route was sitting submerged underneath 11 feet of mud infused flood water.

Two other Parade participants, The Mountain Ice, and Coal Company, located at 511 Elizabeth Street, as well as the nearby Pueblo Gas and Fuel Company had also been cursed with a visit from the King Lumber Yards fiery nemesis, resulting in their own explosions.

The Pueblo Gas and Fuel Company used brick ovens to produce the gas they needed from Coal, but luckily the intense flames were quickly extinquished by the flood waters that had poured into the building and flooded the coal ovens. Unfortunately, this in turn released Coal gas into the air, which quickly ignited after a second floating inferno struck their building, resulting in yet another fire.

And more flaming piles of debris.

On the other side of town, the businesses on Main Street between 2nd and 4th were busy playing a game of floating fire Hockey, as another of the lumberyards numerous blazing piles were threatening to catch their buildings on fire as well.

Earlier that evening, just as the water had first begun to rise on 4th Street, 20-year-old Walter White Munn, a projectionist at the Majestic Theater, began pulling trunks full of costumes out of the basement, which was located underneath the stage, and setting them into the alley. Located at 118 West 4th Street, the Theater shared the alley with the Crews Begg's building who's Manager, 29-year-old George John Henry Schnarre was also busy pulling things up from his store's basement as well.

Grabbing a few stagehands, Walter Munn and his crew were able to hoist a couple of the costume trunks onto the stage before the first wave of water rushed down the alley. Most of the men managed to jump back into the theater to avoid getting wet, but Walter was forced to climb a nearby Telephone Pole to keep out of the water.

With the water quickly receding, Walter jumped down from his perch and helped the men load the now partially wet trunks onto the stage. As a few more trunks were being brought up from the basement, Walter decided that a smoke break was in order and lit up, mentally questioning why the rain just wasn't giving the city a minute of peace.

Which is when he heard a deep rumble.

Glancing towards the sound, Walter Munn suddenly noticed a towering wall of water barreling down the alley, much higher than the first. As the stagehands jumped in through the backdoor of the Theater, Walter was forced to once again climb the Telephone pole, but this time he wouldn't be coming back down.

As the torrent of water began smashing against the sides of the Theater, breaking out windows, and eagerly filling every inch of the one-story tall building, Walter Munn suddenly realized that he was in serious trouble. Hanging onto the Telephone poles top cross beams, and feeling the deep water already licking the bottoms of his street shoes, Walter suddenly realized that somebody was calling out his name.

Looking around, Walter saw a stage hand walking across the roof of the Theater, and when the men made eye contact, the stagehand ran over and instructed Walter to grab his hand. Happily excepting the offer, Walter soon found himself safely up on the roof, just as the floodwaters began flowing over the building's top ledge. Curious how the stagehand had gotten up onto the roof so quickly, Walter was shocked to discover that the man had busted a hole in the Theater's ceiling, clean through to the roof, using tools that he had found inside the now flooded building.

With the rest of the stagehands following suit, Walter noticed that the water was still rising, which meant that the Theater's roof wasn't going to be high enough.

But the building next door was.

The Majestic Theater had been built up against the towering, four-story tall, brick Crews Begg's building, and the men were sure that the building had a fire escape. Unfortunately, the pitch blackness of the storm was making their quest to find the coveted steel ladder quite difficult, as they knew that one wrong step could result in them falling off the roof of the Theater and into the ever rising floodwaters.

As they strained their eyes, they began noticing a welcoming glow developing in the water and praised their good luck, as the mysterious light not only helped them quickly locate the ladder but illuminated their three-story climb up to the building's roof.

But once they reached the top, the men soon discovered what was causing the glow.

Looking down from the roof of the Crews Begg's building, Walter Munn and the stagehands watched in horror as a large floating inferno rode the current of the rising flood, igniting every building it touched. Unknown to them, the large floating torch that had illuminated their view of the fire escape, was just another unexpected visitor from The King Investment and Lumber Company.

As the flaming debris piles floated past the buildings that lined Main Street, between 3rd and 5th, Walter and the stagehands noticed people hanging out of the 2nd floor windows armed with brooms, mops, and pool cues, which they were using to shove the floating inferno's away from their buildings. Unfortunately, their efforts were in vain, as the flaming debris would simply get caught in a whirlpool and end up against the buildings on the opposite side of the street, where it would then be pushed away once again and continue its dance.

As if pushing away flaming piles of debris wasn't enough, the people trapped inside the buildings were also throwing down ropes, sheets, and blankets to the people caught in the torrent, attempting to pull them up to safety, but it didn't always end with a positive result.

Especially when they got near the clock.

Bolted to the corner of the Whitcomb Block building, which housed Fishers Jewelry and Watch repair on the first floor, was a wonderful outdoor clock with faces on all four sides. Securely fastened to the outside of the building, the clock was originally meant as an advertising ploy for the Jewelry store, but right now, it was killing people.

With scores of flood victims caught in the violent current, anyone near the corner of 3rd and Main Street was at risk of being slammed against the protruding clock. One man who survived his encounter was lucky enough to have found a piano to float on, which bumped into the

The Fisher Jewelry and Watch building and the Death clock- Courtesy of the PCCLD Special Collections

clock instead of him. With the timepiece focused on the piano, the man was able to grab hold of a rope that was dangling out of the building's second floor window and was pulled to safety.

Just a block down from the clock, at 4th and Main Street, sat the four story tall Grand Opera house which was full of flood refugees, including one that leaned more towards the dramatic. John Andrew Martin was a 56-year-old man who had seen a lot and had done a lot during his life, and he could definitely spin quite a yarn.

From 1901-1913 John had served as a Colorado Congressman in the United States House of Representatives, before being drafted into the War, where he had commissioned as a Major. As a religious man, he was now spending his time trapped inside the Opera house not only journaling the

John Martin-Authors personal collection

destruction he saw outside the buildings windows but sharing his colorful revelations with the other flood refugees.

"This is a historic disaster and tomorrow the name of Pueblo will be known around the world!" John announced in a booming voice, as he walked around the darkened building. "Like the great flood in Genesis, the waters prevailed exceedingly on the earth. And like the man in the parable, who built his house upon the sands, the rain descended and the floods came and the storms beat upon that house and the house fell and great was the fall of it!"

Suddenly the sound of a woman screaming interrupted John's sermon, as the Opera house refugees ran towards her fearful cry, eventually finding themselves looking out the windows that faced the corner of 4th and Main Street. With their eyes gazing in the direction the woman was frantically pointing, the refugees finally noticed a man in a straw hat tightly holding onto a lamp post.

Located directly across the street from the Opera house and illuminated by the glow of the flaming debris, the refugees could only make out the top of the man's straw hat, as the angry water tried its best to pull him loose from the post and toss him into the torrent.

"My God, look at that man with the straw hat on the lamp post! There seems absolutely no hope for him! I long for the coup de grace, as the French say, that would end his misery!" John Martin began preaching again, as he joined the other Opera house refugees near the windows.

"It reminds me of the testimony of a survivor at the Senate investigation of the Titanic disaster. He said that for a long time after the ship went down, there was a chorus of cries coming from the dark bosom of the sea. He then described how they gradually died out, as an icy chill ran through the Senate chamber, for those voices had died out because rescue was not possible."

"They just threw a rope down! They threw a rope down!" A woman announced with a cheerful tone, as people came running over to her window. As they silently watched, the man in the straw hat grabbed the rope and tied it to the lamp post, before climbing the rope underhanded up into the window. As the glow from the fires continued to illuminate the rescue, the crowd inside the Opera house cheered, while at the same time questioning how the man could have pulled off such a feat.

Their answer soon became clear, after the man finished crawling in through the building's window, while his rescuer pointed out the crowd up on the second floor of the Opera house, who had been watching the entire scene play out. Leaning back out of the window and giving his audience a quick wave, the man's acrobatic feat up the rope was suddenly understood.

The man in the straw hat was instantly recognized as one of the acrobats from the Majestic Theater known as Goulet, who was a little fellow but was all shoulders, chest, and arms. After all the stunts he had performed on stage with his partner Provost while performing their acrobatic comedy act " A Vaudeville Mélange", it appeared that tonight he had really given his audience a show they would never forget.

CHAPTER 8

A storm drenched kitten and the well-built couch

"Hello? Hello? Is anyone there?" the Switchman asked, as he continued walking down the waterlogged tracks above the Grove. "Hello? Anyone?"

As the Switchman continued walking down the railroad tracks, he held his lantern up to each cattle car that he came to, until he saw a pair of eyes reflecting back at him through the darkness. "Well, there you are! I thought I heard voices!" the man announced with a smile, as he pointed down the track. "I've got a caboose down at the end with a fire going, why don't you all just come outta there now and we'll get you warmed up."

Sliding open the door to the cattle car, the Switchman gave the women a warm smile, before helping them down onto the tracks. Waiting until her mother Mary and her sisters were out, Stephanie Blatnick handed her sister Kerstina her box of chickens, before she jumped down onto the tracks herself.

"What are all those lights?" Stephanie asked the Switchman, as she took back the box of chickens from her sister. "I thought the electric was out." Looking back through the storm, the Switchman thought of the best way to explain the fires to the young girl, without scaring her too much.

"Well Honey, a building caught on fire, and then some of that fire started to float down the streets." He explained as he began walking them down the tracks towards the caboose. "But don't you worry none, a lot of people are out there getting people to safety, like how I'm helping you and your family."

Two of those people who were trying to help were 47-year old Joseph B. Roberts, who worked in real estate, and Charles E. Wayland, the Manager of the Kress Department store. The two men had met while trying to secure a rowboat from the Mineral Palace and decided that they would have better luck saving people if they worked together.

Loading one of the rowboats into the back of Charles truck, the men drove down to Greenwood and 8th Street, which sat right at the edge of the flood, and unloaded the rowboat into the water. As a spider web of lightning shot across the rain soaked sky, followed by another round of thunder, the men climbed into their boat and pushed it into the deep water.

As they slowly rowed, they shone their flashlights at every home they passed, looking for anyone who needed help, while loudly announcing that they had a boat and were there to help. At the corner of 8th and Elizabeth Street, the men saw a group of people sitting on the roof of the 8th Street Missionary Baptist Church, waving their arms and pointing down the block.

Stopping at the church, the men discovered that the parishioners didn't want to be rescued, but instead wanted the men to help two women who had fallen into the water. Looking in the direction the faithful were pointing, Charles and Joseph noticed a small, blue boat near a two story house, so they rowed over to offer assistance.

With the current of the water fighting them, the men almost reached the home when they saw the small, blue boat suddenly capsize, tossing the attempted rescuers and the two women into the turbulent water. As Charles and Joseph headed towards them, they watched as the current slammed one of the women into a nearby power pole, while the other managed to climb up into a tree.

Glancing back towards the small, blue boat, Charles watched as the two men it originally contained were sucked into the violent current and vanished from sight, leaving their little boat to drift off on its own. Horrified, Charles questioned his reason for leaving his house as Joseph continued rowing their boat towards the woman who had hit the pole.

"Charles! Charles! Hey, I need you to steady the boat!" Joseph instructed his shipmate, as he tried to reach the woman. "Charles!"

Snapping out of his daze, Charles looked over at Joseph and then down at the young woman who was struggling to reach their boat, all while trying to get the horrific image of the former rescuers possible drowning out of his head. Grabbing the partly submerged power pole for support, the two men were able to pull 23-year-old Inez Edmondson out of the water.

Inez, a colored Vaudeville singer from Chicago who was home visiting her parents, pointed over to a nearby tree where the men were introduced to her mother, a heavy-set, 53-year-old colored woman named Mary McAllister, who was trying her best to stay out of the water.

As Joseph began rowing over towards the woman, Charles grabbed his shoulders and begged him to stop. "We have to leave her! This is how the other men died." Charles pleaded, as he tried to take the oars away from Joseph. "We have to come back for her! Please, listen to me! She is too heavy!"

Pushing him away, Joseph pulled the boat up to the tree, and with Inez's help they managed to get the older woman into the rowboat, but just as Charles predicted her weight turned out to be too much, causing the rowboat to sink under the water and flip over.

Inez (McAllister) Edmondson senior year book photo- Courtesy of the PCCLD Special Collections

Throwing all four of them into the rushing water, Joseph quickly grabbed for Mary, while Charles grabbed for Inez, but when the men finally managed to pull themselves up onto the roof of a nearby house, only Inez joined them.

As the young woman continued to cough up water, the men sat with her along the edge of the submerged house and listened as she cried for her mother, and talked about how she should have just stayed in Chicago. Unfortunately, her mourning period was cut short by the appearance of hot embers raining down into the water, as an odd glow began to light up the night.

"How close are we to the King Lumber Yard?" Charles asked Inez with a nervous tone, as he leaned forward a bit and looked down the flooded street.

"Maybe half a block, why?" Inez answered as she looked up into the sky. "Wait, wait...are you suggesting that this is where all of these embers are coming from? Why would you even think that?"

"Because the King Lumber yard's on fire and it's been on fire for a while", Charles answered, as he pointed towards a single piece of flaming lumber riding the current. An hour before, when he had been up at the Mineral Place, he had seen the fires spreading throughout downtown, and now that he had a close up view of the bright red embers flowing through the air, landing in the water and extinguishing near him with a hiss, it made him wonder what people were facing downtown.

Raymond Lewis was wondering that too, despite being right in the center of it.

Raymond, who was visiting Pueblo with his cousin Bert, had checked into a three-story tall rooming house off South Union Avenue when the levees had first collasped but had fallen asleep on a couch in the lobby. With his hand now sliding off the side of the cushion and landing in the icy water, Raymond woke with a start and instantly smacked his head against something hard.

Confused, he laid back down and as he rubbed his head, he allowed his eyes to adjust to the dim light around him, which immediately created a sour pit in his stomach. The entire first floor of the rooming house was flooded almost up to the ceiling, due to the buildings front windows being knocked out by the storm. Surrounded by floating debris, and listening as the storm howled outside, he questioned how he was going to free himself from this very odd predicament.

As the couch spun around a bit in the flooded lobby, Raymond noticed an odd collection of small search lights shining in his direction. Placing the palms of his hands on the ceiling directly above his head, he carefully turned the couch just enough to see a group of people holding flashlights at the top of the first floor staircase. Seeing that he had noticed them, the men began calling out to him and asking if he was awake yet, followed by laughter.

Leaving his hands on the ceiling, Raymond began gliding the couch towards the lights until he saw two of the men with flashlights lower themselves down into the water and motion for him to keep coming towards them. As his maneuver began to pay off, one of the men grabbed hold of the couch's wooden feet to steady it, while the other helped Raymond onto the submerged staircase. Holding onto the railing for support, Raymond and his rescuers followed the stairs up to the second flood landing, where they were soon treated as celebrities.

Announcing the arrival of the sleeping man, the men introduced Raymond to everyone marooned up on the second floor, who laughed as they informed him that his unusual nap had kept them all entertained. As he handed out fake smiles and insincere handshakes, Raymond quickly headed up the stairs to the third floor where he saw people on their knees, praying for the Lord to save them, while others preached to him that the flood would surely last for days.

Not in the mood for small talk, Raymond felt around in his pocket and pulled out his key, instantly thankful for the privacy of his room, and the ability to take off his wet clothes so he could crawl into a dry bed.

But it was hard for him to fall asleep.

Outside the rooming house, he could hear the sounds of people and animals screaming, as automobiles, furniture, houses, and random debris continually smashed into the buildings outside his window , all mixed in with the crack of thunder and the illuminated dance of lightning. Finally becoming numb to the sounds, Raymond was almost asleep when he heard a terrible crash, which jolted him straight out of bed.

Running to the window, in all of his glory, he looked up and down the street in search of the noise, but every building in his line of sight was still standing, and he was sure that if it was the rooming house that was collapsing, he would hear people in the hallways screaming and he didn't. As Raymond turned away from the window and crawled back into bed, he had no idea that nine people down the street were frantically trying to bust a hole through the ceiling of a one story tall Cigar shop, before they all drowned.

William Riggs Bratton, the 48-year-old owner of The W.R. Bratton Cigar Shop, located at 105 South Union Avenue had headed home when the Arkansas River first began to over flow, but one of his employees who had a spare key chose to seek refuge inside the shop when the levees first began to break.

Joined inside by eight strangers, 32-year-old Otto Wilfred Snapp thought that the Cigar shop would be a safe refuge from the rising water, which it was until the building's front windows shattered. Climbing up onto the shop's display counters, the nine strangers began to panic as the water quickly began flooding the store, prompting Otto to find a way out.

Climbing up onto the store's central glass display case, he ran his hands along the ceiling and questioned if he could actually break through the plaster and get up onto the roof. Screaming over the roar of the flood, Otto called out for the frantic strangers to grab him something tough and sturdy, which luckily a few of them did. As the men joined him in his destructive quest, Otto whispered "I'm sorry William, I truly am", before he joined the other men in pounding a hole into the ceiling of William Bratton's Cigar shop.

With a combination of adrenaline and fear, the men successfully broke a decent sized hole into the ceiling and out through the roof, which unexpectedly caused a wave of rainwater to pour in over the top of them. Seeing the end in sight, and with the water inside the store now almost reaching the ceiling, the nine strangers began squeezing themselves through the hole and onto the roof, where they were hit with an unexpected wave of muddy floodwater.

The W.R Bratton Cigar shop was only one storefront away from the edge of the angry Arkansas River and the building was taking a serious beating. Luckily, their arrival on the roof had caught the attention of the second floor residents next door, at 107 South Union Avenue, who opened up their windows and helped the bruised and bloodied strangers inside and out of the storm.

Surprisingly, the building that had offered the stranger's shelter had originally housed Pueblo's first Jewish Synagogue up on that same floor before the newly constructed Temple Emanuel had opened its doors in 1900, at 1325 North Grand Avenue. Even now, 21 years later, the building's religious teaching still rang true, as the people who resided within its walls unknowingly followed the lessons written within the Jerusalem Talmud when they pulled those strangers to safety.

"Whoever destroys a soul, it is considered as if he destroyed an entire world. And whoever saves a life, it is considered as if he saved an entire world."- Sanhedrin 4:1 (22a)

But while the residents of the former Synagogue were saving lives, the workers inside The Mountain States Telephone Company were helplessly watching a man drown.

Safely up on the third floor of The Mountain States Telephone Company, Night Wire Chief Byron Thady and Chief Operators Josephine Pryor and Margaret Williams were trying their best to calm down the 39 Telephone girls, and one little sister, who were trapped with them inside the flood ravaged building. As Jazz records spun on the turn table and the Lord was prayed to, some of the Telephone girls began to sing, as their arms were held up towards the heavens.

"Rock of Ages, cleft for me. Let me hide myself in thee. Let the water and the blood, from thy wounded side which flowed, be of Sin the double cure and save from wrath and make me pure."

As the women continued to sing, Byron noticed that a reddish glow had appeared a block over, on South Union Avenue, which caused few of the girls to join him at the windows. As the glow continued to spread, the occupants up on the third floor of the Phone Company soon realized that the light was caused by flaming storm debris, and it was setting fire to everything it touched.

Lighting up the night, the floating torches illuminated the flood's destruction, as the eerie sounds of people screaming blended in with the roar of the storm, which prompted the faithful Telephone girls to continue to pray and sing to the Lord. As they did, the girls at the windows informed them that the fires were actually helping the rescuers by giving them the light they needed to save people, which caused the faithful to see the fires as an answer to their prayers.

But the fires were not helping everybody.

Trapped inside the one story tall brick garage that shared the alley with the Phone Company and lit only by flashlights, five strangers were joining forces in order to bust a hole through the roof of the garage before they all drowned. One of these men was Michael Lawrence Valley, a 27-year-old train engineer from Denver had found himself trapped inside the garage after offering to help his buddy get his car out, but instead of driving the vehicle to safety, he found himself standing on top of it.

From his perch, Michael had been introduced to 63-year-old Albert E. Schaubel, who owned a shoe store at 210 South Union Avenue called "The Cut-Rate shoe store", but despite his advanced age Albert had never married, but had a pretty good reason not to.

Albert's father Traugott Christoph Schaubel had practiced polygamy, which resulted in three wives and 21 children, with Albert being the oldest child born to his father's second wife Mary. After being raised in such a large family, Albert decided that he wanted to live a quiet, unattached life with his youngest full-blooded sibling Mary Sprengle and her family instead, while spending his days organizing shoes inside of his store.

But as the flood waters continued to rise around the garage, he didn't even know if his beloved shoe store was even still standing.

As Michael and Albert joined the other men in knocking a hole into the ceiling of the submerged garage, they all watched as the flood water around them continued to rise and questioned what they might be facing once they broke through to the roof. Finally achieving success, the men were quickly drenched in a constant torrent of cold muddy water, as they discovered that the depth of the flood was actually a few feet above the roofline of the garage.

Quickly pulling themselves up through the hole, the men found themselves standing in knee-deep water, and pummeled with heavy rain and hail that threatened to push them off the roof. Fearing that they would soon lose their balance and with nothing to hold onto, Michael Valley spotted a pile of storm debris that was caught against the nearby Telephone wires and felt that it could make a good raft.

Screaming for his companions to climb aboard, Michael helped the men over to the jumbled collection of wood and furniture just as it began floating down the alley that the garage shared with The Mountain

States Telephone Company.

But they were one man short.

In the chaos, they had failed to notice that Albert Schaubel had not been unable to squeeze completely through the hole in the roof of the garage, but Byron Thady did and he was frantic. Hearing the man scream for help, Byron quickly put on his jacket, opened up the door to the Telephone Companies fire escape, and stepped outside.

Taking the staircase down to the level of the angry floodwaters, Byron hung onto the railings as the 10-foot deep water churned and howled in anger below him. Glancing across the alley at the now submerged garage, Byron realized that there was no way for him to safely cross, as the constant flow of storm debris was just too unpredictable.

Excepting that the risk was too high, Byron quickly headed back up the stairs and re-entered the third floor, where he silently stared at the submerged garage until the man's screaming stopped. As Byron walked away from the window, he was unaware that six blocks away another man had not only freed himself from his own garage, but had saved a tiny life in the process.

With the depth of the floodwaters measuring over 14 feet, the areas between North Main Street and Santa Fe Avenue had become a death trap, and no one knew that better than 35-year-old Fred Oral Clasby. Fred was the owner of The Santa Fe Trail Garage, located at 220 North Santa Fe Avenue which specialized in selling the wonder car of the year, The Dort.

The Dort, which came in four styles, was the dream child of Josiah Dallas Dort, who worked as the Vice President of Chevrolet until 1912 when he stepped down to produce his own line of automobiles in 1915. His bottom line automobile, the Fleur-de-Lys Roadster sold for $695, which was a hard sell compared to the Ford Model T, which sold for a mere $395, but owner of The Santa Fe Trail garage in Pueblo was still very proud of its Dort inventory.

Even though it was now underwater.

Crawling up into the rafters of his garage, Fred discovered that the floodwaters inside the building had simply risen up with him, until he couldn't go up any higher. With nothing to light up the darkness but a small

Newspaper Ad for The Dort-Authors personal collection

box of matches he had found in his shirt pocket, Fred lit one and used it to gauge his dire situation. Realizing that he was going to have to punch a hole through the ceiling and climb up onto the roof, Fred looked around at the various pieces of debris the flood had washed into his garage and finally spied a 2 x 4 flooding nearby, which he grabbed just as the match began to burn his fingers.

Feeling around for a flat spot on the ceiling, Fred Clasby began using the board to bust out a hole, which soon produced not only his desired method of escape but the discovery that the pounding rain was waiting to further torment him. Sticking his head up through the hole, he was surprised to discover that he was surrounded by a sea of fire, death, and destruction, as the air was full of not only the roar of the floodwaters, but the screams of people trapped just like him.

Pulling his head back down into the garage, to make sure the hole was wide enough for him to squeeze his slender frame through, he thought he heard a high pitched meow. Striking another match and peering through the darkness, Fred spotted a tiny kitten perched on a piano box that must have floated into the garage when the storm had first broken out his front windows.

Turning his 2x4 around and laying the end on the piano box, Fred lit another match and found that he didn't need to say, Kitty, Kitty more than a few times, before the waterlogged fur ball spotted him, and quickly ran across the board into his waiting arms. Immediately greeted with purr's, Fred held the kitten above his head before squeezing through the hole he had created in the garages roof, allowing both him and his new little buddy to snuggle up and watch the destruction of Pueblo together.

Only a block away and also facing the task of pounding a hole through the ceiling of their own business, was 58-year old George Montgomery Knebel, the owner of Knebel Sporting Goods, and his two sons, 20-year-old Leon and 18-year-old George Jr. Located at 114 West Second Street, the men had found themselves trapped inside the buildings first floor after a large pile of debris had busted out the front windows, causing their store to flood.

With the doorway to the staircase that would lead them up to the second floor located outside the building, and not wishing to swim out into the storm in order to reach it, George and his son's grabbed a few baseball bats off the shelves and punched a hole into the ceiling. After pulling themselves up to the safety of the second floor, George Knebel and his sons went to the windows so they could see the true devastation of the storm.

As the roar of the flood filled the air, they watched Trolley cars and automobiles tumble amongst framed homes, furniture, and what appeared to be the bodies of horses, some of which slammed into buildings before sinking underneath the turbulent water.

Which is when they heard the screams.

Looking towards the noise, they noticed people stranded in the storm and it was then that the two brothers knew what they had to do. With a nod of understanding from their father and a quick hug for good luck, Leon and George Jr. ignored the newly constructed hole in the floor and instead chose to use the second-floor fire escape, in the hopes that they could save at least one person.

But hoping doesn't make it happen.

Holding onto the outside of the building to keep from being washed away, the brothers made their way around to the front of the building, where they dove underneath the deep water and swam back inside their father's flooded store through the smashed out front windows. Popping up inside the showroom, with only a few inches of air available near the ceiling, they saw their father pop his face through the hole that led up to the second floor.

"The rowboats are in the back", he instructed his son's, as he pointed towards the rear of the store.

Wiping their hair back, the brothers swam towards the back of the store where they finally spotted the rowboat, which was almost entirely submerged. With Leon grabbing the rope, and pulling the boat towards the front of the store, George grabbed two paddles and followed right behind him. Arriving at the broken storefront window, George took one of the paddles, dove under the water, and finished busting out the glass in order to make room for the rowboat to slide out of the building and into the storm.

Popping back up for air, the brothers pulled the submerged boat through the window and with a tight hold on the rope, were able to push it up and out of the deep water so it could right itself. With satisfied smiles, George and Leon climbed aboard the little boat, scooped the remaining water out of the bottom, gave their father a quick wave and headed out to save some lives.

Rowing west down Second Street towards Main, the brothers only had to paddle past a few buildings before they were faced with a horrifying sight. Sitting at the corner of 2nd and Main Street was Pryor's furniture store, or what was left of it. The three story tall brick building, located at 127 North Main Street, was quickly disintegrating before their eyes as the strong current was repeatedly smashing a floating freight car into the building over and over, causing bricks, shattered wood, and furniture to crash into the water.

Desperate to avoid getting hit by flying debris, Leon and George quickly steered their rowboat away from Pryor's and onto Main Street so they could be out of harm's way, or so they thought. As the boys headed through the flooded street looking for people caught in the storm, they quickly discovered that the people trapped up on the upper floors of the buildings along Main Street, between 3rd and 5th appeared to be playing a game with large floating piles of fire.

And the Knebel boys were caught right in the middle.

Using pool cues, brooms, and mops, the refugees up on the second floor were hanging out of the windows of the building and frantically pushing away piles of ignited storm debris, as the floating infernos attempted to set fire to everything they touched. Caught in the crossfire, the boys tried to turn their tiny boat away from the piles, but in the confusion, Leon fell overboard.

Quickly caught in a muddy whirlpool, Leon was violently slammed up against the Whitcomb block building, located at 300 North Main Street, and found himself tangled around the large clock that hung off the corner of the building. As he desperately tried to hold on, Leon heard someone scream at him, followed by the end of a rope landing in the water beside him.

Grabbing at the lifeline, Leon was pulled up through a window on the second floor of the Whitcomb building, where he was soon joined by his brother George, who decided to give up on his quest to save people and instead used the rope to tie the boat up to the building until morning.

CHAPTER 9

The butcher knife and a man
named Abraham Lincoln

Perched high and dry inside the upper floors of the Union Depot, Dispatcher Brutus Milton Stearns was keeping a sharp eye on the floodwaters outside of his building, all while making sure that his surprise guests were kept as comfortable as possible. Out of the 75 people who had sought refuge inside the towering red sandstone Train Depot, only about 20 of them were actually passengers who had been left stranded when the flood cut off the arrival of their connecting trains.

Joining Brutus in the Depot's towering perch was 30-year-old Elza Alexander Cress, who was the manager of the Hotel located inside Union Depot. Elza had been a Sailor back before the World War, where he was stationed off the coast of Japan in a Navy ship called the USS Charleston, but even he had to admit he had never seen a natural disaster quite like this.

Peering through the Depots storm drenched windows, the two men watched as the current carried away framed houses, automobiles, animals, furniture, and even train cars throughout the downtown area, which were soon joined by flaming piles of lumber that had appeared from around the corner of a nearby office building. From the glow of its light, the men witnessed a human body whirling around the front entrance of the Union Depot, before it quickly sank down into the mud infused water and disappeared from sight.

But this wasn't the first time a body had been seen outside the Depot.

Twenty years earlier, on April 6, 1901, a 58-year-old express man named William H. Cale suddenly dropped dead right outside the front steps of the Depot just as the clock struck noon. It took a few moments for the people around him to realize what had happened, but when they did Medical aide was immediately summoned, but it was no use. The Coroner, 59-year-old Abraham Lincoln Fugard questioned a few bystanders before coming up with a conclusion of how he thought the man had died.

"I have been informed that just prior to Mr. Cale approaching his horse, it had been startled by the activities of a nearby animal." Coroner Fugard informed the gathering crowd, as the man's body was moved into the back of a wagon. "And it is thought that the excitement caused heart failure, which resulted in him being stricken dead."

But it wasn't the activities of a nervous animal that was spooking the men over at the nearby Power Company.

Located only four blocks from the Depot, at the corner of D and Lamkin Street, sat the partially constructed Arkansas Valley Railway, Light and Power Company building, which was flooded all the way up to its steel rafters. When the water had first begun to rise, 38-year-old Construction Superintendent George Frank Phythian and 25-year-old Steelworker Harry Mitchell had stayed behind to secure what they could and save what might need saving, but now they needed someone to save them.

With the Power plant still in its skeletal form, the two men struggled to find shelter from the rain and pounding hail, but now after hours of clinging to the building's upper rafters, it appeared that the water was beginning to rise once more.

But why?

Back inside the upper floors of the Union Depot, this unexpected phenomenon wasn't going unnoticed as Dispatcher Brutus Stearns quickly went over to the level rod he had obtained from the Division Engineers office and once again checked the water level. Brutus had been using this rod to record the depth of the water about every 30 minutes since 9:05 pm, which had allowed him to document that the water had finally leveled out at almost 10 feet deep just around Midnight.

Unfortunately, as the clocks began chiming out the 3 am hour, the water was once again rising and Dispatcher Stearns had a feeling that something bad was about to happen.

As the dispatcher continued to measure the height of the quickly rising water, the Pueblo residents that lived along the shores of Fountain Creek were in full panic mode. Almost six hours after the Arkansas River and Fountain Creek had combined their forces, and broke through Pueblo's compromised levees, Fountain Creek was revving up for a second strike.

With its normal flow recorded at a minuscule speed of only 100 feet per second, Fountain Creek once again began to swell just around Midnight, quickly reaching a speed of 4,000 feet per second, and devouring not only the surrounding low lying areas but every bridge in its path. By the time 2:30 am had chimed in, the raging water was barreling down the Creek at 12,000 feet per second, covering everything it touched in over six feet of additional water, but it was only getting started.

As the clocks chimed the arrival of 3 am, Fountain Creek had finally crested at the astounding speed of over 34,000 feet per second.

Which was about to severely impact the survival of the train passengers.

After being alerted about the incoming flood from the occupants inside the Nuckolls packing plant, Dallas Cuenin glanced over at the debris field that his fellow passengers from the Denver & Rio Grande No.3 were using to cross over to the plant and began screaming for them to come back to the train.

Choosing to ignore him and instead continue their quest to scale over the mountain of trees, furniture, and lumber, the passengers quickly realized that the debris field had become unstable and was breaking apart. As the water began to rise, both the train and the massive pile of debris began to twist and sway, causing the passengers inside the packing plant to scream for people to run towards them, while Dallas Cuenin was still screaming for people to come back to the train.

As the second flood made its appearance, the water in the train yard rose up to a staggering 16 feet, causing the mountain of debris to rip itself away from not only the edge of the Nuckolls Plant but its connection to the Denver & Rio Grande No. 3. With the thundering roar of the water drowning out the screams of the remaining passengers, the No. 3 found itself once again slamming into the nearby Missouri Pacific No. 14, as both trains bucked and thrashed in the violent current.

Blasting past the submerged train yard, the second wave of water set its sights on the already compromised downtown areas of Pueblo, where it rose the height of the floodwaters well past 20 feet, forcing residents to frantically climb up onto the roofs of buildings in order to survive.

But the two men trapped inside of the partially constructed Arkansas Valley Railway, Light and Power Company building didn't have that luxury.

Climbing up as high as they could, Construction Superintendent George Phythian and steelworker Harry Wilcox quickly realized that the building that they were trapped in just didn't go up any higher. Wrapping their legs and arms around the steel girders and shivering uncontrollably in the icy water, the men tried their best to keep each other calm, as the water reached just under their chins.

But they were alive.

Unlike the infant that 17-year-old Joseph Hubert Abell was currently holding.

When the fire whistle first began to scream out its warnings, Joseph Abell and his friend 21-year-old George Thomas Morrissey Jr had been helping George's parents move office furniture and equipment up onto the second floor of their building using a manually operated service elevator. Located at 300 South Main Street and less than two blocks from the train yards, the Morrissey Carriage Company was not only a family run business, but George Jr and his family also lived in the upstairs apartment.

With help from George's parents, 48-year-old George Sr. and 43-year-old Martha, as well as his siblings, 18-year-old Martha and 13-year-old Albert, the two young men managed to not only hoist up all of the important pieces of office equipment up to the second floor but moved an electric motor onto the elevator as well. Piling more equipment on top of the motor, the elevator's platform was packed rather tight, and not wishing to unload the last of the equipment into the apartment, the exhausted group chose to simply tie the hoist rope to the top of the lift, and knot it for extra security.

As the night continued, the group sat by their apartment's second-floor windows and watched as the flood overtook the city, but with the electricity out and not much else to do, they eventually fell asleep. A little after 3 am, George Morrissey Sr. found himself jostled awake by a repetitive vibration, and sleepily questioned if something might be striking the outside of their building.

Grabbing his flashlight, George quickly got out of bed to take a look, but when he placed his feet on the floor he didn't feel the softness of the rug, but cold water instead. Quickly waking his wife Martha, and alerting her to the problem, George instructed her to wake the children while he walked over to their apartment's front windows to take a look outside at the storm.

As another jolt vibrated the apartment's walls, George Sr. watched as a collection of furniture, automobiles, and ignited wood smashed into the side of their building, causing a wave of water to crash against the windows, with the excess leaking into the apartment.

With the children now awake and holding lanterns, the captives gathered near the windows and silently watched as a large, framed house floated past, riding the angry current with ease. Spinning in a clockwise pattern, the house struck a street light before correcting itself just in time to violently collide with the side of the Morrissey's building.

As the impact vibrated throughout the apartment, the waterlogged house was quickly whipped around by a violent whirlpool and sucked down C Street, where it crashed into the side of the nearby C Street Bridge.

Relieved that the framed house was gone, but with no way to gauge the damage it had caused to their building, the second-floor captives kept a close eye out the windows, fearful that something else might knock into their now compromised building.

Which is when they noticed the rowboat floating down the opposite side of the street.

Fighting the strong current, the little boat appeared to contain both a man and a woman, with the woman holding some type of package against her chest. As the boat continued to ride the torrent, the second floor captives realized that the craft was getting too close to the building across the street, causing the woman to hold out her free hand in an attempt to stop the expected impact.

But she couldn't.

As the man and the woman were thrown into the violent water, the man grabbed both the woman and her package in one fail swoop, while holding onto the edge of the building with his free hand. Frantically searching around for a safe haven, he spotted the second floor captives watching him from their lantern lit window and began swimming towards the Morrissey's building.

As the man and woman fought the quickly flowing current, their clothing snagged on a partially submerged dump rake, as its large metal wheels were sticking out of the debris pile that separated them from the coveted building. Unaware of why the couple had stopped swimming, George Morrissey Sr. opened up their apartment's window and called for the man to continue coming towards them, while George Jr's friend Joseph Abell ran over to the kitchen and began rummaging through the drawers for a knife.

Grabbing a large butcher knife, Joseph ran over to the family's service elevator, and after placing the knife between his teeth, quickly began untying the rope that held the elevator tightly to the top of the lift. With the rope finally free, Joseph took the knife out of his mouth, and while still holding the rope in one hand, leaned over and sliced it as far down to the base as he could, which immediately caused the loaded elevator to slam into the flooded shaft.

As it sank, Joseph gathered up the heavy rope, ran back over to the apartment's front windows and dumped the rope onto the floor. Grabbed one end, he quickly tossed it out the window towards the couple, which prompted his friend George Jr. to quickly ask "Wait, where did you find a rope?"

With no time for small talk, Joseph watched as the man looped it around the woman and with George Jr's help, he quickly pull her in through the window. With the woman safe, Joseph threw the rope back over to the man who then tied it around the unidentified parcel, but when the boy's attempted to pull it towards the window, it became caught in the current and was sucked underneath the water.

"My baby!"

Startled at discovering what was in the package, Joseph and George Jr. frantically began pulling at the rope, causing the baby to quickly pop back up out of the water, only to be thrown towards the building, where it became trapped under a folded awning. Without a second thought, Joseph instructed George Jr. to hold onto his legs as he leaned over the window ledge and using the rope as a guide, lowered himself headfirst into the icy water.

Unable to see anything in the pitch blackness of the flood, and unsure how long he could hold his breath, Joseph managed to free the baby, but he was about to discover that his heroic deed was unfinished. As George Jr. pulled Joseph back out of the water, the apartment's captives looked at the child and discovered that not only was it not breathing, but its face was almost black.

As George Jr. began untying the rope from the child, Joseph flipped the baby over onto his thigh and gave it a few quick whacks, but when no water came out he turned the baby over to discover that its mouth was tightly clenched. Reaching into his pocket, he pulled out his pocket knife and quickly began shoving it between the child's teeth in an attempt to pry its mouth open.

As the child's mother began to scream, Joseph instructed George Jr. to grab another knife, and together the two friends managed to pry the baby's mouth open. Using his free hand, Joseph then reached his fingers into the child's mouth and pulled its tongue forward before flipping the tiny, limp body over his thigh and giving it a few more whacks.

With the child's cries quickly filling the room, the distraught mother fell to her knees as her baby was handed back to her, but as she thanked the boys, they suddenly remembered that there was still a man waiting out in the storm to be rescued. Quickly returning to the window, Joseph threw out the rope and to his relief, the waterlogged man grabbed hold of it while the boys pulled him into the apartment.

But across town, the cries were not of joy, but of despair.

Hours earlier, 47-year-old Joseph B. Roberts and Charles E. Wayland had borrowed a rowboat from the Minerals Palace's Lake Clara and had used it in their attempt to rescue two women near 8th and Elizabeth Street, but after the first one had washed away, the men were left to question the vitality of the second one.

Inez Edmondson, a 23-year-old colored vaudeville singer who had been visiting her parents from Chicago had already been tossed into the raging waters a couple of times and rescued a couple of times before becoming trapped on the roof of her families submerged two story house with her rescuers. Unfortunately, a floating inferno then set the house on fire, which forced Inez and her rescuers back into the frigid flood waters and now she wasn't moving.

When the nearby King's Lumberyard had caught on fire, due to its supply of Quicklime igniting in the rising flood water, it had spawned floating piles of flaming debris which set fire to everything they touched, including the house Inez and her rescuers had been sitting on. Unable to put out the quickly spreading flames, they had been forced back into the icy water, which appeared to of drained the life out of Inez, who they were now unable to wake up.

Holding onto the side of the ignited house, the men took turns keeping her head above water, while looking for any signs of life, but they never saw any. After what seemed like hours, a rowboat finally came into sight, with the men insisting that Inez's body be lifted up first before they boarded. Arriving at the Courthouse on West 10th Street, her body was brought in on a stretcher, while Charles Wayland wrote down her name and the name of her mother Mary McAllister, who had washed away hours earlier, into the ledger before leaving in silence.

As Inez was prepared for transport to the T.G. McCarthy Morgue for embalming, the ledger was only slightly glanced at, with her name being incorrectly recorded as Mary McAllister. Loaded into a truck, Inez was transported to the Morgue where she was laid out on a cold, metal table, but she had something that the other flood victims around her didn't have.

A pulse.

CHAPTER 10

A screaming hog and the waterlogged bananas

As the sunrise of June 4th greeted Pueblo the storm clouds were still evident, but the tiny rays of sunlight that poked through gave people hope that the rain might soon end, as even now it had reduced itself to a mere drizzle. The onslaught of additional water from Fountain Creek, which had added six feet to the flood in three hours had finally leveled out, leaving the depth of the flood around downtown Pueblo at a staggering, but stable 10 feet.

Flood water on the morning of June 4th, at the corner of First street and Santa Fe Avenue- Courtesy of The Pueblo County Historical Society

With daylight beginning to showcase the wrath of the flood, Construction Superintendent George Phythian and steelworker Harry Wilcox, who had been trapped inside the partially constructed Arkansas Valley Railway, Light and Power Company building, finally saw a chance to escape their steel prison. Less than a block away and submerged almost up to its second floor, the two men spied the 3 story tall brick building that sat directly across the street, at 201 Lamkin Street, and it appeared to have life on its upper floors.

Carefully lowering their numb bodies into the cold, debris filled water, and with their teeth locked tight from a night spent being pummeled by frigid rain and hail, the two men forced their stiffened limbs to kick away from the safety of the Power Company's building and prayed that they had enough strength to swim across the street.

As their hypothermic legs burned and throbbed with each jerky motion and in constant fear of drowning, George and Harry finally reached the building, where they used the last of their energy to scream for help, all while struggling to keep their heads above water. Within minutes the two men watched as one of the windows slid open and a pair of hands extended out into the water.

They swore it was one of the most beautiful things they had ever seen.

Over in the train yards, the remaining passengers from the Denver & Rio Grande No. 3 were still sitting huddled together on top of the Pullman car's, just as the sun began to light up the morning sky. All of the remaining passengers from the nearby Missouri Pacific No. 14 had already made their way over to the safety of the Schlitz Brewery Company's building, just as the second flood had hit, but the No. 3 passengers were still too scared to cross the debris field over to the nearby Nuckolls plant.

Seeing that the passengers were hesitant, a few men came over from the plant and crossed the newly formed pile of debris, to not only assure them that it was safe but to help the passengers walk over the piles of logs, fractures buildings, furniture, automobiles, and dead animals.

Seeing that help had arrived, Dallas Cuenin stood up and began rousing the remaining passengers, while the newly arrived men, who appeared dry and well-rested, began helping the battered and exhausted men, women, and children across the debris field.

Unfortunately, when it came time for Dayton Kramer to cross, the sharp wood and pockets of glowing cinders within the debris proved too much for his barefoot to handle. While cursing himself for not tying his shoes in the early hours of the flood, a female passenger informed him that she had seen some foot ware near one of the cars, but when he located the mud filled shoe, he discovered that it was too small. With a shrug, he rinsed out the mud, slipped it on as far as it would go, and carefully tiptoed across the debris field until he made it across.

But not everyone was so lucky.

Out of the almost 60 passengers from the Denver & Rio Grande No. 3 that had spent the night on top of the train cars, not all of them were conscious. With quite a number discovered to be wearing only nightclothes, many of them appeared to be suffering from not only shock but hyperthermia, with some showing no signs of life regardless of how many people tried to wake them.

Not wishing to further traumatize the remaining passengers, the unresponsive were carefully carried across the debris field to the Nuckolls Plant where they were laid next to the fire and wrapped in blankets, in hopes that the spark of life inside them would once again ignite.

As the last unconscious passenger was carried across the debris field and the train cars were checked one last time for stragglers, Dallas Cuenin finally allowed himself permission to cross over to the Nuckolls plant, where he received not only a warm blanket and a hot cup of coffee but a hug from his grateful wife Lydia.

With the rain coming to an end around 8 am, and the sun finally shining down onto the flooded streets, the people of Pueblo once again brought out their rowboats and rafts so they could continue looking for survivors, but one particular raft wasn't going to be used to rescue a person in peril, but a hog that just wouldn't stop squealing.

At the height of the flood, Memorial Hall on North Union Avenue housed many refugees as it sat on the banks of the angry Arkansas River, but one refugee found himself stranded on the roof of a nearby building instead and he wanted everyone within earshot to know that he wasn't very happy about it.

All through the night of June 3rd, and into the early morning hours of June 4th, the constant scream of a squealing hog echoed over the sounds of the storm, driving flood refugees mad with exhaustion, as nobody was about to get any sleep if that hog wasn't happy.

When the first set of rowboats and rafts made their appearance on North Union Avenue, a stranded Fireman inside Memorial Hall opened up a second floor window and motioned for one of the rafts to come close so he could explain his unusual request.

Finding that the men were happy to help, the Fireman climbed out through the window and into the raft, where he directed the men towards the sound of the angry animal. Climbing onto the building's roof, the Fireman preceded to chase the terrified creature around until it was finally tackled and carried kicking and screaming back over to the raft.

With nowhere to drop off the creature, the hog was taken back to Memorial Hall, where he happily walked around the buildings marble lined halls, while the refugees enjoyed some well-earned peace and quiet.

As the raft was completing its hog capture, a rowboat five blocks over had just arrived at the Pueblo Water Works Building, located at the corner of 4th and Grand Avenue in search of 60-year-old John Nittinger. John had been working at the Water Works buildings when the call first came in about a flood heading to Pueblo, which prompted him to begin sounding the building's steam-driven fire whistle, but his family hadn't seen him since.

Entering the flooded building, John was located up near the steam whistle with his arms wrapped around a pipe, and his lower body submerged in the icy flood water. Unable to get himself down, not only because of the hyperthermia but his arthritic knees, his rescuers took extra caution helping him down and out to the boat.

Which is about the same time people started to notice the airplane.

Buzzing around Pueblo was 27-year-old Pilot William Alexander Kimsey who had flown planes in the War, but now he flew newspaper reporters around to cover stories, and he could tell right away that this was going to be a big one.

"From an altitude of about 1,000 feet, the business district of Pueblo looks like a sea of mud and water," William announced to the reporters sitting in the rear of his plane, who were quickly writing down everything he said. "The railroad station looks like an island in a lake, the tracks are completely submerged and the cars are floating about. The waters of the Arkansas River are backed up on the right bank for what appears to be several blocks, and the approximate vicinity of the Vail Hotel is submerged."

"All of the outlying districts of the lowlands appear utterly devastated and for miles around there is nothing but a vast expanse of mud. Dotted here and there I can also see houses perched at some very odd angles." He added as he continued to describe what he saw. "Between Pueblo and Colorado Springs, all of the bridges as far as I can observe are washed out and the city is entirely cut off to the north. It's like the city was cut right in half by the flood."

Looking for a place to land his plane, William finally found a spot at the Mineral Palace Park, where he was greeted by the curious and the desperate, who were hoping for news of loved ones. As William began talking with survivors, the two staff correspondents he had transported, one from the Associated Press and the other from The Rocky Mountain News, exited his plane in search of their stories.

And they found a doozy.

Parked underneath the towering trees which lined Mineral Palace Park, were more than 20 brand new Buick automobiles parked in perfect rows, ranging from the $395 four-door passenger Coupe, to the top of the line seven-passenger Sedan which went for a staggering $2,285. Standing next to the cars and tending to them as a hen would her chicks, was 20-year-old car salesman Ross Harold Edmundson.

When the sirens had first begun to scream out their warnings from the side of the Water Works building and word began to spread that a flood was coming down the Arkansas River, Ross was sitting at home with his widowed mother, 45-year-old Blanch. Worried that nearby Fountain Creek might also flood, and possibly reach the automobile dealership where he worked, Ross walked the one block over to the Colorado Motor Car Company and was surprised to find it deserted.

Fearing the worst, Ross grabbed the keys to the most expensive car on the lot, drove it back home, picked up his mother, and then took the automobile up to the highest point he could think of, which was the Mineral Palace Park. Parking it under a tree and leaving his mother in charge, Ross then ran the six blocks back to the dealership, grabbed the next car, and parked it right next to the first one.

Over and over Ross ran back to the dealership until the flood got too high and the car's waterlogged engines refused to turn over. Admitting defeat, he trudged back up to the Mineral Palace Park and with his mom, stood guard over his collection, hoping that when the disaster was over, his boss would see how committed he was to his job.

Another usual sighting at the Mineral Palace Park was the discovery of an oddly constructed flood levee, between Lake Clara and the railroad tracks that ran past the east side of the park. With the park situated near the banks of Fountain Creek, 29-year-old Park Superintendent Everett Edson Colby had ordered his staff to cut down 13 of the parks large willow trees and use them to build a levee incase Fountain Creek flooded, which it did.

Twice.

As Fountain Creek had risen in power, the pile of downed trees was further fortified with railroad ties and heavy wire cables, which succeeded in keeping the flooded creek at bay. Everett's main objective was not only to protect Lake Clara but the park's beloved flower gardens, which he was happy to report that he had.

With Mineral Palace Park now full of flood refugees, automobiles, and horses wandering around, it was hard to imagine that just two days earlier the Pueblo Newspaper had run a story that focused on how the Police had to patrol the park for "Spooner's".

Sent on patrol day and night, sometimes dressed in plain clothes, the officers were instructed to watch out for minors who would either spoon inside parked cars or be brazen enough as to openly spoon in broad daylight, as the park wanted to be known as a safe place for families to visit.

And for the people of Pueblo to find shelter.

When the flood first began to rise and people began evacuating the low lying areas in search of higher ground, the Mineral Palace had opened its doors to everyone, which is where the newspaper reporters, who had just arrived on the airplane, found five Telegraph operators, as well as a newspaper reporter huddled around a makeshift Telegraph machine.

At 9:10 pm, the night before, 40-year-old Associated Press reporter Howard Hayden had discovered that his Telegraph was no longer giving out its familiar clicks of dots and dashes, which had prompted him to fight the storm to find the nearest Western Union Office. Arriving at the office around Midnight, Howard was introduced to 37-year-old Night Wire Chief Emory Mitchell and together the two men began reconnecting the Telegraph lines before setting up shop inside the Mineral Palace but were only able to send out a few distress messages before the dashes and dots ceased once more.

But it appears to have been enough.

As the newly arrived Newspaper reporters approached the two men and praised them both for a job well done, the reporters began sharing stories about what they had seen from the plane and it was worse than anyone could imagine. Adding into the conversation were four additional Telegraph operators who had also just arrived, after reading the distress message that had come over their wires at 1:30 am, but unlike the reporters, these men didn't have the luxury of traveling to Pueblo by airplane.

The four operators were all part of the Denver Telegraph Division, but only two of them needed to travel from Denver, which was over 120 miles north of Pueblo. Facing deep water, torrential rain, washed-out roads, and bridges that threatened to collapse from the weight of their motor car, 33-year-old William John Bern's and 19-year-old Joseph Henry Hoskins were more than relieved when they finally reached the Mineral Palace Park on the morning of June 4th.

The third operator was a 42-year-old man named Edwin Booth Clements, who faced similar obstacles as he traveled south from Colorado Springs, which was 45 miles north of Pueblo, while the fourth

Telegraph man Edwin Clements- Courtesy of the PCCLD Special Collections

Telegraph man Ellsworth Stapp- Courtesy of the PCCLD Special Collections

Telegraph man Joseph Hoskins- Courtesy of the PCCLD Special Collections

Telegraph man William Berns- Courtesy of the PCCLD Special Collections

operator 35-year-old Ellsworth Logan Stapp traveled over from the nearby town of La Junta.

La Junta, which was around 70 miles east of Pueblo, had caused Ellsworth quite a scare as he had to drive over washed out roads, and unstable bridges, but just like the Post Office, the Telegraph needed to be available in the rain, sleet, snow, or 12-foot wall of floodwater.

But at least all four of the Telegraph men had dramatic stories to tell the reporters who had arrived at The Mineral Palace by airplane.

As the reporters finished filling their notebooks with stories and headed back to their flying chariot, the Telegraph operators and reporter Howard Hayden got back to work. Despite having their makeshift Telegraph once again functional, the men all agreed that one telegraph line wasn't going to be enough to handle the traffic. Unfortunately, the only way to fix this problem was to head down into the heart of the flood and re-wire more of the Telegraph poles.

The main office of the Western Union Telegraph Company was located at 415 North Main Street, which Telegraph operator Emory Mitchell was confident was still surrounded by floodwater, but with the office up on the building's second floor, he was hopeful that it had weathered last night's storm. Unfortunately, the Telegraph Company didn't store their extra equipment and spools of wire inside the building, but down at the Denver & Rio Grande Freight Depot.

Located at 201 B Street, the Freight Depot sat directly across the street from Union Depot and its numerous train yards, which according to the reporters from the airplane, was submerged under about 10 feet of floodwater. This meant that the men were going to have to use a rowboat to get to the Freight Depot, which was almost two miles from Mineral Palace and after they arrived they would then have to haul the Telegraph wire up to the main office on 4th and Main, which was almost 20 blocks north of the Freight Depot.

Confident that some of the roads leading into downtown would be dry, a few rowboats were acquired, as well as trucks to transport the Telegraph men to the edge of the floodwater. As the five men gathered up their supplies and prepared to leave, it was decided that Howard Hayden would stay behind at the Mineral Palace to man the one working Telegraph.

Wishing his comrades good luck, Howard returned to his makeshift Telegraph station and sent out another distress message to both the Associated Press and the Governor.

"Loss of life in the Pueblo Flood Heavy. Body transported in wagons. We need food and water quickly. Need bedding and milk for babies. Conditions here very bad. Rescue work going on. Send every man you can. Hundreds in danger."

As the trucks left the Mineral Palace and headed south towards downtown, the men were able to make it all the way down to 7th Street before they hit water. Seeing that the east side of 7th appeared dry, the trucks began squirreling around any dry street they could find, which allowed them to finally reach 1st Street before once again encountering deep water.

Unloading the rowboats from the trucks, the Telegraph men calculated that they were still almost 10 blocks away from the Freight Depot, and with storm clouds starting to form once again, they knew this wasn't going to be easy. Rowing out into the flooded street, the men were suddenly faced with the horrific reality of the flood's destruction on their city, as they passed piles of floating debris, some of which still smoked with the occasional flicker of flames still deep within them.

Occasionally a human form would be spotted, some stripped bare by the violent waters that had

Flood damage at Second and Main street. Submerged trolley cars can be seen, as well as the collapsed side of Pryors furniture in the upper left hand corner- Courtesy of The Pueblo County Historical Society

tumbled them throughout the night, while others appeared bloodied and torn as they lay tangled amongst the partially submerged piles of furniture and lumber. As the Telegraph men gently used their oars to move the bodies out of their path, they noticed a small dog running back and forth across a floating debris pile, possibly looking for his master while nervously barking at everyone he saw.

Deeper in the bowls of the flood was yet another rowboat, with this one being manned by two young men who thought they had heard a woman calling for help. Turning their boat down D Street, which was only two blocks from Union Depot, the men discovered that

Flooded street near Memorial Hall- Courtesy of The Pueblo County Historical Society

the sound was coming from The Mountain States Telephone's Companies building. As they got closer, they were waved down by numerous Telephone girls who were standing on the building's third-floor fire escape.

"Girls, what can we do for you?" 20-year-old Elwyn Halford Davis asked, as more girls began gathering around the windows.

"Get us something to eat!"

With a tip of his hat, Elwyn, who went by his middle name Halford and his friend William quickly rowed away in search of something to feed what appeared to be an infinite number of girls. Rowing back onto Union Avenue, the two men found a fruit store that had its front windows smashed out, which allowed them to row their boat directly into the store for some drive-through shopping.

Looking for something safe for the girls to eat, the men finally spotted two large bunches of bananas hanging from a hook, with their ends dangling into the deep floodwater. Rowing over, they carefully removed their catch and headed back over to the Telephone Companies building to find the girls still standing outside on the fire escape.

"Oh, lookey, lookey! Here comes the dove with an olive branch!" 18-year-old Wilma Cary cried out, as Halford stood up in his rowboat and carefully handed her the bananas. Knowing that the water around the building was still too deep and unstable to risk rescuing the girls, the men promised that they would return once the water had subsided.

But the Telegraph men didn't have that luxury.

Finally reaching North Union Avenue, and spotting Memorial Hall off to the left, they knew they were only four blocks from Union Depot, which was located on the corner of South Union and B Street. Focusing on the prize, the men continued to row until they finally spotted the Depot and the piles of debris that surrounded it.

Freight cars, household debris, and lumber littered the deep water in front of Union Depot, while the bodies of numerous dead cows casually floated around them, bumping off the debris piles like they were inside of a pinball machine.

Halford Davis bringing bananas to the Telephone girls- Authors personal collection

As the Telegraph men continued down B Street towards the Freight Depot, they soon spotted the three-story-tall Arcade Hotel off to their right, which they had heard was a brothel, or least used to be. Unfortunately, with no red lights flickering in the windows to prove the rumor, the Telegraph men had to come to their own conclusions, just as the Denver & Rio Grande Freight Depot finally came into view.

The one story tall brick building was over two blocks long and contained numerous large freight doors that faced the street, which were opened from the inside, as well as a two-story-tall office

Union Depot submerged in flood water. The Arcade Hotel can be seen on the left side with a freight car leaning against the front door-Courtesy of the Pueblo County Historical Society

building attached on one end. Rowing the boats up to the office building, the Telegraph men could see that despite it being perched on a set of raised stone stairs, the floodwaters had still partially submerged the first-floor windows, as well as the main door, so it was decided that shimming open a window would be the easiest way to enter the building.

Looking through their supplies, Emory Mitchell located a knife, as one of the other men handed him a flashlight so he would be able to see once inside the building. Using the knife, Emory was able to unlock the window, but when he slid it open water quickly began to pour into the once dry office building. As a feeling of guilt washed over him, Emory quickly grabbing his flashlight, and scrabbled inside, closing the window behind him.

Looking around the vacant offices and rifling through their files, Emory was finally able to not only discover which storage area was rented by the Western Union Telegraph Company but where the keys were stored as well. With a celebratory swing in his step and the coveted key in his hand, Emory clicked his flashlight to life before heading down the dark hallway towards the prize.

Locating the door, and sliding the key into the lock, Emory took a deep breath before opening up the storage room, which revealed not only a stockpile of supplies but spool after spool of Telegraph line. With a sigh of relief, Emory began looking through his bounty using not only the light from his flashlight but the sunlight that was shining in through the upper windows of the exterior door.

The exterior door.

Glancing around the room once again, Emory suddenly remembered that the depth of the floodwater outside was above the level of the loading ramp, which meant that the storage room would flood as soon as he opened the exterior door. Setting down his flashlight, he moved as many of the supplies up onto shelves as he could, before condemning the rest to an onslaught of floodwater.

With one last glance back, Emory raised the exterior door, which allowed over a foot of murky, debris filled water to engulf the room.

Cheering Emory's success and their good fortune, Ellsworth Stapp, Edwin Clements, William Berns, and Joseph Hoskins rowed their boats in through the now open door and joined him inside the storage room, where they all discussed not only how they were going to move all of the needed equipment into two rowboats, but how they were going to re-establish the connection with so many damaged Telegraph poles.

With about 4,000 feet of spooled Telegraph wire sitting inside the storage room, the men all agreed that it was going to take every inch of it to reconnect the city, which would leave no room for any of them inside the rowboats. With a shrug of their shoulders, the men began to load the spools of wire and equipment into them, as they glanced over towards Union Depot trying to decide which Telegraph pole they should climb first.

As the last spool was loaded into the rowboats, Emory Mitchell sat down on a nearby box and began untying his shoes, which he quickly slid off, before removing his shirt, pants, and underwear, which he folded and set aside, before sliding his shoes back onto his feet. As Emory began retying his shoes, Ellsworth, Edwin, William, and Joseph began following his lead, with each man eventually dressed in nothing but their shoes and hat, as a man is always considered properly dressed when he is wearing his hat.

Finding a canvas sack inside the storage room, the men placed their clothes inside before tying it tight and tossing it into one of the rowboats, just as Emory began slowly lowering himself down into the debris filled water. As his naked body adjusted to the frigid temperature, he began pushing the debris away from the rowboats as his comrades joined him, minus the one who stayed inside the storeroom so he could lower the exterior door and leave back through the office window, which he respectfully closed behind him.

Unfortunately, just as the men began shimmying up the first Telegraph pole in all of their glory, the dark storm clouds that covered the sky began to release a fine mist of rain over the group, which gave them the feeling that Mother Nature was trying to stop them from reconnecting the Telegraph. Not to be defeated, and already wet from their swim, the naked men swam over to the next pole, while questioning if the incoming rainstorm could possibly bring on another surge of water.

Which might have unintentionally caused a Jinx.

As the Telegraph men continued to work, a Dam that sat over 30 miles North West of Pueblo was unwillingly excepting this same onslaught of rain, but it was reaching its breaking point.

And its walls were beginning to crack.

Sunbathing rattlesnakes and the bestial monster

Towering 14,115 feet above sea level, the mountain known as Pikes Peak had been a historic beacon for Gold prospectors who dreamed of striking it rich years before Colorado was even a state, as well as being named after a man who never even tried to reach its peak. Lieutenant Zebulon Montgomery Pike had been hired by President Thomas Jefferson to survey the new land acquired through the Louisiana Purchase of 1803, but when Pike headed out to visit the towering mountain in 1806, which he named Grand Peak, he accidentally climbed the wrong one.

After climbing neighboring Mount Rosa instead, or perhaps by accident, Lieutenant Zebulon Pike and his men spent a chilly November day standing in the waist deep snow that covered the base of the correct mountain and quickly decided that their summer attire and lack of provisions made the peak unobtainable. Heading south, the party built a shelter for the winter but were unfortunately captured by the Spanish who held them captive until July 1, 1807.

In 1820 Major Stephen Harriman Long, who later helped design the steam locomotive, took a team up to "Pikes" Grand Peak and after his Botanist, Edwin James reached the top, he officially renamed the mountain James Peak. Unfortunately, despite James actually being the first American to ever reach the top and with history understanding that Zebulon Pike never even attempted the climb, the mountain was still re-named Pikes Peak in 1890.

Regardless of its history, one thing that can be agreed on is the large amounts of snow that accumulate on the towering mountain. Every spring, when the snow begins to melt, the run off fills numerous lakes and river beds nestled around the base of the mountain, such as the ones located near the tiny farming towns of Glendale, Toof, Juniper, and Woodruff.

The river bed that watered the town's orchards is known as Beaver Creek and in 1907 a businessman from Colorado Springs, named Spencer Penrose bought up all of the water rights from 73-year-old farmer Newton D. Schaeffer and created The Beaver Land and Irrigation Company. The icing on the cake for Mr. Penrose's new business venture was the construction of a Dam to catch the water that flowed down Beaver Creek, which he named The Schaeffer Dam after the farmer.

Built by a crew of over 400 mostly Spanish workers, the men found themselves working in an area infested with dozens of rattlesnakes who would continuously sun themselves not only on top of the sections of metal pipe used for the Dam's construction but inside them as well.

As the Dam was nearing its completion in 1910, eleven Steam locomotives were stripped and dumped at its base for stability, but not even a team of decommissioned Iron Horses would be able to hold back the water if the Dam up the river from The Schaeffer Dam ever ruptured.

Over ten miles upstream from the Schaeffer Dam, near the mining town of Victor, sat yet another Dam, but unlike The Schaeffer Dam, which was built for irrigation, this one was built to create hydroelectric power. Completed in 1901, The Skaguay Dam and Power Plant, also known as the Pikes Peak Power Company, produced electricity not only for the mining town of Victor but also for the nearby gold town of Cripple Creek.

Built by around 500 men, the construction of the Skaguay consisted of three crews, with one building the Dam, another building the pipeline from the Dam to the Power Plant five miles down the mountain, and the third to build the Power Plant. The reservoir behind the Dam was constructed by packing 13,000 pounds of explosives into a nearby Granite mountain top and lighting the fuse.

Just like The Schaeffer Dam, The Skaguay was also built to contain the snowmelt that poured down from towering Pikes Peak, but the same cloud busts that had caused the city of Pueblo to flood, on June 3rd had also added an excessive amount of rain to the reservoirs behind both Dam's and the water was beginning to crest.

At 4:30 am on June 4th, around the same time that Fountain Creek was adding six feet of additional flood water to the already swollen Arkansas River in Pueblo, it was discovered that the Schaeffer Dam had water pouring over its top. In order to relieve the pressure, the spillway was opened, which caused the excess water to quickly rush down Beaver Creek and pour into the Arkansas River at a point between the Portland cement plant and the town of Swallows. Fortunately for the residents of Swallows, the town had been evacuated almost 12 hours earlier.

On the night of June 3rd, before the flood waters took over the city of Pueblo, the enraged Arkansas River had pounced upon the tiny farming town of Swallows, which caused its terrified residents to run for the hills. As the angry Arkansas River began to overtake their town, the flood managed to skate right past Cabin Springs Community Park and leave it untouched.

Built in 1870 by 45-year-old Corporal Robt Eugene Spaulding and his 36-year-old wife Bell, following his release from a Louisville, Kentucky Military Prison on May 9, 1865, the name was derived from the soda spring the family discovered on their newly acquired property. While the Corporal was fighting against the Confederacy up in the Eastern states, and eventually captured along with his men on June 18, 1863, his wife Belle watched over their son's, 10-year-old George and 8-year-old Steven, as well as 5-year-old John who unfortunately wouldn't survive to see his father's return.

Settling for the quiet life of a farmer in Swallows, Corporal Spaulding, who had acquired the nickname Rufus during his travels, surrounded his soda spring with a white picket fence, beautiful trees, and rose bushes before inviting the town to walk around his newly constructed community park. As Corporal Spaulding grew older, he began studying to be a scientist and in 1895 at the age of 70, created a flying machine.

Made of wire frames and wrapped in strips of woven silk, Corporal Spaulding took his flying machine up to Denver, Colorado so he could demonstrate his unusual invention, which was meant to allow a man to fly like a bird, which he successfully demonstrated to a captive audience.

The Corporal died in 1902 at the age of 77, and his wife Bella kept Cabin Springs full of flowers until her own death in 1920 at the age of 86, when the little park was gifted to the town of Swallows. Seen as a treasure, the town's people continued to care for Cabin Springs which for now had been spared from the wrath of the flood.

But the cracks in the Schaeffer Dam were getting bigger.

As the excess water from the Dam continued to pour into the Arkansas River and flow past the flood ravaged town of Swallows, it mixed in with the water that still held the city of Pueblo hostage and added to its grief. As Pueblo's residents began to pull themselves out of their flood ravaged homes, they began seeking shelter inside one of the newly opened refugee centers, of which there were many.

One of these centers had been set up in the Courthouse by the Pueblo Chamber of the Red Cross on the morning of June 4th, and since hundreds of people had already sought refuge within its walls, it just seemed the logical choice. As Red Cross members 19-year-old Ella Wilder and 36-year-old Rosetta A. Booth, as well as 41-year-old school teacher Saraphine Omeara, 31-year-old Episcopal Minister Reverend Benjamin Dunlop Dagwell from the Church of the Ascension, and 25-year-old Boy Scout Commissioner Oscar Charles Alverson walked into the Courthouse at 6:30 am, they were faced with a somber sight.

Covering what appeared to be every inch of available floor space were hundreds and hundreds of people, some of which had the appearance of being deceased. Hovering around collections of belongings which represented the few things they had left, dirty tear stained faces glanced up at the Red Cross team and immediately began filling their ears with requests for food and inquiries about lost loved ones.

As the team started to talk to the refugees, they suddenly heard what sounded like a voice of authority, and gravitating towards it they quickly found themselves in room 135, which to their surprise held several hundred babies and their traumatized mothers. The voice they had heard was that of Doctor F.J. Peirce, who had been assisting the refugees since the flood has first broken through the levees the night before, along with a handful of Boy Scouts and a constant trickle of volunteers.

Seeing the new arrivals, the Doctor quickly explained to them that he had already delivered three babies, two boys, and a girl and that he had two other women in active labor. He needed food, milk, clothing, and a room set up somewhere in the Court House that he could use as a makeshift hospital, as well as supplies so they could wash the babies.

As the newly arrived team began an awkward scramble, 27-year-old Florence Mishou, who was well known in the local Vaudeville circuit as a Musician and a dancer, ran past them and with a smile offered her services to the overwhelmed Doctor. Seeing that two of the women she had just passed were dressed in Red Cross uniforms, she quickly took charge and asked them for canned milk, soap, washcloths, towels, tubs, water, and any clean clothes they could find.

Snapping into action, volunteers were quickly rounded up and assigned tasks, with some sent to nearby homes and businesses to ask for donations of clothing, food, and supplies, while others clamored into automobiles in search of more refugees.

Since the infants and their mothers had already laid claim to room 135 on the first floor, the two women in labor and the injured were moved up to the third floor, which was soon set up as a hospital and would be run by volunteers until proper nurses could arrive. On the second floor, the courtrooms were divided up into a men's dormitory and a woman's dormitory, with the excess being sent to nearby churches who were just beginning to open up their doors.

Within the hour, housewives began arriving with coffee pots full of freshly brewed coffee, food,

Florence Mishou and one of the many babies she cared for- Courtesy of The Pueblo County Historical Society

clothing, and blankets, while a Casualty and Missing Person Bureau was set up to take reports of all reported deaths and to compile lists of the missing, which would be run by J.W. Wagner.

As the supplies began to arrive, all of the canned milk collected was sent to room 135 for the babies, which was a Godsend, but now volunteer Florence Mishou was faced with an unexpected problem. Despite most of the babies being covered in dirt and wearing soiled clothing, some of their mothers were objecting to having their children bathed, which lead to a few members of the Pueblo Unit of the National Guard being called into the room and engaging in forceful arguments to get the babies washed.

With more volunteers needed to care for the refugees, a second wave of Boy Scouts soon arrived, which had been rounded up and driven to the Court House by 19-year-old Assistant Scout Master Frank Allman. The Scouts were instructed to visit nearby homes and businesses to collect clothing, food, and supplies, as well as help to clean and bandage the wounded up on the third floor hospital wing.

Surprisingly, while some of the Boy Scouts were busy helping the Doctor, the fourth baby to be born in the Court House in the last 24 hours made his arrival into the world. Lupe F. Lazo was born to 25-year-old Sofia Diaz Delgado after she had spent a harrowing night caught in the wrath of the flood.

Sofia had been discovered stranded on the roof of a house by a 17 year old boy who carried her on his back until they reached the Courthouse. Covered in mud and slime, the boy had no idea that Sofia was in labor when he carried her, as he just assumed her failure to walk was caused by exhaustion.

Unfortunately, not everyone was so lucky.

Inside Centennial High School, located at 2525 Mount View Drive, a few members of the Pueblo Unit of the National Guard were carrying in a mud covered woman and her newborn infant, who were both on the brink of death. As Doctor Ratty Woodward accepted his newest patients, the men explained that while they were out looking for survivors in the squatter towns they had discovered the woman buried up to her armpits in mud and floodwater, all while holding her newborn infant above her head.

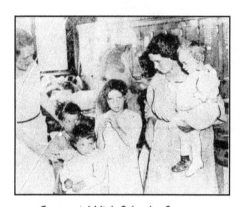

Centennial High School refugees.
Lockers can be seen behind them-
Authors personal collection

Flood damaged house in one of the squatter towns
-Courtesy of The Pueblo County Historical Society

Taking the pale infant from its mother's hands and wrapping it in a blanket, the men had begun digging the mother free of her confinement, as she struggled to explain to them what had happened. It appeared that she had gone into labor around the time that the Steam whistle first began to blow, but being alone, she had no one to help her to safety and had become trapped.

With the last of her energy spent, she faded from consciousness just as the men finally managed to free her, but by the time they reached the Centennial High School building, neither her nor her newborn showed sustainable signs of life.

But one man who showed a lot of life was Denver Post's Editor Frank E. White

Desperate to get a story about the Pueblo flood for his newspaper, but not really sure the extent of the damage or the severity, Frank gathered up 35-year-old Bruce Albert Gustin, A.W. Stone, and Charles E. Lounsbury, all reporters for the Denver Post, and took the next train out of Denver. Unfortunately, when the train arrived in Colorado Springs a few hours later, they were informed that it would not be continuing onto Pueblo, so they would have to find another mode of transportation.

Asking around at the train station in regards to renting a car, the men learned that no automobiles had been seen coming up from Southern Colorado for hours, and rumors abound in regards to possible washed out roads and collapsed bridges. Not willing to give up that easily, Frank White and his reporters inquired about renting a vehicle and were informed that one would be available first thing in the morning.

Confident in his choice to wait until first light , as he had convinced himself that any other reporters would have to do the same, Editor Frank White arranged for him and his men to stay in Colorado Springs until the following morning.

But some reporters were more eager than others.

As the Denver Post Editor was busy finding rooms to rent for his men , Denver News and Times Photographer Harry Rhodes was driving his automobile past Colorado Springs in his own attempt to get to

The Army Rangers following the train tracks to Pueblo. Photo taken by Harry Rhodes-Courtesy of The Pueblo County Historical Society

The Army Rangers posing while following the train tracks to Pueblo. Photo taken by Harry Rhodes-Courtesy of The Pueblo County Historical Society

The Army Rangers crossing over a makeshift bridge. Photo taken by Harry Rhodes-Courtesy of The Pueblo County Historical Society

Pueblo. Finding the road washed out due to Fountain Creek running over its banks the night before, Harry knew that he had to get creative and he knew just what to do.

While driving towards Pueblo he had noticed that while the roads were washed out, the train bridges appeared to be intact and since he hadn't seen a train coming up from Pueblo since he started his trip, he turned his automobile around, found a railroad crossing, and carefully drove up onto the tracks.

To space his vehicle, Harry set the driver side wheels on the inside of the track, while the passenger side wheels were set on the outside of the track and extremely satisfied with his ingenuity, he began slowly driving towards Pueblo. Despite his slow pace, Harry had traveled quite far before he noticed a group of automobiles stopped up ahead of him. Slowing down, he was surprised to find that he had just caught up to the Army Rangers.

Parking his automobile a respectable distance away, Harry walked up to the Rangers and discovered that they had stopped due to a damaged railroad bridge. With 43-year-old Major Paul Paschal Newlon in command, Harry discovered that not only were the Rangers moving their vehicles and equipment over a makeshift bridge, but they were also willing to move his automobile across as well.

As the Army Rangers and their new companion continued down the tracks towards Pueblo, they were unaware that Martial Law had just been implemented in the flooded City, with Sheriff Sam E. Thomas deputizing dozens of men so they could stand guard over the ruins of the downtown area, mainly to help prevent looting.

Undersheriff Kenyon was put in charge of the Southside of the City, while Deputy Sheriff Fiscus was put in charge of the Northside, with the Pueblo Unit of the National Guard and the Pueblo Post of the American Legion stepping in to help in any way they could.

But the Elks Lodge had already stepped up.

Before the Court House was officially made a refugee center by the Red Cross in the early morning hours of June 4th, the towering three story tall Elks Lodge at 426 North Santa Fe Avenue had already opened its doors.

As the levees began to break on the evening of June 3rd, the Elks Lodge members had already started a fire outside of their building in order to warm cold bodies, while also brewing coffee, and making sandwiches, all while the Pueblo Police force began setting up a makeshift command center inside their building.

A line of flood refugees circling the Elks Lodge-Authors personal collection

And around 1 am on June 4th, they brought in 3 men in handcuffs.

But surprisingly, the arrests were not related to looting, but instead to illegal gambling.

Sitting inside a small rented room on Walnut Street and snitched on by their neighbors around midnight, three traveling salesmen, who had no train to catch, were arrested by Officers Lee West and Jeff Taylor for playing a dice game called Craps.

F.E. Williams from Denver, as well as R.J. Caster and Leo Thompson from De Moines, Iowa were found with a pair of dice and about $10 in cash, which appeared to of been put up as a stake. Sent before Judge Sarchet early on the morning of the 4th, the men explained to the Judge that despite their rented room only being 100 yards from the Police Station, they believed that the raging floodwaters and lack of electricity made them safe from detection.

The men were each fined $10 each, plus costs.

As the Pueblo Police force continued to make themselves at home inside the Elks Lodge, the Pueblo Unit of the National Guard began establishing their headquarters up on the buildings third floor, where they began issuing passes which authorized people to enter the flooded areas, while an emergency food depot was set up downstairs.

With the number of refugees quickly beginning to multiply, the Elks Lodge members set out tables and rounded up volunteers to hand out sandwiches, hot coffee, and soup to not only flood refugees but emergency and military personnel as well. To keep the large kettles of soup and coffee constantly boiling, a tent was erected in the back lot of the building to act as the kitchen.

But while Pueblo was starting to put things in motion, the men in charge of the Skaguay Dam up near the mining town of Victor were in a panic.

The President of the Beaver Park Land Company, 32-year-old Charles Leaming Tutt was busy gathering up a group of men, and rushing them up to the Dam to check on the water level. It had been raining off and on since June 3rd and with the summer snowmelt from Pikes Peak added to the mix, he had a really bad feeling.

Reaching the Skaguay, the men noticed that the water was about nine inches from the top of the Dam, but its reduced depth was the result of his men opening up the spillways just hours before.

Feeding the refugees outside the Elks Lodge- Courtesy of The Pueblo Historical Society

Constructing tents next to the Elks Lodge before Camp Shoup was built- Courtesy of The Pueblo Historical Society

Understanding that any excess water that was released from the Skaguay traveled down the mountain and emptied into the Schaeffer Dam near Glendale, Charles Tutt and his men headed down the mountain to check on the condition of the other Dam.

But it wasn't good.

When Charles Tutt and his men arrived at the Schaeffer Dam, they were greeted by Mr. C.E. White, who was the Superintendent of the Water Division of the Beaver Park Irrigation Company, and the news he told them was grim. Not only had the Schaeffer Dam been developing cracks, but all of their attempts to patch them had failed.

"So yesterday, despite all the rain, the water behind the Dam was about seven feet below the spillway level, but this morning around 4:30 a.m., after your men released the excess water from the Skaguay, the water began running over the top of the spillway." The Superintendent explained to the men, as they walked around the Schaeffer Dam. "Now around 7:30 this morning we did open the outlet gate about halfway, in order to release the excess and the level of the water is beginning to drop, but it's the cracks were are really worried about."

As the men talked, they agreed that the outlook for both Dam's was very concerning. The Skaguay Dam up near Victor, which was the smaller of the two, held back around 90 acres of water, while the Schaeffer Dam held back 135 acres of water, but the rupture of either Dam would be catastrophic.

If the Skaguay Dam failed, the release of water could not only destroy the Power Plant, which was the Dam's sole purpose for existing, but the Schaeffer Dam as well, as it would not be able to hold the additional water.

As the men continued to discuss the condition of both Dam's and curse the occasional rainstorm that passed overhead, rescue efforts remained constant in Pueblo, as the deep water covering the downtown area slowly began to subside. As night fell, and the clocks chimed in at 9pm, the Army Rangers, as well as their tag along Harry Rhodes, a photographer for the Denver News and Times, finally arrived at the Pueblo Elks Lodge to a much appreciated dinner of sandwiches and soup.

Taking out his notebook, while sipping his coffee, Harry wrote down his description of the flood damage that he had seen so far, all while showing his passion for creative writing. "It was as if some bestial monster had chewed up the city, taken a gigantic gulp of muggy brown water, then sickened of his diet, spewed the whole sorry mess on the ground."

As the Army Rangers began setting up their command center, one group of men who could really use a meal and hot cup of coffee were the Telegraph men who were still rewiring the lines, as well as fighting the weather that was trying its best to halt their progress.

Western Union Telegraph operators Emory Mitchell, Ellsworth Stapp, Edwin Clements. William Berns and Joseph Hoskins had been swimming through deep floodwater since early afternoon, all while pulling two rowboats full of not only Telegraph wires and supplies, but a tied burlap sack full of their clothes. Unfortunately, as soon as the sunset behind the mountains, the sky darkened and the rain began to fall.

While one man positioned himself high up on the Telegraph pole to connect the lines, another would balance himself on the opposite side of the pole to shine a light on the task at hand, using either the lantern or candles, but the storm did its best to extinguish both. Holding his hat over the flame to block the rain, the other three telegraph men remained below them in the deep, icy water to roll out the wire and hand up any supplies that they needed.

Reaching dry land alittle after midnight, the Telegraph men were now forced to unload their supplies from the rowboats they had been pulling and carry them, all while rolling the large spindles of wire down the street.

But at least they were finally able to get dressed.

With daylight beginning to show its face on June 5th, the reporters from the Denver Post rose from their beds in Colorado Springs, still confident that if they couldn't have made it to Pueblo the day before then nobody else could of either. After a hardy breakfast, a few of the reporters began searching for not only supplies for their trip, but a Taxi driver who would take them to Pueblo, as they were still unable to find a vehicle to rent.

As reporters Bruce Gustin and A.W. Stone tried their best to inspire reluctant Taxi drivers to take them into a flood zone, Editor Frank White headed out to purchase pocket flashlights, while Charles Loonsbury purchased sandwiches for the trip.

Finally finding a willing driver, the Newspapermen happily piled into the taxi but were disappointed to discover that they were only able to travel a little over 7 miles before they hit the washed out bridge at Sand Creek. With the water receded just enough to leave a muddy mess, the Reporters tried to convince the Taxi driver that he could easily jump the 20-foot wide stream bed, but instead of attempting the stunt, the driver asked the reporters to get out of his vehicle.

Disappointed with the driver's lack of enthusiasm, the reporters exited the Taxi, paid the man for his time, and began walking across the flooded stream bed to the other side. As they continued towards Pueblo, they soon spotted a Railroad bridge that had survived the washout, which they eagerly walked towards. Congratulating themselves on their discovery, the reporters were soon following the tracks and felt confident that they would reach Pueblo by nightfall.

Only 39 more miles to go.

As they continued on their journey, the men noticed an automobile driving towards them on the tracks and were soon introduced to 57-year-old Wilbur F. Cannon who was the Pure Goods Drug Commissioner for the State of Colorado. After a round of introductions, the reporters were pleased to discover that not only was Wilbur heading back to his home in Denver, but he was willing to call up the Denver Post and give them a story on the Pueblo flood once he got there.

Another group of men, who were having a great morning, were Emory Mitchell, Ellsworth Stapp, Edwin Clements, William Berns and Joseph Hoskins from the Western Union Telegraph Company, as they had finally reached the Western Union office after almost 24 hours of wading naked in debris filled floodwater and climbing up every Telegraph pole they could find.

Opening up the exterior door to the building, the men happily climbed the stairs up to the second floor and unlocked the door to the office at 415 North Main Street just a little after 9 am.

Despite being exhausted, wet and hungry, the men diligently worked to connect the last of the wires, being rewarded at 10 am with a response from the Denver Office. Taking the first shift was Edwin Clements, who quickly began sending out appeals for help, while his comrades napped in the corner of the room.

As Edwin continued sending out his familiar dots and dashes, the little towns that sat below the Schaeffer Dam found that they were unable to use their Telegraph to send out any appeals for help, as they were too busy running for their lives.

CHAPTER 12

The aerodynamic speeder and a lake full of bodies

"The Dam's collapsing! Get to higher ground!" Ernest Callen screamed as he rode his horse to every ranch he could find around Glendale. "Get to higher ground now!"

All of the ranches along Beaver Creek had been preparing for this, after noticing the large amounts of water that the Schaeffer Dam had been releasing from its spillways, but they still prayed that it would hold. The nearby hills were dotted with household goods, farm equipment, and livestock, as the residents of Glendale, Toof, Woodruff and Juniper waited to see if the Dam would hold.

Mr. White, the Superintendent of the Beaver Park Irrigation Company and his men had been working around the clock to not only fix the cracks but to relieve the pressure from behind the Dam. At 5:30 pm the night before, after the spillway had been opened halfway, the water inside the Dam had dropped 9 inches and it was felt that the danger had passed.

Unfortunately, only two hours later, at 7:30 pm the water was once again flowing over the spillway and rising at a rate of 3 inches an hour. At this point, it was decided to completely open the large outlet gate, as well as the Pass gate and by 9:30 am, on the morning of June 5th, the water had only slightly dropped, while the cracks in the Dam had become more evident.

As Ernest Callen made his desperate ride to warn his neighbors around Beaver Creek of the Dam's imminent collapse, he had no idea what was happening 10 miles up the mountain at the Skaguay Dam near Victor. Unlike the Schaeffer Dam which was built for irrigation, the Skaguay provided both the towns of Victor and Cripple Creek with hydroelectric power. The power not only ran homes and businesses but the Gold mines as well, which meant the entire area depended on this Dam remaining intact.

Around 9 am, on June 5th after many attempts to release the excess water through the Skaguay's many spillways, the choice was made to do whatever was necessary to save the Dam and the livelihood of the two mining towns. Gathering up dynamite and setting the fuse, the overflow flashboards were blown at 9:30 am, releasing over 90 acres of water into Beaver Creek, but in the chaos, no warning was given to any of the towns near the Schaeffer Dam that would soon be impacted by the influx of additional water.

Hitting the Schaeffer Dam only a few minutes later, the water put so much pressure on the Dam that it ruptured, releasing not only the 135 acres of water that it normally held but the 90 acres of water that was rushing down from the Skaguay Dam.

Acting as the Paul Revere of Glendale, Ernest Callen was still riding his horse to warn people about the Dam when he heard an odd rumbling sound, combined with what sounded like branches breaking. Stopping his horse so he could look around for the noise, he noticed a mountain of water coming straight for him, taking out every cottonwood tree in its path as it did.

With a quick kick in its side, Ernest was able to get both him and his horse up onto a nearby ridge where he found 50-year-old George E. Reigel and his family silently watching the destruction of their farm. As they all stood in silence, a wall of water 75 feet high and 20 yards wide filled Beaver Creek, carrying with it houses, barns, livestock, and the two automobiles owned by the Reigel family.

"I just couldn't get them up the hill." George Reigel explained to no one in particular, as he watched the destruction unfold before his eyes. "Both me and my son Edmond tried. We really did, but we just didn't have the time."

Another family had been sitting inside their home eating breakfast when the Dam first broke, but was ready to leave on a moment's notice. The horses were already hooked up to the wagon and their household goods and animals sitting up on the ridge, when the man heard his son call out "Here it comes daddy!"

Running out to the wagon, the man's wife and children held onto the sides as they helped push it up to higher ground, but the height of the water rose so fast that the man began grabbing the children and putting them into the wagon instead, while the horses continued trudging through the ever rising water. Counting his children, the man suddenly realized that one of them was missing.

"My God Mama! Where's the baby?"

"You're holding the baby!"

With the wall of water continuing down Beaver Creek and racing past the numerous farms that lined its shores, it carried with it uprooted trees, homes, barns, farm equipment, livestock, and even boulders before smashing into the last farm on Beaver Creek, which belonged to the Toof's. With the flood water's now only 35 feet high, but about half a mile wide, the Toof's farm didn't stand a chance, and neither did the Beaver Station Train Depot.

As the wave of water smashed into the Toof's farm, it obliterated not only the family's barn but their two story stone house, as it continued towards the steel bridge at Beaver Station. Ripping it from the embankment, the bridge and a mile of track were quickly washed away as the torrent finally poured into the Arkansas River, where it set its sights on the town of Swallows.

After Swallows had been hit by the June 3rd flood, 14-year-old Irene Church and her 12-year-old brother Russell were sent to live with their Grandmother high up on the cliffs that overlooked the town, which unfortunately gave them a front seat to the incoming second flood. Hitting Swallows at 11:30 am the children watched as the wall of water smashed into what remained of their town, picking up stores, framed houses, and about 20 boxcars that were stored on a side track near the Swallows Depot.

Leaving only the town's community park of Cabin Spring's intact.

As the children continued to watch the uprooted buildings bounce along in the raging current, snag on a section of upended train track, and spin around like tops, the town's Sheriff was quickly sending a Telegraphed message to Pueblo, which was received by Western Union Telegraph Operator Emory Mitchell.

"Wall of water rushing towards Pueblo. River 4 feet higher than June 3rd"

With the Phone lines still out, but with the Water Works building only around 3 blocks away, Emory quickly sent a Boy Scout over to the building at 4th and Grand Avenue with instructions to either hand the Telegraph over to someone who would be willing to blow the steam whistle, or for him to blow it himself.

One of the jobs issued to the Boy Scouts, since the arrival of the first flood, was to deliver Telegrams all over town, and when this Scout arrived at the Water Works building, he luckily found numerous employees who were busy digging out mud and debris. Running up to the first man he saw, the Scout handed the message over, but none of the men were happy with the warning it contained.

With John Nittinger home resting, after being trapped inside the Water Works building during the first flood on June 3rd, a workman quickly put down his tools, climbed up to the steam whistle, and pulled down the lever. Everyone understood that one blast meant there was a fire, and two blasts meant it was over, but with no set blast for a flood the man chose to simply blow it three times, which definitely got everyone's attention.

Unfortunately, with the phones still out all over Pueblo, Telegraph Operator Emory Mitchell did the next best thing and sent Telegrams to each of the refugee centers.

As the Telegram recipients began preparations for what would now be the third flood to hit Pueblo in three days, a newspaper photographer was planning on heading out of Pueblo in order to deliver his flood photos by using a tiny train vehicle called a Speeder. Also known as a Jigger or a Trike, the gas powered vehicle is primarily used to inspect sections of the track and to transport the people who are working on them, but it's only built to hold 4 people.

And right now, seven people wanted a ride out of Pueblo.

In the early morning hours of June 4th, 31-year-old Pueblo Chieftain Emergency Photographer James Thurman Kinch, along with his bodyguard 27-year-old Floyd Arthur Banning obtained a rowboat and entered the flooded areas to document the destruction of downtown Pueblo for the newspaper. As the water began to recede, James and Floyd were able to walk over the piles of flood debris and train wreckage, which is when they discovered a Speeder sitting on a raised rail bed.

Approaching the vehicle, they were soon spotted by 38-year-old Louis Justus Hausman and 43-year-old Henry M. Clifford, who were both dispatchers for the Denver & Rio Grande railroad, as well as 40-year-old James N. Austin, and A. Ooley who were both trackman for the Santa Fe Railroad. After a bit of small talk, the men agreed to help James get the Speeder onto an undamaged piece of track, so he could get his photos to Colorado Springs but only if they could come with him.

With a smile and a handshake, the men arranged to meet at the Canon Junction, on the Santa Fe track.

As Pueblo Chieftain Photographer James Kinch was preparing to leave Pueblo on a small, gas-powered train vehicle, the Editor of the Denver Post and his reporters were still walking down the tracks from Colorado Springs, in their attempt to reach Pueblo.

"Remember, you might get a great story, but it is no good at all unless you get it to the office!" Editor Frank White reminded his reporters once again, just as one of the men spotted a road off in the distance. Deciding to leave the tracks and walk across a large field in order to reach it, the men found that their gamble was paying off, as they soon spotted several automobiles coming down the road behind them.

Waving them down, a vehicle driven by 42-year-old Rowland Griffiths Edwards stopped and offered the men a ride. As they drove towards Pueblo, the reporters discovered that Rowland was both a Director and an Actor for the Universal Film Manufacturing Company, and finding himself in the area, he wanted to go check out the flood for himself.

But one group of men had already checked out the flood, and now they were on their way out.

Meeting at the arranged time, Pueblo Chieftain Photographer James Kinch was surprised to see that the number of people who wanted to leave Pueblo on the Speeder had just increased by two. Standing next to the four railway men were 45-year-old Anton Christie Washington Wiegel, who was the Manager of Mail and Express Traffic of the Denver & Rio Grande, and 38-year-old Edward S. Shacklett, a businessman from Colorado Springs who just wanted to head home, as he knew his wife Eva would be worried sick.

In regards to Anton Wiegel, he was extremely eager to get to Colorado Springs because in his satchel he had a list of the missing, dead, or presumed dead from the Denver & Rio Grande Train No. 3 and he needed to get it up to his superiors. As of that morning, after interviewing the survivors inside the Nuckolls Packing plant, Anton's list contained the names or descriptions of over 30 deceased or missing passengers, but he was sure there were more.

The Nuckolls packing plant-Courtesy of The Pueblo County Historical Society

With everyone accounted for, the group of seven men climbed aboard the seven foot long Speeder and headed north down the tracks eight miles to the train stop of Bragdon, where they discovered that they had to pick the speeder up off the tracks and carry it over to the nearby Denver & Rio Grande tracks. With the Speeder lined back up on the rails, the men continued for another 18 miles until they spied the steel bridge near the train stop of Buttes, but as they got closer, they discovered that they had a problem.

Speeder-Courtesy of The Pueblo County Historical Society

The track leading up to the steel bridge was lined with automobiles and trucks for almost a mile, from both the north and south side, as they all waited for their turn to cross. Shutting down the Speeder and choosing to walk towards the bridge for a closer look, Pueblo Chieftain Photographer James Kinch and a few of his travel companions questioned a man

*Vehicles leaving the flood zone- Courtesy of
The Pueblo County Historical Society*

about the holdup and were introduced to Denver News and Times Photographer Harry Rhodes.

Harry had driven to Pueblo the day before, with the help of the Army Rangers and now was on his way back to Denver to deliver his flood pictures to his Editor. As the men talked, James learned that the hold up at the bridge was due to a large truck loaded with food, which was heading south to Pueblo to help with the refugee camps, and it was having a very difficult time crossing the bridge.

Thanking Harry for the information, James and his comrades returned to the Speeder and after a quick meeting about their options, decided that they had no desire to wait. Piling back onto the Speeder, the men put it in reverse and backed it up about a mile or so until they could see the parallel Santa Fe track in the distance.

Lifting up the Speeder, the seven men carefully carried it across the open field where they set it down onto the Santa Fe tracks, all while congratulating themselves for discovering a way around the blocked truck and the miles of traffic. Starting up the Speeder, the men rode the rails north towards Colorado Springs for almost 18 miles without a single soul in sight, before they discovered why nobody else was using this particular track.

The bridge was washed out

As then men turned off the Speeder and went to check the damage, the Denver Post reporters, who were still heading to Pueblo from Colorado Springs had driven up to yet another washed out automobile bridge, after they had hitched a ride with Universal Film Manufacturing Company Director and Actor Rowland Edwards.

Stopping his car at the remains of the bridge, Rowland and the men exited the vehicle and after confirming that there was no safe way for the vehicle to cross, the reporters thanked him for the ride, jumped the culvert, and continued to walk down the road towards Pueblo.

But Pueblo Chieftain Photographer James Kinch and his comrades didn't have the luxury of simply carrying the Speeder over a muddy culvert.

Walking up to the washed out Santa Fe Train Bridge, the men discovered that it was so badly damaged that the tracks were only held together by the railroad ties, creating the image of an old fashioned rope bridge. Glancing below the dangling track, the men watched as the angry current of Fountain Creek kicked and bucked as it threatened any man who might attempt to cross it.

With a confident look, Santa Fe trackman Ooley informed his comrades that the Speeder could make it across, but with only one passenger, not seven. As the men looked back over the edge of the still swollen Creek, they reminded Ooley that the gulch appeared to be at least 70 feet wide.

Sporting an ornery smile, Ooley shrugged his shoulders before heading back towards the Speeder. Realizing that his new friend was serious, James Kinch ran up and stopped him before he started up the engine of the little train vehicle. "Wait, wait! Let me at least try to walk across what remains of the bridge first, before you do anything stupid".

With a second of deep thought and the pleading eyes of his companions staring into his soul, Ooley agreed.

Breathing a sigh of relief, James turned around and walked up to the edge of the washed out bridge, where he carefully placed one foot on the first railroad tie. As he felt it sway under his weight, he looked back at his friends and saw not only the worried looks on most of their faces but the smug look he was getting from Ooley, who uncrossed his arms just long enough to coax him forward with the sarcastic wave of his fingers.

The washed out bridge the railway Speeder crossed- Courtesy of The Pueblo County Historical Society

Turning back to the task at hand, and taking a deep breath, James slowly lowered himself down onto his knees and began carefully crawling across each wooden plank, stopping only when he encountered a gap where a plank had fallen into the raging creek below him. With the remains of the bridge gently swaying from side to side, and the high water below him continually splashing up onto his shoes, James glanced up to see how much farther he still needed to go which is when he noticed a group of people watching him from the other side and they appeared very nervous.

Finally reaching dry land, and receiving not only applause but a few pats on the back, James motioned for his six remaining comrades to make their crossing, leaving only Santa Fe trackman Ooley left to attempt to get the Speeder across.

Climbing aboard the little train car, Ooley started it up, threw it into reverse, and backed it down the track until he felt the distance was acceptable before he hit the throttle. With bated breath, Ooley's six comrades, as well as the small audience that had formed on the opposite side of the raging creek, all stood in shocked silence as the Speeder reached the edge of the broken train bridge, slid across the remaining train rails like a professional ice skater going for the gold, before triumphantly coming to a stop on the other side.

As Ooley was swarmed with smacks on the back and around of much deserved applause, his stunned friends climbed back aboard the Speeder and together they continued following the tracks the last 15 miles north to Colorado Springs, As they pulled the Speeder up to the Train Station, which resulted in quite a few odd looks, the men were unaware that it wasn't only Fountain Creek that was raging again.

But the Arkansas River.

With the steam whistle on the side of the Pueblo Water Works building screaming out it's warning of a third flood, Telegraph operator Emory Mitchell was still stunned with this unexpected turn of events. After receiving the news, Emory had sent a Boy Scout down to the Water Works building with instructions to either find an employee to pull the lever for the steam whistle, or for him to pull the lever himself, but the Scout luckily had found a nervous but willing participant once he reached the building.

Down at the numerous refuge centers, volunteers had quickly spread out to check on any residents that might be left in the low lying areas of the Grove and Pepper Sauce bottoms, while the search for bodies and survivors using rowboats and rafts was put on hold.

Unfortunately, since most of Pueblo missed watching the first two floods strike the city, due to either the pouring rain, the hail storms, or the late hour at which they arrived, hundreds of people swarmed the remaining bridges to watch the third flood make its appearance.

But it wasn't going to put on the show its audience expected.

When the Schaeffer Dam had first ruptured around 9:30 am, it instantly released a 75 foot wave of water that destroyed everything in its path before it slammed into the Arkansas River. Setting its sights not only on the Train Depot at Beaver Station but the farming town of Swallows, the extra water was able to spread out into nearby fields, which was easy to do since the flood of June 3rd had already washed out the river banks.

The ability of the Arkansas River to flood the fields and towns along its banks, instead of following a direct path to Pueblo, had the added benefit of reducing not only the height of the water but its strength. With the additional flood water still needing to travel down the Arkansas River 25 more miles before it hit Pueblo, the people swarming the bridges expected to see a violent swell of water strike their city, but instead they stood by and watched the still swollen river rise only about four feet around 2:15 pm.

With the newly arriving surge quickly pouring itself through the numerous gaps in the river levees, the excess water easily added itself to the already saturated downtown areas before finally settling in a newly formed body of water tragically called Death Lake. Situated near the Grove, just south of the Santa Fe train tracks and East of Santa Fe Ave., the 10 acre lake had formed in a low lying area of Pueblo that sat near the original channel of the Arkansas River.

Wait... Just wait one minute!

Are you saying that Pueblo moved the River?

When did this happen?

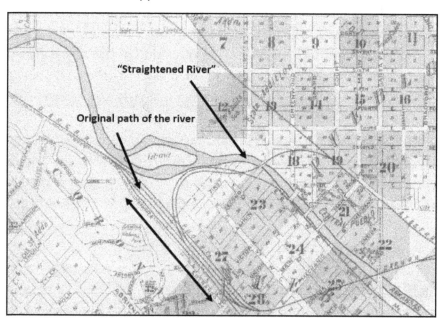

"Straightened River"

Original path of the river

Map of Pueblo's straightened section of the Arkansas River-Authors personal collection

On April 14, 1874, the Pueblo City Council approved a measure to "Straighten" the Arkansas River, to protect the site of the city's future Water Works filtering well. Ironically, the river was already fairly straight and nowhere near the proposed Water Works, but it was actually in the way of the city's future site of their desired Train Depot.

To keep up the farce, 16 foot piling were inserted eight feet apart at a combined cost of $7.60 each, to construct a 600 foot wall near the proposed Water Works well, while the Colorado Central Improvement Company, who was in charge of planning out the Arkansas River's new channel decided on the best way to curve the river.

Choosing to dramatically force it to flow in the shape of a half-circle, the newly formed river channel would now arch up and over 20 city blocks before it was allowed to nestle back inside the safety and security of its natural course. To stabilize the un-natural curve of the river, extra pilings were added to force the Arkansas River to bend to the will of not only the Mayor but the City Council as well.

As the new channel was dug out, the silt, rocks, and dirt that the workers removed were to be used not only to fill in the original river channel but to build up the surrounding areas against future flooding. Unfortunately, the Colorado Central Improvement Company ran out of fill dirt when it came to filling in the low lying area that would one day house the squatter towns of the Grove and Pepper Sauce Bottoms.

Ironically, after the Arkansas River was "Straightened" in 1874 the City of Pueblo flooded seven times, with each onslaught of water not only killing countless numbers of people but always settling in the same low lying area that Pueblo felt wasn't necessary to fill in. With history once again repeating itself after the flood of 1921 hit the city, the low lying area near the Grove become a catch-all for not only flood debris but bodies.

A lot of bodies.

As the rescue boats halted their search for the dead on June 5th and headed for higher ground, just as the 3rd flood headed towards Pueblo, it was quietly understood that more bodies lay under the abyss. As the arrival of the flood finished its expected surge, a group of six men returned to the Grove and went back to digging a ditch at the edge of Death Lake in hopes that it would help it drain and aide in their recovery efforts.

Within view of the dig site, the men could see the steel Santa Fe railroad bridge, which still stood proud despite everything the floodwaters had thrown up against it, while the Denver & Rio Grande railroad bridge was literally standing on its head. With one end of the bridge stuck fast in the center of the Arkansas River and the other slanted high up in the air, the railroad bridge still fared better than the nearby Santa Fe Avenue automobile bridge which had totally disappeared, leaving only its base sitting on the shore.

As the men continued looking for bodies

Death Lake-Courtesy of The Pueblo County Historical Society

Family posing next to a flood damaged house in the Grove-Courtesy of The Pueblo County Historical Society

in Pueblo's Death Lake, Denver Post Editor Frank White and his reporters continued their grueling walk from Colorado Springs to Pueblo. With their supplies gone and facing exhaustion, they kept their eyes out for anyone who might offer them a ride.

The Santa Fe train bridge still standing proud-
Courtesy of The Pueblo County Historical Society

With the blaring summer sun finally beginning to dip down behind the mountains, the men noticed a farmhouse sitting off the side of the road. Hoping for a ride or even a hot meal, the men pushed themselves to walk towards the barn, where they discovered a man milking a cow. After a quick round of introductions and a brief rundown of their quest, the farmer agreed to drive the reporters to Pueblo but skirted around the issue when it came to a possible meal.

"You boys just go and take a seat. I'm not going anywhere until I'm done milking my cows", the farmer announced, as the reporters sat down on the floor of the barn, with some of them quickly dozing off. As the sun finally set, leaving only the light of the moon to illuminate the sky, the farmer led the men over to his Ford model T and attempted to crank the engine of the truck, but it refused to start.

"She's been sitting in the rain for two days." The farmer shrugged, as reporter Charles Loonsbury offered to take a look.

Flipping open the engine cover, and poking around a bit, Charles asked the farmer for a kettle of boiling water, which the man was happy to provide. After 20 minutes of cranking the engine while pouring the hot water onto the trucks carburetor, it finally started.

Piling into the back bed of the truck, the reporters quickly found themselves dozing off again as the farmer drove them towards Pueblo, but after only 18 miles they were jostled awake when the truck came to a sudden stop. Getting out of the vehicle, the farmer walked over to the edge of what used to be a bridge and quickly announced that he couldn't take them any farther.

"Where are we?" reporter Bruce Gustin sleepily asked, as he grudgingly climbed out of the back of the truck.

"Well, I'm pretty sure there is one of those train stops just on the other side of this creek, so if I'm right, then you only have about 16 more miles to go before you get to Pueblo", the farmer replied, as he headed back to his truck.

"16 more miles! Oh, man!" the reporter whined, as Editor Frank White thanked the farmer for the ride and bid him a good night. Clicking on their flashlights, the reporters reluctantly began wading across the swollen creek, but as it was full of rapidly moving water, they quickly lost their footing and soon found themselves not only drenched but covered in mud.

Pulling themselves up out of the creek and finding their bearings, the wet, muddy, hungry, and cold reporters continued to walk down the road towards Pueblo for what felt like hours before they finally saw headlights heading towards them. Frantically waving their arms and shining their flashlights at the vehicle, they were soon introduced to 40-year-old Albert William Marksheffel, who was a car salesman from Colorado Springs.

Albert had driven to Pueblo earlier that day to look for some relatives, but was now out in search of a jug of freshwater, as Pueblo's water supply was contaminated due to broken sewer lines. Happy to offer the reporters a ride to Pueblo, the men quickly noticed a problem that needed a creative, but potentially dangerous solution.

The automobile was a four passenger Cadillac, but the vehicle already had someone occupying the passenger seat and there were four men who needed a ride. As the Editor of the Denver Post, Frank White decided that he should be the one to sacrifice his safety and comfort for the good of his three reporters, especially after all the hell he had been putting them through.

Shoving his three reporters into the automobiles back seat and forcing the door closed, Frank put his feet on the back wheel of the vehicle and pulled himself up onto the hard top of the Cadillac. Sitting down with his legs crossed, and grabbing hold of the edges of the vehicle's roof, Frank leaned forward and tapped on the windshield to indicate that he was ready for his unconventional ride into Pueblo.

Surprisingly, the drive was quite uneventful until they reached the edge of Pueblo, where the mud got so deep that the hub caps of the Cadillac were barely visible. As the vehicle continued to inch along, the men encountered numerous washed out bridges that had just enough wood remaining to allow the Cadillac to pass, before coming face to face with a squad of Army Rangers who were guarding the entrance to the city.

After a heated discussion concerning the fact that none of the men in the car lived in Pueblo, or had any valuable skills to offer the flood ridden city, the Rangers soon gave in and not only allowed the automobile to pass but gave the men directions to the only working telephone in Pueblo. Thanking the Rangers with a tip of his hat, Frank White and his men soon pulled up to the front steps of the First Baptist Church at 9th and Grand Avenue a little after midnight.

Walking into the church, the reporters found a few volunteers that led them down into the church's basement, where a Telephone booth room was located. This room had been set up to allow the general public to make phone calls without tying up the telegraph lines, which were all located on the church's upper floors. The booth had been set up in the corner of the basement that was normally used as a Sunday school class called "Amoma", which meant helpful in Greek.

"You will need to send all of your press releases out before 6 am, as no press releases are sent out or received during the day", one of the volunteers explained to Denver Post Editor Frank White, as he led the men over to a group of children's craft tables. "You can set up down here if you like."

After saying goodbye to Albert Marksheffel and once again thanking him for driving them into Pueblo, the reporters headed back upstairs where they were all given temporary night passes. "Now, when you're out walking around tonight, make sure you head over to the Elks Lodge. When you get there, head up to the second floor and ask for an offical night pass. It will allow you to go anywhere in the city that you want."

Full of energy and hot coffee, the reporters quickly walked the seven blocks over to the Elks Lodge, at 426 North Santa Fe Avenue, where they easily acquired their night passes, as well as a few interviews with the issuing officers. As the reporters headed back downstairs to begin touring the flood-ravaged city, they decided to scatter out and meet back at the First Baptist Church in two hours, that way they could still send out their stories before the 6 am cut off.

As the reporters headed off in different directions, Editor Frank White decided to walk over to the Courthouse so he could not only find out what the Red Cross was doing with the flood victims but possibly grab a bite to eat while he was there. With only the light of the moon to guide him, as well as the dying batteries in his handheld flashlight, he was relieved to find that the courthouse was lit up with lanterns and candles, which would allow him to conserve what little life his flashlight had left.

Far from quiet, Frank discovered that the first floor of the Courthouse was not only filled with the sounds of snoring, loud whispers, and angry babies crying to be fed but the shuffling of bodies, as hundreds of refugees tried their best to get comfortable as they slept in any available space they could find. As Frank tried his best not to disturb anyone, he walked past a woman wearing a Red Cross Uniform who not only agreed to be interviewed but also directed him to where he could get a bite to eat.

With a full stomach and a fresh cup of hot coffee, Frank happily began filling his notebook with stories from not only some of the Red Cross workers but a few of the refugees as well, which is where he learned about 38-year-old Reverend Frederick Henry Zimmerman's heroic deed.

Reverend Zimmerman was the Pastor of the First Methodist Church, at 9th and Main Street, and had been informed of the birth of his church's newest member during the early morning hours of June 3rd. The baby boy had been born to 49-year-old Carpenter Leary Oliver Herring and his 39-year-old wife Eva, who both already had a seven-year-old son named Oliver, but the boy had been sent to stay with friends when Eva first went into labor.

As the rain continued to fall throughout the day and the fire whistle began to scream from the side of the Water Works building, Reverend Zimmerman began to worry about the safety of the family, as they lived only five blocks north of the Arkansas River. As he went along with his day, the Reverend couldn't stop thinking about the family and they stayed in his thoughts as the levees broke.

Despite the downtown areas beginning to flood, the Herring family had chosen not to evacuate and instead lit candles, but all that did was illuminate the water that was beginning to seep into their little one story house. Removing a wooden slat from the bed, Mr. Herring punched a hole in the bedroom ceiling and with the help of his wife's nurse, they hoisted Eva, and the new baby into the attic, before they both followed close behind.

Unfortunately, the water level soon topped the first floor and with no way out of the attic, the family found themselves trapped. As Mr. Herring tried to figure out how to save his family, they suddenly heard what sounded like something scraping across the roof of their house. Holding the lit candle up towards

Special Pass approved for John William McClary and his wife Mary in order to check on the Burch Tent and Awning Company at 111 South Grand Avenue- Courtesy of The PCCLD Special Collections

the sound, the family soon saw the face of their Pastor looking back at them through a newly formed hole in their roof.

With the floodwaters outside the house continuing to rise, and the attic beginning to fill with water, Reverend Zimmerman continued prying the sheeting off the roof until the hole he had peeked through was large enough to help the family and the nurse escape. Once free, he helped them into the rowboat and took them back to his house.

"Wait a minute, wait a minute. Where did the Reverend get a rowboat?" Denver Post Editor Frank White asked the Red Cross volunteer, as he lowered his pencil. "I'm pretty sure he doesn't just carry one around in his back pocket."

"Well, the Mineral Palace Park and Lake Minnequa have more than enough rowboats, so I guess the Reverend just popped over and grabbed one." The volunteer explained to Frank, who responded to her answer with an accepting nod of approval.

"Ok, but how did the Reverend break through the roof?" Frank White asked, with a suspicious tone, as he pointed to the volunteer with his pencil. "Try to answer that one!"

"He used the oar from the rowboat to pop off the wooden shakes." An older man replied, as he walked out of the shadows and over to where Frank was conducting his interviews. "See, the roof of these older homes is nothing but a few rafters joined with wooden slats, and then covered in wooden shakes. If he shoved the edge of the oar under the shakes, especially with the nasty storm that was brewing that night, they would have just popped off."

As an understanding expression crossed Frank's face, he completed his interview, thanked everyone for their help, and headed back to the First Baptist Church.

Arriving at the Church and heading down into the basement, Frank White was pleased to see that his three reporters had not only returned but were already telling their stories to the Denver Post. Finally, after two hours and exhausted of any further news to report, the reporters ended their call, stretched out on the floor, and quickly fell asleep.

CHAPTER 13

The glass-filled china hutch and a box of oranges

With no more Dam's left to break and a cloudless blue sky finally greeting the residents of Pueblo on the morning of Monday, June 6th, people walked out of their front doors expecting to face a fresh, new day but instead took a whiff of a scent that was so nauseating that it burned the back of their throats.

Which is why Pueblo was quickly dubbed, "The City of a thousand smells."

As the summer sun began to bake the mud that held together mountains of debris, and the stagnant floodwaters continued to infuse itself with the raw sewage that had been leaking out of the Cities broken sewer pipes for the past 58 hours, the city took on a smell that was more than most people could bear.

But it still needed to be cleaned up.

With the refugees at the Elks Lodge beginning to line up outside for breakfast, 81-year-old Michael Clera Studzinski headed up to the buildings second floor to conduct a very important meeting, as the city needed to discuss the best way to clean up the mess left behind by the flood.

Michael, who immigrated to the United States from Germany when he was 48, was also the Commissioner of Safety and Highways for Pueblo and had been laying out a plan with not only the Pueblo National Guard, the Elks, The American Legion, and the Army Rangers, but with the Pueblo Police Department.

"We have thousands of tons of mud filling our streets and another thousand tons of debris, ranging from sawdust, huge trees, automobiles, household items, and hundreds of dead animals and people that need to be removed." Commissioner Studzinski explained, as the collection of men studied a map of Pueblo. "Now, to prevent an epidemic of disease, we need these bodies collected as soon as possible, with the animals taken out of town and burned."

"As of this morning, I was informed that around 20 human bodies have already been brought into the numerous Morgues and refugee centers around the City and I'm sure more will arrive today. We also have about 500 people in temporary hospitals around the city, with people suffering from Typhoid, Pneumonia, and Diphtheria as well as one or two from insanity. Now, we do feel that many of the people suffering from a disease acquired it before the flood, as it was reported many days ago that the Squatter towns were infected, but regardless of how it started, we don't need it to spread any further than it has."

"We also need a telegraph sent over to the newspaper, so they can get the word out that the water is not safe to drink and will need to be boiled, and with no ice available, any milk used for babies will need to be used immediately." The Commissioner added as he turned to speak to 29-year-old Army Captain Durbin Vanlaw. "If you and your men would so kindly take over the cleanup, I would be much obliged."

"Yes Sir, I will begin rounding up volunteers." Captain Vanlaw announced, as he quickly put on his hat and headed downstairs to gather his men. With one topic taken care of, the subject then turned back to their plans for stopping the spread of Typhoid.

"To help prevent the spread, I would also like oranges, lemons and grapefruits handed out to everyone, which will be used as a fever preventative as well." Commissioner Studzinski added, before the meeting was adjourned.

With the information regarding the fruit and the boil water order handed over to the Telegraph operator on duty, the Pueblo Chieftain soon received the information and quickly added it to the evening edition of their daily paper, which was now more like a small pamphlet.

The Pueblo Chieftain, located at 111 East Fourth Street, had been publishing their paper twice a day since the flood stuck the night of June 3rd, but with no electricity, the men were forced to dust off their old handset machine and crank the papers out the old fashioned way.

Called Letterpress printing, the news stories were painstakingly constructed by hand, one letter at a time using tiny metal or wood blocks of individual letters and numbers. Once the page was complete, the little blocks were then locked into place on a metal tray, rolled with ink, and then pressed onto paper using a large hand crank mounted on the side of the machine.

By the light of tallow candles, the employee's at the newspaper had been spending all day and night setting each letter and number just to ensure that their reader base was up to date on not only the boiling water order but for any official or military news that came to them over the telegraph.

With the newspaper now busy setting up the next set of stories and guidelines, Army Captain Durbin Vanlaw, on orders from Commissioner Studzinski, had finally finished gathering up every available man he could find and headed them downtown into the heart

The Pueblo Chieftain newspaper leaflet handed out after the flood-Courtesy of The PCCLD Special Collections

of the flood ridden city. As he walked, he checked that the guards were still set up at every street corner and down Main Street with strict orders to not only check everyone's nighttime passes after 7 pm but to shoot anyone caught looting.

This order had been issued by Colonel Paul Newton of the Army Rangers after their arrival on the evening of June 5th and after a couple of looters had been killed, the cases of looting had dropped dramatically but unfortunately had not stopped.

As Captain Vanlaw continued to walk the flood damaged streets, he discovered many store owners standing outside the remains of their ruined shops shaking their heads, unsure where to start. After confirming that the men in question did indeed own the businesses, they were then offered a few volunteers and a guard to help them salvage what they could.

One of these store owners was 51 –year-old George A. Lotts, who was checking out his grocery store at 602 West Third Street, not only to see how it held up to the flood but to see if the thief was still inside.

George's building not only contained his family's apartment up on the second floor, and a mechanics garage off to the side, but a Grocery store on the street level. He had worked for years as a member of Hook and Ladder Company No. 1 so that one day he could own his own shop, but when he found a thief inside his building on the night of June 3rd, he wasn't about to let him leave without a fight.

As the fire whistle had begun letting out its screams from the side of the Water Works building, George's wife Mineola became nervous about the approaching flood and had insisted that her husband drive her up the hill to the Hinsdale School, as their home and business on West Third Street was only one block from the Arkansas River. After driving his wife to higher ground, George Lotts drove back to keep an eye on his Grocery store, which is when he noticed that his front door had been pried open.

Walking inside, he heard what sounded like someone rummaging around, but when he called out, the noise stopped. Angry that his newly stocked store was being targeted by looters, and unable to locate the thief, George eventually walked back outside, secured the front door behind him, parked his automobile outside the front door, and waited for the thief to immerge.

As he waited, he noticed that the storm was beginning to intensify, resulting in the water around his vehicle now reaching almost halfway up his tires. With one more glance at his beloved store and still not seeing anyone at the windows, George finally had to admit defeat. Putting his automobile in drive and heading towards Hinsdale School, he angrily muttered to himself about how he never caught the looter who he was sure was robbing him blind.

But he had.

When George arrived to check on his building on the morning of June 6th, he discovered that it had unfortunately shifted a bit off its foundation due to the force of the flood, but it was still standing somewhat straight. As his newly assigned volunteers began helping him pull piles of debris away from the front of the building, he discovered that the floodwaters had smashed out his front windows, resulting in the inside of his store looking extremely mangled.

Curious to see how bad his store really was, George carefully began making his way inside, but as he stepped over a pile of debris, he discovered the body of a drowned Mexican man. Calling the volunteers over to help him move the body out of his store, it was soon confirmed that the dead man had been his looter, as they watched money and valuables fall out of his pockets as they carried him outside.

Flood damage at 319 North Union Avenue-Courtesy of The Pueblo County Historical Society

Flood debris outside Jagger Grocery and Market at 238 West first street-Courtesy of The Pueblo County Historical Society

Flood damage inside The White and Davis Department store at 301 North Main Street-Courtesy of The Pueblo County Historical Society

Flood damage inside Union Depot-Courtesy of The Pueblo Historical Society

As the volunteers continued helping George Lotts remove the thief from his store and load the body into a nearby truck, Captain Durbin Vanlaw was still walking around Pueblo's flood ravaged downtown and assigning volunteers to help out store owners, but the more he walked the more stories he began to hear.

And some of the stories were so incredible, that they simply boggled the mind.

Over at Union Depot, a casket had been sitting in the open bed of a pickup truck outside the Depot's baggage room, as it was to be loaded onto the train. Unfortunately, when the flood hit during the evening of June 3rd, the men who had placed it there sought refuge inside the upper floors of the Depot and then watched from the windows as the coffin floated away.

Caught in the swirling floodwaters, the men watched as the coffin traveled in all directions, but when the water finally began to recede, it was found once again resting in the back of the truck.

A Grocery store, located at 208 South Union Avenue, was cleaned out from one end to the other by the turbulent floodwaters, but when store owner Frank M. Smith finally got back inside his store to check out the damage, he found an odd site. Over on a peg and barely hanging on, he discovered an automobile wrench, while on the other side of his store he found two light globes sitting on a counter right where he had left them before the water arrived.

The 3,000-pound safe belonging to the Morrissey Carriage Company had been ripped from the building and deposited 200 feet away, while the Forbush Coal Companies safe was carried all the way across Union Avenue.

Sam Nelson's Furniture Company, at 107 South Union Avenue, had all of its stoves and ranges carried through the entire length of its store and deposited outside the buildings demolished storefront, while a china cabinet sat unharmed. Still sitting upright and filled with glass and other delicate wares, not a single item suffered any damage.

At the Whiton Mortuary, located inside the Labor Temple building on North Union Avenue, a steel casket was carried out of their building by the floodwaters, which was discovered over a mile away at the A. S. & R. Company's Plant. Also discovered at the plant were two dairy wagons, two dead horses, a pile of household goods piled 15 feet high, a cooking range, and 18 inches of mud.

On the 1100 block of West 8th Street, a framed house was ripped from its foundation and carried by the floodwaters nearly a mile before it crashed into the side of Black's Garage, located on Victoria Avenue. When the floodwaters subsided, a bottle of milk, a bottle of wine, and an egg were found in perfect condition sitting upright on the dining room table near a Phonograph, which was also unharmed.

About 9 miles east of Pueblo, on the north side of the Arkansas River lies a farm owned by Andrew Smithour, who had been faced with an expensive, time-consuming task that the floodwaters took care of for him. Most of Andrew's farmland was rather swampy and the task of draining it and filling it in with usable soil would have set him back around $1,000, but when the flood swept over his land it deposited three feet of fertile soil and fixed his swamp problem overnight.

The Silver State Music Company at 306 North Main Street, which was managed by 28-year-old George Nicodemus, suffered the destruction of 65 piano's, which now sat buried underneath 5 feet of mud, as well as a $350 Victrola, which had been sitting in the store's front window. Inside the building, the manager found a dead pig, part of a jewelers repair kit, and numerous items from a tailors shop, as well as the store's $25 Phonograph, which was in perfect condition.

But it was 32-year-old Army Ranger Captain John Lee Dennis that found the biggest prize.

As the Rangers were busy inspecting the flooded area's and issuing work order's, Captain Dennis and his collection of volunteers headed down to the train yards, where they discovered huge tree's pulled up by their roots, downed fences, deep gully's still partially full of water, the remains of a small cottage half-buried in the mud and dozens of box cars piled in a heap.

Army Rangers looking over piles of flood debris-Courtesy of The Pueblo County Historical Society

Pullman train cars washed off the tracks. Notice how the windows are broken out-Courtesy of The Pueblo County Historical Society

Pullman train cars with a freight car upside down in front of them-Courtesy of The Pueblo County Historical Society

The Denver & Rio Grande No. 3 Engine with the Missouri No. 14 laying on its side
in front of it-Courtesy of The Pueblo County Historical Society

The Missouri Pacific No. 14 Engine laying on its side- Courtesy of The Pueblo County Historical Society

Walking towards the boxcars, in search of either survivors or bodies, the men began hearing an odd whining noise coming out of a coal car, which was then followed by a type of shallow squeal. Following the unusual sound, the men soon found themselves looking at a bright pink, newly born family of piglets, and one mud covered mama.

Knowing that the animals would be hungry, a few of the men managed to get the mother pig down from the train car, where a rope was used to construct a type of leash, while the rest of the men were left carrying unhappy piglets back to the Army truck. As they approached the vehicle, Captain Dennis noticed that there was a large cage already sitting in the back, making all types of racket.

"You found chickens?"

After making room for the piglets and tying the mama pig up to the bumper of the truck, Captain Durbin Vanlaw and his group started to laugh, as they told the men their story.

"So, we were down by where those little squatter towns used to be when we heard this cackling, followed by a weird hiss noise. Each time the cackle happened, the hiss would follow. So, we finally locate this half-buried chicken coop, with 10 live chickens in it …and a cat!" the Captain explained, as the men started to laugh again. "We are just keeping the cat in there so we can get her back to the Elks lodge, so she can get something to eat."

"You're keeping her in there so she doesn't attack you!" a man joked, which prompted Captain Vanlaw to glance over at a group of approaching Rangers, who all appeared rather pleased with themselves.

"Aww, are those kittens?"

After hearing the story of how these two little fluff balls were discovered on top of a cottage, which was lodged up against one of the piers of the Denver & Rio Grande Train Bridge, Captain Vanlaw announced that he needed to get these animals back to the Elks Lodge, as the truck was getting pretty full. Hoisting the mama pig up into the back with the chicken coop and holding the piglets in their arms, three Army Rangers drove out of the flood district with their catches of the day.

Arriving back at the Elks Lodge and dropping off their charges, the Ranger's headed upstairs to the Police Department to ask if anything new had come over the wire, before heading back into the flood district. While they were there, the Rangers were greeted by a Police Officer who informed them that a large number of bodies had been brought into each of the refugee centers, as well as more injured survivors, so if the men could help with transports, it would be quite helpful.

As the Ranger's headed downstairs, the officer headed back into the meeting room where the leaders of Pueblo were busy drafting a letter to the Governor of Colorado, who had just recently moved his Denver office to Colorado Springs to be closer to the carnage in Pueblo.

In hopes of securing funds for their city, a letter was being composed by 54-year-old James Lee Lovern -the President of the City Council, 50-year-old Frank Steven Hoag - the chairman of the newly created levee repair committee, 65-year-old Charles King McHarg -the President of the Arkansas Valley ditch Association, and 38-year-old Ernst Edmund Withers who was not only the President of the Pueblo Water Works, but also the Vice President of the Iron City Fuel Company, a Trustee for the Northside Water board, a thirty-second degree Mason, and a member of not only the Knights of Pythias, but the Rotary club, just to name a few.

Despite being the best looking man in the room, the charismatic Ernst Withers- who pronounced his name "Airnst"- was a wonderful family man who had married his high school sweetheart Noma in 1902, and together they had three sons, who Ernst hoped would follow in his footsteps as they got older. Any chance Ernst had to include his son's in his many obligations, such as writing this letter to the Governor, was just another chance to help his children learn the meaning of responsibility.

As the men finished writing the letter, they all agreed that it was rather short, but they all felt that it covered every point they wished to convey.

Honorable Oliver H. Shoup, Governor, Colorado Springs,

Late estimates of total property and crop damage between Canon City and the state line is from 15-20 Million dollars. Damage in Pueblo city and county alone will total 6-8 Million dollars.

The Federal Government expends millions of dollars to improve and repair levees in all sections of the county. We now ask for the government to appropriate the sum of $5,000,000 of which the sum of $2,000,000 may be immediately available for purpose of repairing and improving Arkansas River and Fountain River levees and removing debris from cities damaged, of which Pueblo would have at least 1½ million dollars immediately.

Impossible to ascertain loss of life owing to the impossibility of removing debris without great financial assistance, but Pueblo alone will show several hundred people drowned when debris removed.

And the dead just kept coming

As the cleanup continued and the roads were being scraped by slips pulled by four-horse teams, the volunteers watched as motor cars moved up and down Main Street with mud encrusted bodies tied to their fenders, adding to the bodies that were quickly piling up inside the morgues and refugee centers.

One man had discovered 18 bodies in just 20 minutes, which he piled up in the back of his truck like lumber, before bringing them to the Court House. Covered in a yellowish slime, mud, and debris, the bodies were carried in by volunteers as the man informed everyone that he was heading out to go find some more.

Another arrival of a body at the morgue was discovered draped across the lap of a man's wife after they drove over 10 miles to deliver the body. Upon being questioned, the woman didn't appear upset and instead asked for a rowboat so she and her husband could help retrieve more bodies.

But some deaths were more heartbreaking than others.

Lying in the back of a pickup truck and covered in a thick layer of yellowish-gray river mud was the body of nine-year-old Neal J. Kendall, the last of his family. Identified by the two missing fingers on his right hand after being electrocuted when he was seven, he was the eldest child of 38-year-old Professor Edwin Pomeroy Kendall, who was not only the principal of the South Avondale School but also drove trucks for the Colorado Fuel and Iron Company.

The Kendall's home and dairy farm sat right along the shores of the Arkansas River on a street called Goodnight, but when the flood of June 3rd hit the family's farm, it wasn't a goodnight for anyone. Nobody knew if the family was aware of the incoming flood or if they even tried to reach higher ground, but it was obvious that none of the family made it out in time.

With hopes now dashed that at least one member of the family had survived, the body of the mud encrusted nine-year-old soon joined the bodies of not only his father but his 42-year-old mother Edna Gertrude, his 75-year-old grandmother Nancy Catherine Jackson and his three siblings, six-year-old Elwin, four-year-old Catherine Grace, and three-year-old Albert.

Another family struck by the flood of June 3rd didn't all die from the high water, as a few had died because of the hazards of wearing a long, fashionable dress near a barbwire fence.

As the floodwaters blasted down the Arkansas River and followed its natural channel out of Pueblo, it continued east towards the Colorado/ Kansas state line, where it tore apart every town it encountered along the way. One of these towns was La Junta, which is Spanish for "The Junction" and was so named due to the fact it was built at the intersection of the historic Santa Fe Trail and an old wagon road the pioneers had used during the gold rush.

Thanks to Telegraph Operator Emory Mitchell and reporter Howard Haden's heroic quest to reconnect the Telegraph line up to Mineral Palace Park, all the towns east of Pueblo had received their flood warning a little after 1:30am on June 4th.

As the Mountain States Telephone and Telegraph girls in La Junta received Emory's emergency message, they jumped straight into emergency mode and began calling every home in the area which resulted in a rush of activity as people scrambled out of bed, threw on their shoes, and headed up to the hills above the town as fast as they could.

One of the ranches contacted was owned by 59-year-old Francis Thomas Lewis, who was also the City Engineer for La Junta and his 60-year-old wife Frances Mary Lewis, as well as their two adult daughters Mary and Hester, who both worked as High school teachers in the area. When the alert first went out about the flood, the family began assisting their farmhand Frank White in moving all of their animals to higher ground, before attempting to find safety for themselves, which unfortunately proved to be their downfall.

With Lewis's adult daughters Mary and Hester already halfway to La Junta in one automobile, their parents Francis and Frances, as well as Frank White's wife, infant child, and five-year-old niece Gertrude headed out in the other. With no room for Frank inside the vehicle, he instead chose to jump up onto the back of his horse just as the automobile headed towards La Junta at around 10 am, which is when they all spotted a terrifying sight.

Coming down the Arkansas River at a breakneck speed, was an eight-foot wall of water and it was heading right towards them. As Frank White quickly stopped his horse in anticipation of Francis Lewis turning the vehicle around, Frank was forced to watch as Francis turned too sharply on the wet road, overcorrected and then rolled the automobile into a ditch.

A ditch that ran right alongside the already engorged Arkansas River.

In a panic, the women were able to pull themselves and the children free of the vehicle and run towards a nearby hill, but when they tried to crawl through the barbed wire fence, their long dresses snagged. Hearing the women scream, Frank White turned his horse towards the sound and found his wife, and 5-year-old niece Gertrude, as well as his employer's wife Frances Lewis, tangled in the barbed wire.

Just as Frank began to dismount his steed to free his wife, he heard the horn from Mr. Lewis's overturned automobile bellow out a warning. Turning towards the sound, he saw not only the sight of

Mr. Lewis struggling to free himself from his vehicle but the wall of water licking the bumper.

"Frank! Frank!"

Turning back towards the sound of his wife's voice, he saw the fear in her eyes as she hoisted their infant child into the air towards him." Take the baby! Take it!"

Leaning off the side of his horse, Frank White was able to grab the corner of the child's gown just as his panicked steed quickly turned and began sprinting up the hill to avoid the incoming water. As Frank cradled his child, he turned back towards the rushing water and noticed that both his wife, niece and Mr. and Mrs. Lewis, as well as the automobile, had all disappeared.

When the floodwaters finally subsided and the rescue efforts began on June 6th, 32-year-old American Legion Commander Ralph Leonard Hufford led a search party for Mr. Lewis and his traveling companions and what they found was heartbreaking.

The body of Frank White's wife was found first, nude except for her stockings and shoes, as the barbed wire fence appeared to of kept her garments as a trophy when the floodwaters sent her down the river. Located face down under some bushes near the edge of the Arkansas River, her body was covered in numerous bruises, as well as sporting a deep gash in her skull, while her finger still held her heavy gold wedding ring.

But now Ralph Hufford had to figure out how to get her body back to their truck.

Glancing around for something to strap her to, the men quickly gathered up some loose boards that were floating nearby and drug Mrs. White up onto them. Tying her onto the boards with rope, to keep her body taunt, they finally lifted her free of the water, but since the ground was so unsteady Ralph and his crew fell into the rapidly flowing river numerous times before they finally reached the truck.

Mrs. White and her makeshift stretcher were soon slid into the back of the vehicle right next to the body of a mangled young boy, believed to be that of 10-year-old Bert Waters, but his bruised and mangled face and head had made him hard to identify.

As the search party continued to comb the banks of the river, the body of Francis Lewis was discovered 500 yards away from where his automobile had first overturned, but the bodies of his wife Frances and Frank Whites 5-year-old Niece Gertrude were nowhere to be found.

But La Junta wasn't the only town downstream from Pueblo to feel the wrath of the flood.

Sixty miles east of Pueblo and only 12 miles west of La Junta, sat the small farming town of Rocky Ford. Known around the nation for its abundance of watermelons and cantaloupe, the town's people normally focused their attention on farming , but on June 6th produce was the last thing on 19-year-old Nettie's Darr's mind, as all she wanted to do was find the bodies of her children.

Wearing dry clothing that wasn't hers and holding a single baby shoe in her trembling hands, Nettie begged anyone within earshot to please find her boy's. "I have to bury them!" She wailed, as she began cradling the tiny shoe against her chest, "My children...they just, they just... slid out of my hands...right out of my hands..."

Nettie's heart wrenching ordeal had begun around 9 am on June 4th, as the flooded Arkansas River barreled past Pueblo and headed east in search of new towns to conquer. With no warnings coming their way and hints of a blue sky finally peeking out from around the storm clouds, Nettie's 30-year-old husband Arthur William Darr, who preferred to be called Art, was spending the morning talking with his 59-year-old father Jacob Franklyn Darr, who preferred to be called Frank, about moving the carnival from the railroad tracks. As he continued to speak to his father, Art was suddenly distracted by an extremely large flock of birds flying overhead, seemingly on a quest to get as far away from Rocky Ford as possible.

Turning to see what might have spooked the birds, but not seeing anything out of the ordinary, Art just shrugged his shoulders as he walked over to his wife and took their wiggling 10-month-old son Charles out of her arms. "My dad wants us to spend the night in town tonight, so I can help move the carnival, so I'm going to head over to John's and have him milk the cows for us while we're gone. I figure we will head out after dinner."

Sitting the baby down in the grass and watching as his children played with the neighbor's cat, Art thanked his lucky stars for Nettie, as she had fallen in love with his boys almost instantly. When his first wife Era died during the Flu epidemic of 1918, her passing had left him with three little boys to tend to, but luckily he had met 18-year-old Nettie, who he married in January 1920 and was soon blessed with little Charles Franklin within the year.

As Art walked off to work on his chores, Nettie was surprised to see that the cat that the children had been playing with had suddenly become startled and with a quick twist of its fuzzy, furry body untangled himself from their grasp, gave a hiss of warning and took off towards the trees. Curious what had scared the little animal, Nettie looked behind her and noticed one of their neighbors riding by on horseback and when they made eye contact, he began waving his arms frantically in the air.

Waving back and giving the man a friendly smile, Nettie quickly turned away and headed towards the chicken house to get a roaster for dinner when she heard what sounded like hooves beating on the ground behind her. Turning around, she was surprised to see horses, cattle, and even rabbits rushing past her, which is when she noticed the eight-foot wall of water heading straight towards her.

Nettie Darr-Authors personal collection

Arthur and Richard Darr-Authors personal collection

"Grab Delbert and Leedew!!" Nettie screamed to her husband's 14-year-old niece Vera who was collecting eggs, as she herself grabbed her baby and the hand of 8- year-old Richard. "Head to the house! Go! Go!"

The family's home, which sat on a small strip of land between the Arkansas River and the Fort Lyon Canal Companies ditch was built of stone, with two additional wooden rooms off the side and it would be those rooms that would prove to be their downfall.

Entering the home, Nettie and the children quickly braced themselves against one of the interior stone walls just as the flood water smashed into the house. As the children screamed, the torrent set its sights on the two framed rooms, which it began to tear free from the house.

"Mrs. Darr! Mrs. Darr! What are we going to do?" Vera begged, as the water inside the home began to rise. Looking around, Nettie spotted the kitchen table, and with her baby Charles firmly attached to her hip, as he had no intention of letting go of his mama, she quickly grabbed the table and pulled it over to the stone wall. Instructing Vera and the older boys to climb up onto it, Nettie used her body as a brace to hold the table steady until it appeared the water was finished raging.

Finally dropping to around 3 feet deep, Nettie released her grip on the table and waded over to the homes windows, where she looked towards the welcoming hills. "The ditch is only about a quarter of a mile north of us and past that is a hill. We need to get to higher ground."

Looking back over at Vera, Nettie could see the fear on the child's face. The girl's parents had both died during the War, which is when her husband's first wife Era had taken her in at the age of eleven and then the poor girl had to watch her Aunt Era die of the flu, so the last thing Nettie wanted to do was force the girl to watch her remaining family drown.

With Vera taking hold of Richard and his six-year old brother Delbert's hands, Nettie grabbed five-year-old Leedew, and with baby Charles still on her hip, the group began wading through the water towards the ditch. Unfortunately, after walking only 50 feet, the water quickly began to rise once more, forcing them back to the house.

Once inside, they noticed that the furniture was now floating around which gave Nettie an idea. Grabbing hold of the bed, she pulled it towards her and put all four of the boys in its center, as she glanced up at the remains of the homes framed rooms, which were barely held on by a thread.

"Vera, I need you to climb up onto the flat top of the rooms and tell me if they are stable," Nettie explained, as the young girl nervously looked up at the damaged section of the home before shaking her head no.

"I can't! I just can't" she wailed, as the fractured wooden walls continued to twist and buckle against the violent floodwaters.

"Vera, honey, listen to me. We need to get up onto the roof and that's the only path we have, so I need you to be brave for me, ok?" Nettie pleaded as the water continued to rise around her at an alarming rate.

Glancing back over at the boys, Vera watched as yet another wave of water splashed up onto the bed and realized deep down that she was the only one who could do this. Turning back to the wooden addition and trying hard to ignore the raging river around her, Vera carefully climbed up onto the flat roof of the two framed rooms.

"What do you see?" Nettie yelled over the roar of the water, as the wild torrent continued to batter the house. "Can we get the boys up onto the roof?"

Glancing back down at her Aunt Nettie, Vera wrapped one arm around a beam before she lowered her free hand down and motioned for the first boy. One by one Richard, Delbert, and Leedew were pulled up onto the roof of the home, with Nettie and her very clingy 10-month-old following close behind.

And it wasn't a moment too soon.

As the violent current continued to batter the stone home, the wooden addition finally gave up the ghost and allowed the raging water to finally tear it free from the side of the house, which immediately caused the roof of the home to become unstable. As Nettie and the children frantically tried to find something to hold onto, the roof began to buck, spin and twist until it finally snapped free from the house entirely.

With their makeshift roof raft now caught in the current and riding the waves down the river, Nettie soon felt confident that the roof would hold and began to relax a little. As they continued downstream, the unexpected sailors floated past Vera's Grandparent's house but were unaware that her Grandmother had already been killed by the violent water.

Margaret Catherine Platz and her husband Mendhous, both 64 years old had been caught off guard by the flood, but unfortunately, it was only Mendhous who washed up onto a nearby riverbank alive when the water decided to recede.

As Nettie and the children continued down the river, their raft soon encountered a swift side current that had formed right at the point where the head gate of the Fort Lyon Canal joined with the Arkansas River. As the roof raft hit the edge of the rapid, it was quickly caught in a whirlpool, which spun the raft directly into a large cottonwood tree, with the impact causing both Nettie and baby Charles to slide into the angry water.

With Vera holding onto the older boys and screaming for her aunt, Nettie frantically trying to ride the violent torrents towards her baby, but was only able to barely touch the edge of his little dress before he was pulled away from her forever.

With shock taking over her body, she unwillingly watched as her baby disappeared under the waves, only to be snapped out of her trance by the sound of Vera screaming at her over the crash of the water. Turning towards her voice, Nettie saw Vera's hand reaching for her from their roof raft.

Climbing up onto the raft and scampering towards its peak to join the children, Nettie quickly held the youngest boy tightly in her arms, as she suddenly felt naked without her infant son against her body.

As the raft floated along for almost two more miles, the sailors finally spotted the Rocky Ford Bridge, on which was standing 31-year-old farmer Lester Swink and his 27-year-old wife Grace. As the couple lowered a rope down from the center of the bridge, Nettie felt a sense of relief swarm over her, but when she prepared herself to grab the rope, she instantly realized that she had a very important decision to make.

The roof raft that she was riding on with the children was not slowing down, which meant that only one person could be lifted to safety before the sailors continued on their voyage down the raging Arkansas River. If Nettie allowed herself to be lifted up, then she would be condemning the children to certain death, but if she had one of her stepson's grab the rope, they surely wouldn't have the strength in their little hands to hold on long enough to be pulled up onto the bridge.

So she handed the rope to 14-year-old Vera.

As Lester Swink and his wife began pulling Vera up, Nettie and the boys held onto their roof raft as it dipped underneath the steel bridge, which gave them a front-row view of an image that would be burned into Nettie's memories for the rest of her life.

Only inches from the railing of the Rocky Ford Bridge, Vera was unexpectedly ripped free from the rope by a rogue wave and fell into the raging torrent.

As an icy chill ran down to her very soul, Nettie screamed for the young girl as she scanned the water around her, but she never saw Vera again.

As Nettie began comforting the boys for the loss of Vera, who they had only known as their big sister, the sailors continued floating down the river for almost three more miles before the roof raft slammed into a tree and broke apart, sending its passengers into the angry floodwaters. Nettie managed to grab hold of a log, which allowed her to stay afloat, but like her infant son, the boys were gone.

And she was truly alone.

After covering a total of nine miles down the river and having her clothes ripped from her body by barbed wire, debris, and tangles of branches, Nettie was finally able to pull herself ashore where an elderly woman found her and wrapped her in a blanket.

**Vera Ellen & Margaret Platz
Both drowned in Pueblo Flood**

*Vera and her Grandmother Margaret Platz
-Authors personal collection*

Desperate to learn if her husband survived, Vera was driven back up to Rocky Ford where she learned that her husband Art had perished. After the Arkansas River finally calmed itself down enough to allow people to search for loved ones, Nettie's 8-year Stepson Richard's body was found tangled in a barbwire fence, while her husband and infant son were found buried in river silt. Unfortunately, the bodies of 14-year-old Vera, six-year-old Delbert, and five-year-old Leedew were never found.

But Nettie's family were not the only flood victims found buried in river silt.

Discovered over 80 miles east of Pueblo, near the town of Las Animas and buried up to her armpits in silt, rescuers began digging out what they thought was yet another body, that was until the woman opened her eyes.

Suffering from not only starvation but hypothermia as well, the woman told her saviors that she had been thrown into the river when the flood struck the train she was on back in Pueblo. She went on to explain that after being battered by debris and tumbled by the river, she must have been knocked unconscious, because when she finally awoke, she found herself stuck in the silt.

As the men quickly began digging the woman free, the search for another person from the train was underway back in Pueblo, but this search was fueled by greed, not honor.

With a $250 reward offered for the whereabouts of 41-year-old Elijah Bruner, Conductor of the

Manifest Freight Train No. 62, numerous people were drawn to the hunt as his 37-year-old wife Maude and 12-year-old son Glenn prayed that he would be found alive. She described her husband as being 6 feet tall and around 220 pounds with a light complexion, adding that he was also missing the large toe on his right foot and that the thumb on his right hand was crippled.

After an extensive search around Pueblo's flooded areas, the treasure hunters began to fan out and head east, in hopes that perhaps Conductor Elijah Bruner's body had washed up along the shore of the Arkansas River or had become tangled in a tree or fence line.

As the men continued to drive around, they suddenly discovered a large island of debris sitting in the center of the Arkansas River near the town of Boone, which was around 25 miles east of Pueblo, and it was constructed of everything their minds could imagine. Piled high with timber, furniture, uprooted trees, automobiles, and dead animals, the treasure hunters felt certain that it also contained the remains of human bodies.

Like Conductor Bruner's.

To keep the hunt fair and to stop the men from fighting if and when the Conductor was found, each group of treasure hunters was assigned a recently deputized Police officer to help keep things civil. One particular hunt was also being monitored by not only Constable S.A. Curran, but a few men from the Santa Fe train line, as someone in the group needed to be able to positively identify Elijah Bruner since none of the fortune seekers had nver even met the man before.

The first island the group decided to search was situated around 200 feet from the shoreline of the Arkansas River, but with the current still quite strong, the men were afraid to cross it. As the group discussed what to do, they soon noticed that a Mexican man who had joined the hunt was quickly removing all of his clothes, which he was piling up on a nearby rock.

Intrigued, the treasure hunters continued to watch as the man pulled a rope out of his bag and tied one end around the bumper of one of the group's automobiles, before placing the other end in his teeth and lowering himself into the rushing water. Fighting the strong current, the man then swam over to the island of debris, tied the rope to a partially embedded piano, and began looking for the missing conductor on his own.

Not wanting to lose out on the prize money, the rest of the search party clambered over to the rope, lowered themselves into the rapidly flowing currents, and with a tight hold, crossed over to the island to continue their hunt.

But Conductor Bruner wasn't there.

Another group of treasure hunters, who had not only secured a rowboat, but a National Guard member to keep the peace, had just discovered survivors on another island in the middle of the swollen Arkansas River, but to their dismay, neither of the men turned out to be Conductor Bruner, but they had been on the trains.

Originally on the Missouri Pacific No. 14, 37-year-old Frank Dillon Spicer explained to his rescuers that he had followed a group of his fellow passengers across the tops of the submerged Pullman cars in order to reach the engine, during the flood of June 3rd, but after the engine capsized he was thrown into the water and washed downstream. He went on to explain that he had then managed to climb up onto the roof of a shattered house, which he rode down the Arkansas River until it eventually collided into the island of debris that he was currently standing on.

The second man was 35-year-old Edward McMahon Harrison, who had been a second Lieutenant in the War and during the flood of June 3rd had been a passenger on the Denver & Rio Grande No. 3. He had managed to escape the Pullman car he was in and then grabbed hold of a log which he clung onto until he was tossed up onto the island with Frank.

Happy that they were finally being rescued, Edward quickly walked over to a section of the island, lifted the lid off a crushed trunk, and pulled out a small box, which he handed over to one of the members of the National Guard. Opening it, the guard discovered a life insurance policy for a woman named Mary Fuyda, as well as other personal papers.

Satisfied that the box was now in good hands, Edward climbed into the rowboat, while Frank reached into another box and pulled out a few oranges, some of which he tossed over to Edward before joining him in the boat. "An entire case washed up onto the island during the flood and it's all we've had to eat since we got here" he told their rescuers with a smile.

As the two flood survivors were taken back to Pueblo, their rescuers told them the story of a man who had single handilly saved 17 people from the angry Arkansas River in the early morning hours of June 4th, as well as four more the following day.

In the town of Sugar City, which was a little over 60 miles east of Pueblo, 34-year-old Russian Immigrant Peter Markus received a phone call from nearby Olney Springs that a terrible flood had hit Pueblo and that people were being washed down the Arkansas River in droves.

Quickly loading his fishing boat into the back of his Ford truck and heading the 16 miles down to the Arkansas River, he was suddenly faced with a terrible scene. Lowering his boat into the violent river, Peter immediately began pulling men, women, and children down from the tops of trees, as well as pulling them up out of the water as they floated by.

Once his boat was full, he would then head over to the shore, where people were waiting to take the victims to the home of Olney Springs County Commissioner John H. Cowden, so they could rest.

Returning again and again, Peter managed to rescue 17 people from the river before night fell, but the darkness that followed made it impossible for him to navigate the angry river safely. Still hearing the sounds of people begging for help, but unable to see them, Peter Markus regrettably loaded his boat back into his truck and drove home to rest, but awoke at 4 am the next morning to continue his rescue mission.

As the sun began to rise, Peter scanned the river but was only able to rescue four more victims of the flood, who he found high up in the trees. Dropping them off on the shore, he then lowered his boat into the river once more, but this time he rode the flood water's east for over 60 miles until he reached the head gates of Fort Lyon.

As he traveled towards the historic Military Fort, he searched every debris pile and tree that he came across but was unable to find any more survivors.

But now he could rest.

With night finally falling over Pueblo and the day of June 6th coming to an end, thousands of volunteers and Army Rangers happily put down their shovels, buckets, and rakes and left the piles of rancid, debris filled river mud for another day. As the men went searching for a meal and a good night's rest, the day time guards were changed out, so the men on the night shift could have their turn protecting the streets of Pueblo.

Placed on each street corner downtown and stationed sporadically throughout Main Street and Union Avenue, the guard's job was to prevent looting and to make sure that anyone out after 7 pm had a valid pass that gave them a good reason to be downtown.

Everyone knew that the night guards were a bit jumpy and that you dare not challenge them when they asked you for your pass. Anyone out after dark knew that it was best to walk down the center of the street with your pass pinned to your hat and to stop the instant you heard the words "Halt! What are you doing out here? Come on up slow and easy! Let's see your pass!"

The guard would then shine his flashlight in your face, before ever reading the pass, as though he wished to temporarily blind you while he checked to see if you had permission to be out at such a late hour. After confirming that you were clear to proceed, the guard would then shove the pass back to you with an irritated attitude, as if he was hoping to find your arms full of mud covered merchandise instead.

And if you did, maybe, just maybe... you would then take off running, and give the guard a reason to use his rifle and bag yet another looter.

But unlike when a man is out on foot, the game becomes quite unpredictable when a twitchy night guard is trying to stop an automobile.

After a late night meeting with the Northside Water Board Association, Ernst Withers was heading home with his 16-year-old son Granville, who preferred to be called Grant, sitting in the passenger seat of the families Pierce-Arrow seven-passenger touring car. The two had just spent hours listening to board members discuss the best way to restore freshwater to the city, and with Ernst being on the board of Trustees, it was his duty to attend the meeting, so he had brought Grant along for some father and son time.

Finally able to head home, Ernst Withers turned his automobile onto Grand Avenue at around 11:30 pm, where he immediately found himself following another vehicle whose driver was also out after curfew. As both vehicles reached the intersection at 7th and Grand Avenue, their combined headlights caught the attention of a night guard, who ordered them to stop so he could check their passes.

With the vehicle in front of them quickly slowing down, Ernst began applying his brakes but his response, unfortunately, wasn't fast enough to appease the impatient night guard. Assuming that the second car was refusing to stop, the guard readied his Springfield rifle, pointed it at Ernst Withers car, and fired.

CHAPTER 14

A blood-covered teenager and the hand of God

With Ernst Withers foot no longer applying pressure to the brake or the clutch, the Pierce-Arrow touring car quickly began to shutter and buck as it attempted to gain power despite no longer being in gear.

"Dad! Dad!" Grant screamed as he watched his father's hands quickly slide off not only the automobile's steering wheel but the shifter as well. "Dad! Wake up!"

Glancing through the windshield and seeing that the vehicle in front of them had already made a complete stop, 16-year-old Grant grabbed the steering wheel in an attempt to avoid a collision, but it was too late. As the Pierce-Arrow stuck the back of the automobile, Ernst Withers body slammed into the steering wheel with a sickening thud, before quickly sliding over onto the shoulder of his terrified son.

Ernst Withers- Courtesy of The Pueblo County Historical Society

Pushing his father off of him and pinning him up against the driver's seat, Grant was still unaware of the severity of his father's injuries until another vehicle drove past. As its headlamps illuminated the touring car's interior, Grant was suddenly faced with something that his young mind had trouble understanding.

As blood continued to pour out of the area that used to contain the top of his father's skull, Grant quickly removed his hands off his father, but now with nothing holding him upright, Ernst Withers once again slumped over onto the shoulder of his son, who let out a horrified scream. Now covered in his father's blood, Grant immediately wiggled free of the vehicle, but in his fear, tripped over the running board and landed on the road with a thud.

Glancing back up at the vehicle, as if to confirm that this experience had truly happened, Grant watched as his father's lifeless body fell over onto the passenger's side of the Pierce-Arrows bench seat, but stopped short on the armrest. Unable to turn away, Grant suddenly realized that the weight of his father's arms and shoulders were

Grant Withers Senior Yearbook picture- Courtesy of The PCCLD Special Collections

slowly pulling his body toward the floor of the automobile, which eventually caused his head to hang down at a ghastly angle.

As yet another automobile drove past, and unknowingly lit up the horrifying details of Ernst Wither's injuries, Grant silently watched as the remainder of his father's blood poured from his horrifying head wound, and onto the vehicles running boards, before it dripped down onto the dirt road near Grants feet.

While scooting away from the ever growing puddle of blood, Grant began glancing around the immediate area, which is when he spotted a night guard standing nearby with a rifle at his side. As he watched, Grant noticed how calmly the guard was checking the night pass of the other driver, who appeared terrified, but what really bothered Grant was that the guard didn't appear to be bothered by the fact that he had just killed a man.

In what felt like mere seconds, the sounds of hurried footsteps began filling the air as members of not only the Army Rangers, but the Pueblo National Guard began running towards the two automobiles, while the Night

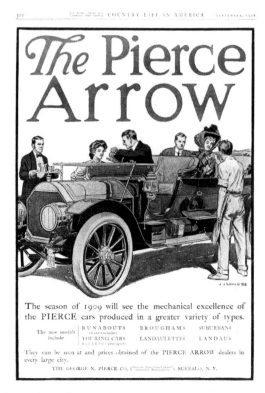

Pierce Arrow Touring Car-Authors personal collection

Guard who had murdered Ernst Withers' quickly disappeared into the darkness. As the Rangers and National Guard members got closer, Grant recognized the face of his older brother, 17-year-old Newton Wayne Withers who was a member of the Pueblo National Guard, and began screaming for him.

Running over to his brother, Newton unexpectedly found himself faced with not only the task of calming down his younger sibling but witnessing the horror of his father's lifeless body hanging out of the family's automobile. Confirming that his blood-soaked brother wasn't physically injured, Newton Withers led him over to the front steps of a nearby house, where they both sat down and waited for the Coroner to arrive.

As they sat, the brothers began talking about the night of June 3rd and how happy their parents had been in the hours before the levees broke and all these problems began.

Despite the talk around Pueblo of a possible flood, Ernst Withers had taken his wife Noma out to a dinner party at their Country Club and Newton had taken his girlfriend Leona Voorhees's to a show at the Opera house, all while Grant and his eight-year-old little brother Ernst Jr. chose to spend a quiet night at home.

After going to bed, Grant had heard a knock on his home's front door and discovered his neighbor J.E. Creel asking him for help, as he was worried that the floodwaters would ruin all of the merchandise he stored in his building's basement. Agreeing to help, Grant informed his little brother that he would be right back, before he slid on a pair of thick, leather knee-high boots and headed with Mr. Creel to the Dean & Creel Furniture Company, at 200 North Main Street.

Unfortunately, while Grant was helping to load furniture from the store's basement onto the service elevator, the flood suddenly struck the building, which began to quickly take on water. Flipping up the lever that would send the elevator up to the second floor, Mr. Creel and Grant ran up the stairs after it, only to witness the turbulent water blow out the buildings first floor windows and cover them both in shards of glass.

Wading through the rising water, Grant followed Mr. Creel to the stairs that would lead them up to the buildings second floor, which is when he noticed that his thick boots had been slashed to ribbons by the glass, which he carefully picked out of the leather to avoid any further damage. As the water began to take over the second floor, two men climbed up onto the building's roof, where they looked for a place to get out of the pouring rain.

As they glanced around at the nearby buildings, Mr. Creel and Grant watched as a small, wooden railway section house crashed into the side of Pryor's Furniture store, before spinning around and disappearing under the waters violent swell.

"Grant! Grant! Follow me! The Saddle shops roof has an overhang!" Mr. Creel yelled as he tried his best to be heard over the sounds of the pounding storm. Climbing up and over the short wall that separated the buildings, the two men quickly ducked under the overhang and got out of the weather the best that they could.

From their viewpoint, they watched as people floated by on pieces of wood or furniture and at one point they even saw a Collie swimming and made bets on whether the dog would find something to climb up on or drown.

Finally seeing a bolt of fabric float by, Grant grabbed it and threw it towards the dog, who snagged it with its teeth and held on tight. Like a big fish fighting you at the end of a line, Grant and Mr. Creel managed to reel the exhausted dog up onto the roof with them, where he stayed until morning. When the sun finally came up, Grant lowered himself into the deep water and swam home to the loving arms of his family.

Family.

Seeing that the Coroner had just arrived caused both Grant and Newton Withers to become deathly quiet, as the man's appearance brought back the image of their father's untimely death. As they watched 28-year-old Coroner George Francis McCarthy get out of his car, the brothers suddenly realized that their mother and younger brother didn't know that their father had been murdered.

As it was now after midnight, the remains of their family would be waking up in a few hours to a whole new reality, one that Grant and Newton had to now experience all over again.

Seeing the two young men sitting on the steps, Coroner McCarthy, from McCarthy & Brown Undertaking shone his flashlight towards them, which is when he noticed that not only was Grant's face and hair splattered in blood, but most of his clothing was stained a dark maroon.

"Has he been examined? Has anyone examined him? Are you injured?" he asked Grant with a worried tone, as he motioned for an Army Ranger to step forward.

"No sir, I'm not injured. This is my father's blood." Grant replied as tears began to run down his crimson stained cheeks. "It's all of my father's blood."

As a medic began to check over Grant and helped him clean some of the blood off his face, Coroner McCarthy interviewed the brothers about what had happened and he wasn't happy with what he heard. Closing his note pad and putting his pen back into his pocket, the coroner finally stood up and asked them if they were ready to re-visit the scene and identify the body of their father.

Responding with a silent nod, the brothers were lead back over to their family's car, where they were once again faced with the image of their father's bloodied body, this time lit up with the bright beam of the coroner's flashlight.

With the body now drained of blood, the wounds to Ernest Withers's head were much more evident, with the light illuminating the fact that the entire top of his head was missing, as well as part of the left side. The headlights of their families automobile still shone brightly, which added to the grisly scene as the light bounced off the car in front of it, casting an eerie shadow across their father's face.

After Grant and Newton finished identifying the body and Grant gave his statement once again, the brothers were driven home by a uniformed officer who had the unfortunate task of informing Noma Withers that she was now a widow.

But who killed Ernst Withers?

With Grant and Newton heading back home, a swarm of activity continued to buzz around not only the body of Ernst but the automobile he was driving. As 46-year-old Colonel Patrick J. Hamrock, the Adjutant General of the State National Guard and Captain Dennis of the Colorado Rangers, as well as a score of guardsman, Rangers and Pueblo Police officers watched as the body of Ernst Withers was removed from the front seat of his Pierce-Arrow touring car, they looked for the bullet that killed him but didn't find it in or on his body.

After obtaining permission to move him to the Morgue, Coroner George Francis McCarthy and his associate loaded the remains of Ernst Withers into the back of their truck and headed over to McCarthy & Brown Undertaking, located at 210 West 8th Street to begin their autopsy, while the vehicle was searched once again.

Using every available flashlight they could find and shining light both inside and outside the automobile, a steel-jacketed bullet was finally located inside the vehicle, which caused accusations to run wild, including the theory that perhaps the gun had been discharged from inside the car by none other than Ernst Wither's own son Grant. At that, 32-year-old Louis W. Biele, the President of the Newton Lumber company stepped forward and offered the men proof that their theory was wrong.

"Gentlemen, my name is Louis Biele and I live just a few houses down from here, at 721 Grand Avenue and when I heard the shot fired, I slipped on my shoes and ran down to see what had happened. It was then that I witnessed Grant exit his father's car, covered in blood and screaming!" Mr. Biele explained as he pointed to the bloody shoe prints on the street just outside the car.

"I ran over to Grant and as I'm a friend of his father's he knew me and trusted me with the true account of what had happened. All the boy kept saying was that a guard that was checking passes shot his father and I believe him."

"I can also prove that the boy is innocent." Announced 31-year-old Sargent Johnathan Edwin Griffith, who was from Troop C of the Colorado National Guard, as he walked up to the group. "I was doing guard duty over at Ninth and Grand, which is only one block away from here when I heard a challenge of "Halt!" followed almost instantly by a shot."

As the accusers began to accept that perhaps their theory about Grant Withers was wrong, the search of the automobile was completed and with no weapon found, Grant Withers was declared innocent.

But if Grant didn't kill Ernst Wither's...who did?

When the sun rose a few hours later and announced the arrival of June 7th, the Elks Lodge was bustling with activity as each night guards' gun was not only inspected for signs of discharge, but their bullets were inspected and counted. As Colonel Patrick J. Hamrock and Captain Dennis continued inspecting the guns and ammo, they quickly realized that none of the Colorado Rangers or the Colorado National Guards used Steel Jacketed bullets, but the Militiamen did.

And one of them never checked in.

The Militiamen consisted of hundreds of men from Pueblo who had offered to help Captain Sinclair on the night of June 3rd and in turn, were deputized before being sent out into the storm. The volunteers were made up of Fireman, Elk Lodge members, Railway men, Steelworkers, and in the case of the missing night guard, a Navy Veteran.

With the people of Pueblo now beginning to question the mentality of the Militiamen, the arrival of Lieutenant Colonel William Goff Caples on the afternoon of June 7th was just what Pueblo needed.

At around 12:30 pm the Lieutenant Colonel and a few of his men headed up to the second floor of the Elks Lodge and offered their assistance with restoring the sanitary conditions around Pueblo. After a round of introductions, the Colonel inquired about the condition of the city and what still needed to be done.

"Well, we have plenty of food, water, and shelter for the thousands of people affected by the flood and we also feel that the danger of any type of pestilence has passed, as the Squatter towns where much of the disease originated were all washed away during the flood." Doctor F.J. Peirce explained as he had been on the front lines since the early morning hours of June 4th.

"We also have hundreds of people cleaning mud and debris out of stores and moving what feels like thousands of dead animals out of town and onto trucks to be burned." Colonel Patrick J. Hamrock added, as took another sip of his coffee. "Almost 500 dead horses have been discovered so far, along with cows, hogs, dogs, cats, and even chickens, but with limited manpower, they are just rotting in the streets and the stench is simply horrid."

As the men continued talking about the conditions of the city with Lieutenant Colonel Caples, a Telegraph operator walked into the room with a disappointed look on his face. "Sorry to interrupt Sir, but we just received a Telegrammed response from President Warren Harding, but it isn't what we expected."

Drown horses in the street-Courtesy of The Pueblo County Historical Society

Dead horses being loaded onto a truck near 712 Court Street-
Courtesy of the Pueblo County Historical Society

The surviving cows from the Manifest
Freight train being rounded up down
town-Authors personal collection

Two men out looking for bodies and instead finding a dead cow from the Manifest
train No. 62- Courtesy of the Pueblo County Historical Society

"It has come to my attention that an overwhelming disaster has come upon the people of Pueblo and the surrounding district. Realization of their suffering now and in the days to come prompts me to issue an urgent request to all whose sympathies are awakened to assist the labors of the American Red Cross which has quickly organized to cope with the first great need and will stand by until homes and home life can be re-established there.

Contributions may be sent at once thru the office of any chapter or directly to Red Cross headquarters at Washington for use in the stricken Territory."

- President Warren G. Harding

"The President isn't helping us. He isn't doing anything." The Telegraph operator declared in a hushed tone, as he looked around at the faces of the men standing around the table. "I thought he would help us."

"Well gentleman, it looks like I got here just in time!" Lieutenant Colonel William Caples announced with an encouraging smile. "Young man, why don't you direct me to your Telegraph station so you and I can get started."

Leading the Lieutenant Colonel over to his station, a smile of hope quickly began to spread across the operators face. In total three Telegrams were sent, with all of them requesting trucks, wagons, and mules, in order to remove dead animals and human bodies from the downtown flood district.

The Lieutenant Colonel also requested an apparatus for sterilizing water, and trucks to haul mud and debris, as well as asking that all companies that send men also bring enough food rations for 15 days, as not to put pressure on Pueblo to feed them.

The first Telegram was sent to the Army Post of Fort Sam Houston, which was located 820 miles south in San Antonio, Texas, and was the base that that Lieutenant Colonel was assigned. The second Telegram, which was identical to the first, was sent to Fort D.A. Russell, which was located 213 miles north in Cheyenne, Wyoming, while the third was sent to Fort Meade, which was located 1,708 miles east of Pueblo in the state of Maryland, as they were the only ones who could supply Pueblo with Tanks.

Walking back into the meeting room, Lieutenant Colonel Caples asked Dr. F.J. Peirce, who had been christened Pueblo's Sanitary Officer in the early morning of June 4th, if he would be willing to organize a new relief camp to relieve the strain on all the nearby churches and homes that were providing shelter and he happily agreed.

Heading over to the Telegraph station to begin putting Lieutenant Colonel Caple's plan into action, Dr. Peirce was thrilled to discover that he could now make a phone call instead, as phone service had just been re-established at the Elks Lodge. Quickly grabbing the receiver, the Doctor happily asked the Telephone girl on the other end to connect him to the Fitzsimons Army Medical Center in Aurora, Colorado, which was located 112 miles north of Pueblo.

After explaining his request to the head of the Hospital, Dr. Peirce was delighted to learn that they would not only deliver 250 tents and all the necessary equipment but send along 85 personnel members to staff them. With this new information, the new camp was set to be erected at 23rd and Court Street and its construction would soon be underway.

As Dr. Peirce hung up the phone, he also learned that The Mountain States Telephone Company, which still had its main office inside the First Baptist Church at 9th and Grande Avenue was now connected to not only the Elks Lodge but The Congress Hotel, The Mineral Palace Park Pavilion, the lobby of the First National Bank, The Vail Hotel, Frey's Drug store, and Dundee's Pharmacy.

But getting the phones back up and running wasn't an easy task.

Two days prior, in the early morning hours of June 5th, countless truckloads of Mountain States Telephone Company employees were heading south towards Pueblo from Denver and Colorado Springs, all loaded to the brim with switchboards, telephone wire, magneto equipment, and every tool they thought they might need in order to re-connect Pueblo with the outside world.

As they drove, one group of Mountain States Employees were set to stop at every telephone pole along the way, to check the connection and fix it if need be, while the second group headed on to Pueblo, where they fought washed out bridges, gully's full of water and deep mud holes before they finally reached Pueblo around midnight.

But now that they had arrived, where were they going to set up the temporary switchboards?

With the main Telephone Companies building at 112 West D Street still full of mud and debris, as well as missing all of its first floor windows, the newly arrived Telephone repairmen began asking around Pueblo for a new location, but all they received was rejection.

That was, until God intervened.

Hearing about the men's plight, they were approached by 35-year-old Reverend Frank Eugene Eden, who was the Pastor of the First Baptist Church at 9th and Grand Avenue, but he didn't just offer them a single room inside of his church, but use of the entire building.

"God has been good to us. He has spared us and while the waters reached within a few feet of our edifice, it was not washed away. Come, take what you need and set up your Telephone boards, as the world outside is longing for news from our city and they want to hear from friends and relatives. How may we help you?"

As the first group of Telephone men began setting up the switchboards in the basement of the church, the other was down at the Phone Company's main building on D Street to help a group of volunteers clean out the building, which is when they discovered a heartbreaking sight. In the back of the building was not only the remains of a small framed house but an elderly Jewish woman who was trying her best to dig through the debris.

Putting down their equipment, a few of the men approached the woman and asked her if they could be of any assistance. "I lost my husband during the flood and nobody has been able to find him, but I have found our house. I would like my candlesticks, they were a wedding gift from my husband. Can you please help me?" She asked as she held up her mud covered hands.

In an instant the elderly woman was sat down on a random box and cleaned up, while numerous men began digging through the thick mud that filled what remained of her house, eventually handing over her beloved candlesticks. As the smile that crossed her face filled the hearts of the Telephone men, the image of another face filled a young woman's heart with shock and despair.

During the height of the flood, 25-year-old Helen Welsh had been helping out her uncles at the Colonial Theatre on Union Avenue when the levees first broke but had managed to seek shelter inside the third floor of the Labor Temple building only a block away. Battered and bruised, Helen and her family were rescued by a rowboat the next day, which took them to Central High school's refugee center for hot coffee and a much needed meal.

After the flood water's receded, Helen had followed her Uncles back down to their Theatre and was heartbroken to see that only the outside walls of the building remained. The two buildings on either side of the Theatre appeared to of caught on fire during the flood, while a nearby rooming house had collapsed, but what she found inside her Uncles Theatre turned her stomach.

As Helen and her Uncles walked inside the area that once held the Theatre's lobby, Helen noticed the bodies of two dead horses, a spring water wagon, and a lot of lumber, and as the sour heap baked in the hot summer sun, Helen announced to her Uncles that she needed some fresh air.

Curious what the rest of the downtown area looked like, Helen began walking down Union Avenue towards Union Depot, which is when she spotted a lot of activity over at The Mountain States Phone Companies building. Not wanting to be in the way, but still eager to see what all the commotion was about, Helen decided to walk through the remains of a garage that sat just across the alley from the phone building, but her decision would lead to a gruesome discovery.

As she carefully walked around the automobiles that still occupied the garage, Helen noticed sunlight shining in through a good-sized hole in the ceiling. As she stepped closer, she noticed that an oddly shaped form was hanging directly underneath it, and being of an inquisitive nature, Helen decided to climb up onto an overturned automobile to take a peek.

Balancing on the side of the overturned Model-T, Helen was not only able to rise above the debris that filled the garage, but to hold onto the ceilings metal girders for support, as she carefully made her way over to the form.

Which is how she found herself face to face with the body of 63-year-old Albert E. Schaubel.

Oddly tangled around the steel girders of the garage, with his pocket flashlight still faintly shining onto his ghastly pale face, was the owner of The Cut Rate Shoe store located at 210 South Union Avenue. The barrel sized hole above his head had been punched into the ceiling to allow Mr. Schaubel to escape during the flood, but it appeared that he had been unable to squeeze through it in time.

As Helen carefully reached up to turn off the flashlight, which was still

Flood damage at the Cut Rate Shoe Store owned by Albert E. Schaubel, located at 210 South Union Avenue-Courtesy of The Pueblo County Historical Society

tightly gripped in Albert Schaubel's cold dead hand, Lieutenant Colonel William Caples was back at the Elks Lodge asking the Boy Scouts to turn on another type of light.

Despite the Telephone system being operational in a handful of buildings, there was still no direct communication with the south side of the city, namely the refugee center that was sitting two miles away inside of Pueblo's Central High school. Built in 1906 in the Neoclassical style, the beautiful stone building stood a towering five stories tall, which gave Lieutenant Colonel Caples the brilliant idea of using its towering roof to install a Heliograph, in order to send Morse code communications back and forth to the north side of Pueblo.

A Heliograph is a wireless Telegraph that uses sunlight reflected onto a mirror, to send Morse code across long distances. Invented in Germany in 1821, the device consists of a tripod with a mirror attached to the top which is used to reflect the sun, with a small lever on the side that is used to tilt the mirror up slightly, for the user to produce the required dots and dashes.

At night, when the sun ceased shining, a spotlight would be used to send the signals, which is the method that the Boy Scouts would be using, regardless if it was day or night. Needing a multi-story building on the north side to complete the code, the three-story-tall Y.M.C.A building only two blocks from the Courthouse was chosen, as it had an additional tower that would give the Scouts the extra height they needed to send the signals.

The Y.M.C.A building also conveniently sat right in between The Elks Lodge and The First Baptist Church, with one located three blocks north and the other 3 ½ blocks west, which was quite beneficial as both buildings had working Telephone communications.

But where will the Boy Scouts find spotlights?

As Lieutenant Colonel William Caples walked outside the Elks lodge to discuss his plans with the Boy Scouts, he glanced over at the numerous Model-T Fords parked around the building and smiled. Mounted right below and off to the side of the windshields of the automobiles, the Lieutenant noticed that each had a second set of lights, which looked a lot like mining lanterns.

Originally designed to illuminate street signs or house numbers, the extra lights were quite a helpful feature on the automobiles, but today they were exactly what the Lieutenant Colonel was looking for.

Obtaining two lights from a patriotic citizen, as well as a few Dry cell batteries to run them with, the Boy Scouts split up into two teams. The first group, which was assigned to set up their Heliograph on the roof of Central High School was comprised of not only 30-year-old Deputy Commissioner John Donald Price but 17-year-old Scouts Hallie August Sorenson, Paul Pedrick McCord, and John Howard McGill.

The second group consisted of 19-year-old Assistant Scout Master Frank Jackson Allman, 16-year-old Assistant Scout Master John Creader Risher Jr, and 20-year-old Scout Walter Wilson Munn, as well as 14-year-old Scouts William Edward Gammon and Thomas Bearden O'Kelly, who all headed over to the Y.M.C.A. to set up their Heliograph.

Since the Y.M.C.A was located only a few blocks from a working telephone, it was decided that five Scouts would be assigned to that location, instead of the three assigned to Central High School, as the additional two Scouts would be needed to relay the messages from the Y.M.C.A building over to the Elks Lodge.

With the Heliograph's finally set up, the Scouts pulled out their official Boy Scout International Morse Code pocket signal disk and began relaying the first set of messages a little after 6 pm, just as the lights inside the halls and corridors of the Courthouse began flickering back to life. As cheers and applause echoed throughout the halls and corridors, the refugees and the Red Cross celebrated the return of the electric, unaware that it was made possible by Pueblo's own Colorado Fuel and Iron Company.

After arranging connections with the cities lighting system, the Fuel and Iron Company was able to divert a limited amount of electricity from its own electric plant to turn on a few downtown street lights, The Elks Lodge, the Courthouse, The Congress Hotel, and The Pueblo Chieftain building, so that the newspaper could finally use electricity to power their press instead of laying out the type by hand.

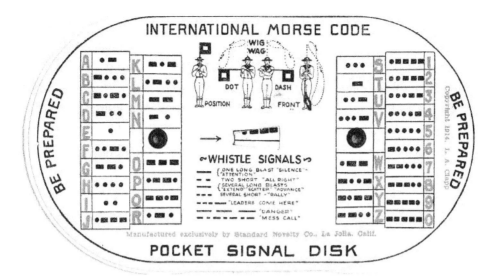

Boy Scout International Morse Code Pocket Signal Disk-Authors personal collection

The Gas Company also had their preparations nearly complete for supplying light and heat, but only in areas where the pipes had not been destroyed, while the Cities Water Plant announced that a newly installed water purifier would begin preparing 5 million gallons of clean water starting the morning of June 8th, which was now only six hours away.

But how should the people of Pueblo celebrate?

What about drinking 50 gallons of whiskey, courtesy of The Federal Prohibition Commissioners office in Washington D.C.?

Even though Prohibition had taken effect in Colorado on January 1, 1916, which prohibited the sale, manufacture, or transportation of alcoholic beverages, the men of Washington D.C. had arranged for an unlimited supply of whiskey to be dispatched immediately to Pueblo, as they felt that it would help stop the spread of diseases such as Diphtheria and Scarlet fever.

With the news delivered by 52-year-old Colorado Federal Prohibition Director Frank Joseph Medina, Pueblo was informed that all liquor restrictions were to be lifted for 30 days and that an unlimited supply of whiskey would begin arriving the next day, which was June 8th. Ironically, the decision came just in time for some of the cities closet drunks, who had been seen drinking from flood-ravaged Lemon extract bottles in order to get their fix.

As the sun rose on a bright and sunny June 8th, Doctor William Alhanan Buck, the 49-year-old Chief of the Pueblo Health Department and Pueblo's Sanitation Officer Doctor F.J. Peirce greeted the arrival of the volunteer Physicians from the Fitzsimons Army Medical Center in Aurora, Colorado. As the Army Rangers began taking the truckloads of their donated supplies over to the location of the new relief camp, which was four blocks north of the Mineral Palace Park at 23rd and Court Street, the Doctors took the newly arrived Physicians on a tour of the City.

"Our first task was to discover the whereabouts of the people who had been quarantined for Diphtheria before the flood, as they had all scattered around the city when the first flood hit." Doctor

Buck explained as he drove the men past what remained of the squatter towns. "When we finally located them, we discovered that the number of infected had exploded into 80 cases, but they refused to leave the homes where they had sought refuge during the flood to be quarantined."

"Now, since they wouldn't come willingly, we had to use the strong arm of Military Law to get them segregated into Hospitals and colonies. We also continued doing throat cultures on the people they had sought refuge with and if they also tested positive, they were also quickly placed into quarantine. We also discovered six cases of Small Pox's, with four being from the same family and they were also moved into quarantine."

"Oh, and we also implemented the Swat the fly Campaign, to help stop the spread of disease." Dr. Buck added with a smile as he watched the expression on his guest's faces turn from one of approval to one of confusion.

The Swat the Fly Campaign was created after the Health Department had noticed large swarms of flies hanging around the pools of stagnant water that had been left behind after the flood waters had receded and it was feared that they would cause a pandemic.

After handing out five thousand fly swatters, as well as flyers explaining the dangers of the airborne insects, the city decided to also spray the flooded district with formaldehyde to not only disinfect everything but to greatly improve the obnoxious odor that was emanating from the piles of rotting debris.

As a further preventative, residents and store owners were asked to put screens up around windows, as well as a screen in any outside toilets, while also removing or burning all trash and draining flooded cellars. Additionally, the Pueblo Chieftain chose to educate the public on the nature of the fly, and using a mathematical twist, they hoped that their readers would understand how just one fly can cause major problems.

Pumping flood water out of the White and Davis Department stores basement-Courtesy of The Pueblo County Historical Society

"Flies are the fastest multipliers known, with a single female fly laying batches of 120 eggs six times each season, which will hatch in exactly 10 days. If each of those flies survives and lay their own eggs, by September their dependents would total four sextillion, 353 quintillion, 564 quadrillion, 672 trillion, with scattered billions, millions, thousands, and hundreds thrown in for good measure."

"If this number of flies were pressed together they would make a mass as large as the Woolworth building, which is the tallest structure in the world."

But as Doctor William Buck was busy explaining the Swat the Fly Campaign to the volunteer Physicians from the Fitzsimons Army Medical Center in Aurora, Colorado, talk around Pueblo had shifted to shouts of joy over the discovery of a well-known horse stuck in a tree.

Discovered 15 miles east of Pueblo, in the town of Avondale, the popular life-sized Papier Mache display horse was the pride of R.T. Frazier's saddle shop, as it was always seen sporting one of Mr. Frazier's custom made saddles on its back, all while attracting customers to its owner's world-famous saddle shop. The horse was a familiar sight, as it stood either on the sidewalk outside the saddle shop, located at 115-117 West 2nd Street or on cold, rainy days, inside the store's front display window watching the world go by through its painted eyes.

R.T. Frazier's Papier Mache horse-Authors personal collection

On the night of June 3rd, 71-year old Robert Thompson Frazier and his 54-year-old wife Katherine, who went by the name Kittie, brought the horse inside once the rain started and when they left the store when the fire whistle began to scream, they never thought that a flood would destroy their store or wash away their horse. When the floodwaters finally receded, the Frazier's dug through the remains of their store and mourned the loss of their horse, that was until a truck pulled up to their house with a mud-covered horse in the back a few days later.

The men who returned the horse explained that they had found it stuck in a tree that hung over the Arkansas River and recognizing it, risked their lives to free it from the branches so they could return a smile to Mr. Frazier's face.

Which it did.

Adding to the smiling faces around Pueblo were the families of 50 Centennial High school students, who just returned home after being stranded in Colorado Springs since June 3rd.

And boy, did they have a story to tell.

CHAPTER 15

An angry waterfall and shoes filled with barley sprouts

On the morning of June 3rd, despite being cloudy and spitting a little rain onto the grass that surrounded Pueblo's Centennial High school, a collection of 50 students were happily piling into a convoy of automobiles, as it was finally time to head up to the Bruin Inn for the annual last day of school picnic.

Located at 3440 North Cheyenne Canyon Road in Colorado Springs, which was a little over 50 miles north of Pueblo and nestled at the base of a glorious 35-foot waterfall, the trip up to the historic Inn had been a yearly tradition.

The Bruin Inn had originally been built as a private residence for Edward P. Tenney, the President of the Colorado College in 1881, but he was fired three years later for frivolously spending the Colleges money on things such as building the Bruin Inn. After his departure, the building became a caretaker's residence and welcomed students who wished to visit the nearby waterfalls, which were later named after author and Native American activist Helen Hunt.

A widow and a mother whose two sons both died before reaching the age of 10, Helen had visited Colorado Springs in 1873 in an attempt to cure her Tuberculosis. After spending time at the area's waterfalls and writing a poem about them, the falls were christened The Helen Hunt Falls following her death from stomach cancer in 1885, at the age of 52.

But the students from Centennial High School didn't care about any of that, they just wanted to see the waterfalls.

As the students and their chaperones arrived at the Bruin Inn, they noticed that dark, menacing storm clouds had filled the sky, which threatened to not only ruin their picnic but their chance to hike the trail up to the top of the falls. As the rain began to pounce upon them, they quickly grabbed their lunches and gathered inside the Inn to wait for the rain to subside, but this particular storm wasn't about to give up that easily.

Helen Hunt falls received its water from the melting snowpack of Colorado's towering Pikes Peak and the rainstorm, which was now adding to the mountains seasonal runoff, was causing the waterfalls and the river that fed them to rage. As the storm's strength intensified, the river began to tear at its shorelines and grabbed every tree and boulder it could find, which it hurtled down the mountain.

As the storm used its immense power to blacken the sky as though it was the witching hour, the Inn's caretaker received an urgent Telephone call that cast more gloom over the group. As the man hung up the phone, he informed the chaperones that the automobile bridge below the falls had just washed away, which meant there was now no way they were getting their vehicles back down the mountain.

Curious how bad the road really was, a few of the students drove out into the storm to check on the condition of the road themselves, but were quickly forced to return to the Bruin Inn, as the water flowing over the road had threatened to overtake their vehicle.

With the Inn ill-prepared for such a large number of overnight guests, the seats were pulled out of the cars so the girls and female chaperones wouldn't have to sleep on the hard, wooden floor, while the boys laid down where ever they could find room. With their coats under their heads or over their shoulders for warmth, the group tried their best to get some sleep.

The next morning the students awoke to discover that the rain had ceased, but Helen Hunt falls was still displaying quite a tantrum as it rushed down the mountain towards Colorado Springs, where it collided with the already engorged Fountain Creek.

Which, unknown to the students, was helping to flood their home town of Pueblo.

With the automobile road still un-drivable and un-walkable due to the washed-out bridge, the caretaker at the Bruin's Inn offered the chaperones an unexpected option. "If you like, I can lead you and your group up the hill to the Cripple Creek Short Line railroad tracks, and from there you can just follow them to the Dixieland Resort, which is located right at the base of Helen Hunt Falls," he explained, as he began to pour himself another cup of coffee. "From there you can just hop back onto the train to Pueblo."

"How far of a walk do you think it is from here?" one of the chaperones asked, as the offer was sounding very appealing.

"Ehhh, I'd say maybe three miles. Maybe more, maybe less."

After the initial shock of the unexpected hike wore off, the chaperones gathered up their students to give them the news, but quickly questioned their decision to take the caretaker up on his offer. Laced up saddle-backed shoes and cap toed Oxfords graced the feet of not only all 50 of the students but the chaperones as well and this type of footwear was not meant for mountain climbing, but perhaps if they stuck to the tracks, and walked on the wooden ties, their shoe heels and lack of traction wouldn't be a hindrance.

As the students began assembling in front of the Inn, in order for roll call to be taken, one of the chaperones used the caretaker's phone so she could call the representative for Centennial High School, but the phone call wouldn't connect. The night before, when the chaperone had called the representative about the washed-out road, she had been informed that the fire siren was screaming out it's warning about a possible flood heading to Pueblo.

And now with the phones out, she understood what had happened.

Hanging up, she looked over at the students and decided that the upcoming hike should be the only thing on their minds right now.

The news about the flood could wait.

Grudgingly following the caretaker halfway up the hill and onto the train tracks, the student's spirits were not especially high, but it's amazing what a little fear can do to add a little spunk to your step. After walking less than a mile down the tracks, the group began hearing an odd rumbling noise coming from the top of the hill, which was sprinkled with what sounded like twigs snapping and it was getting louder.

Stopping on the tracks and looking around for the source of the noise, a rock suddenly rolled down the hill and landed on the tracks in front of them, followed by another which was larger than the first.

"Run!"

With their chaperones close behind, the students began sprinting down the tracks until the terrifying rumble that followed faded into the distance. Slowing back down to a brisk walk, the group began glancing behind them to see if they were out of danger.

Finally coming to a complete standstill, some of the girls began to cry as the chaperones pulled out their list of students and began taking roll call, relieved that everyone was accounted for.

Curious what had actually happened, one of the chaperones took some of the more inquisitive students back near where the two rocks had originally hit the tracks and they were shocked by what they saw. Covering the coveted spot was a pile of mud, boulders, and trees easily 20 feet deep and 150 feet wide.

Fearful of more mudslides, the students kept their ears perked up for any more tattle tale sounds, but as they continued on their quest to find the Stratton Park Dixieland Resort, they began to realize that the tracks they were following were simply winding around the mountain, not going down it.

Curious, the group stopped walking and looked over the side, which is when they spotted something in the distance. Sitting in the middle of a clearing was a cluster of buildings with a raging creek running right along alongside it.

A creek that they would have to cross.

With a collective sigh, the exhausted group looked down at their traction less footwear and understood that getting down the mountain wasn't going to be easy. As their shoes began sliding in the mud, the students carefully began making their way down, but when they reached the bottom, the group found themselves facing North Cheyenne Creek.

The creek, which they had first encountered when they watched it explode over Helen Hunt Falls, was running faster and wilder than they had expected, but they still needed to get across it. Taking some of the older boys, one of the chaperones began walking along the side of the creek in an attempt to find the safest place to cross, but there wasn't one.

Returning to the group with a defeated expression, the chaperone glanced across the angry creek one more time before gathering up all of the older boys and explaining what she had in mind. Across the creek, the group could see the outline of the buildings that they all hoped was the Dixieland Resort, and with no way to avoid crossing the swollen creek in order to reach it, the chaperones plan went into action.

With arms locked, the boys began to lower themselves into the icy, turbulent water to construct a human chain from one end of the creek to the other. With the waves of water bearing down on them, the boys stood strong, knowing that it was their responsibility to ensure that the rest of their classmates got safely across.

And thanks to them, they did.

Walking towards the buildings, the group was relieved to discover that the cluster of buildings was indeed the Dixieland Resort, but once the group arrived, their happiness turned to fear, as one of the chaperones sat them all down to tell them some terrible news.

"The deep, quickly rushing water that we all just went through is part of a flood that struck Pueblo last night." She explained as the students grew silent. "We can't go home right now, but what's important is that we are all safe."

After being made aware of the dire situation, The Dixieland resort quickly sent out requests around Colorado Springs for assistance and soon all of the stranded students and their chaperones were wearing dry clothes and eating a hot meal. To add to their good fortune, the group also discovered that they were allowed to stay at the resort free of charge until they were able to take the train back to Pueblo, which finally happened on the afternoon of June 9th.

But June 9th wasn't a good day for everyone.

In the flooded downtown district of Pueblo, a group of men who were helping to clean up the city had just discovered a very sticky, gooey mess in the alley between the Post Office and The Grand Opera House that was definitely not brightening their day.

A large bucket of tar.

The gummy, tacky substance had been washed up against the corner of the Federal Building's lawn at 421 North Main Street where it ruptured and poured out its contents which many were finding very hard to clean up. After many attempts to remove the sticky nuisance, the volunteers finally resorted to rolling it up like a great blanket until it was no longer possible to move, then cutting off the chunk before attempting to roll it again.

But it wasn't just tar the city of Pueblo had to deal with.

All around the flood district thousands of men, including City employees, Army Rangers, The National Guard, and even the Pueblo Calvary were moving tons of mud and debris, which included automobiles,

A train car laying against debris in an alley- Courtesy of The Pueblo County Historical Society

Clean up crews removing mud and debris. The Vail Hotel can be seen on the right, while Memorial Hall can be seen in the rear of the photo. - Courtesy of The Pueblo County Historical Society

*Cleaning up after the flood-
Authors personal collection*

*Dynamite being used to break up the flood debris-
Courtesy of The Pueblo County Historical Society*

furniture, sawdust, straw, and huge tree trunks as well as hundreds upon hundreds of dead animals.

Mud covered horses, cows, hogs, goats, chickens, cats, and dogs were being piled high in the back of trucks and taken out of town to be burned, while men stood by the piles all day pouring oil on them to keep the fire as hot as possible, as more truckloads

J.S. Brown Grocery Company cleaning out their damaged stock at 305 Santa Fe Avenue- Courtesy of The Pueblo County Historical Society

of animals continued to arrive. Unfortunately, not all of the drowned animals were easily removed from the mud and had to either be dug out with considerable effort or dynamited loose, as was the case along the shores of the Arkansas River.

But how could the workers safely walk around the flooded areas with so many bridges washed away or damaged?

To aid the workers, several footbridges were constructed out of the lumber found within the debris piles, with one bridge spanning the length of an entire city block.

While the men on the outside worked on cleaning up the streets, there were also numerous men on the inside trying to clean up the cities food and water supply to stop the spread of disease, with one of those men being Chief Sanitarian Officer John C. Cornell.

To make the city's water safe to drink, without it needing to be boiled, the water pipes were being pumped

40,000 Cans of Fruits and Vegetables At Prices You've Never Seen

Part of the flood stock of the J. S. Brown Wholesale Grocery Co.

By buying these goods you not only save 50c on the dollar, but you are also assured of the same high quality you always bought. You run no risk, as every can is positively guaranteed and we will replace those that do not open up to your entire satisfaction.

TOMATOES, No. 2 cans, 7c; dozen 78c
TOMATOES, No. 3 cans, 3 for 25c; dozen............. .....95c
KUNERS' PORK AND BEANS, can 7c; dozen 80c
BABY GRAND COUNTRY GENTLEMAN SWEET
   CORN, No. 2 can, 3 for 25c; dozen 95c
P. V. BRAND CUT STRING BEANS, No. 2 can,
   3 for 25c; dozen 95c
COUNCIL BRAND CANNED MEATS, 4 cans 25c; doz. 70c
CAMPBELL'S SOUPS, assorted, 3 for 25c; doz.........95c
LOG CABIN SYRUP, small cans 28c; medium
   cans 55c; large cans ....A............ ....$1.10

J.S. Brown Grocery Company's Newspaper advertisement-Authors personal collection

out so they could be cleaned and disinfected with chlorine before chlorinated water was pumped back through them. When it came to fruits and vegetables, including oranges, lettuce, onions, and all other foods that are not usually cooked and that may have been touched by the floodwaters, the Sanitation Officer had ordered that it all be destroyed.

All milk was also to be inspected and marked with a small symbol on the paper cap. The number four would appear above a small star, with the number 2 appearing beneath it and everyone was reminded to demand the presence of this symbol to ensure the milk was safe to drink. When it came to canned goods, they were considered safe to eat, but the stores were instructed to label the cans as "Flood hurt" while disposing of any cans that contained a bulge, rupture, or any evidence of fermentation.

Any flour that has been touched by the floodwaters was to be turned over to the bakers, so the bread it produced could be put on the public market, while all wet sugar was to be turned over to the Candy Kitchens. When it came to any meat that had been covered or touched by the floodwater, except those that had been previously cured or pickled was to be immediately destroyed.

After another full day of cleaning up the city, the sun finally set and the workers wearily picked up their shovels and headed home. Setting their sights on a good meal and a soft bed, their desire for a quiet evening, unfortunately, would not be in the cards. As the men laid down their heads and tried to sleep in peace, their rest was interrupted by an unexpected chorus that filled the air and echoed throughout the city's flood-ravaged streets.

Frogs.

With many sections of the downtown area still full of water, the frogs began to rejoice over the conversion of the business district into a swamp and filled the air with their song, much to the dismay of many people who just wanted a peaceful night's sleep. Unfortunately for one family, it wasn't the frogs that were keeping them awake, but instead it was the combination of the sorrow of burying a loved one and the knowledge that they could soon come face to face with the man who killed him.

The pre-funeral viewing of Ernst Withers, who had been killed by a guard on the night of June 6th, had been held at 1:30 pm at the family's home, with only close friends and family in attendance. The graveside service was held later that afternoon and was attended not only by his friends and family but the people of the community as well.

As the church choir stood by his grave, accompanied by a piano, the women sang "Nearer my God to thee" and "Jesus, lover of my soul", while "Forgive me Lord", which the deceased greatly loved, was played on a Victrola record player as his coffin was slowly lowered into the ground.

"To one and all who were so kind and good and helpful to the bereaved family of Ernie Withers, in the hour of their great sorrow and trouble, the death of a beloved husband, father, son and brother. The sorrowing ones desire to return their most sincere and heartfelt thanks for the loyal, loving service so kindly extended to them, in their great and irreparable loss"

- Reverend Hubert M. Walters-Pastor of the Episcopal Church, Boulder, Colorado

With dawn breaking on the morning of June 10th, the Pueblo Courthouse was a bustle of nerves and emotions, as witnesses, Police Officers, Military officials, the Coroner, and the family of Ernst Edmund Withers would soon be arriving to hear testimony regarding the murder of one of Pueblo's most prominent citizens. With the new flood victims Relief Camp already up and running a few blocks north of The Mineral Palace, many of the refugees had been moved out of the Courthouse, which allowed the hearing to be conducted inside one of the courtrooms.

As the invited began to enter, several newspapermen and close friends of Ernst Withers attempted to join them but were stopped at the door. Despite their best protest, the men were informed that this was to be a closed hearing, as Coroner George Francis McCarthy did not want the shooter's name to be released to the public. As the men continued to plead their case, the rest of the Civilian Board arrived and squeezed past them, just as the door to the 11 am hearing was closed.

Seated on the first bench was the Wither's family, which consisted of 66-year-old Granville Gustavus Withers and 65-year-old Mathilde Caroline Withers, who were not only Ernst's parents, but Granville was also the president and publisher of the Pueblo Chieftain Newspaper, which caused quite a stir in the courtroom. Seated next to them were Ernst's 37-year-old wife Noma, as well as his son's 18-year-old Newton Wayne, 16-year-old Granville Gustavus-who went by Grant- and 9-year-old Ernst Edmund Wither's Jr.

Also seated in the courtroom was Coroner George Francis McCarthy, from McCarthy & Brown Undertaking, and Colonel Patrick J. Hamrock, as well as Major Christopher F. Cusack, Captain Richard, A . Talbot, Captain John L. Fitzgibbon, and J. Will Johnson, who were all members of the Civilian Board.

The first witness called up to speak was Major Christopher Cusack, who after greeting the group informed them that it was he who had interviewed the shooter.

"After locating the gunman, who had fled the scene after the shooting, he did confess to firing the rifle that killed Mr. Wither's but claimed that he was shooting towards the vehicle's tires, not directly at the driver. This man is no longer in Pueblo for his own protection and was not a member of the National Guard or the Army Rangers, but did inform me that he had served in the Navy during the War."

"The man also informed me that he was one of the many men who was deputized in the early hours of the flood before being put on duty as a guard and I strongly believe his claims that the shooting was an accident" Major Cusack explained, as the echo of disagreement versus agreement quickly began filling the courtroom.

"Silence!" Chairman J Johnson demanded, as the room quickly lowered its tone, but continued to quarrel. "We will be hearing from everyone before a decision is made!"

The next to speak was Coroner George Francis McCarthy, who after greeting the group pulled out his tablet and began reading his notes from the crime scene. "When I first arrived on the scene, I witnessed Mr. Ernst Wither's young son Grant covered in blood, as well as his father's body hanging out of the passenger's seat of his automobile."

"After interviewing young Mr. Grant, I then transferred his father's body to my funeral home where I conducted a thorough autopsy. There I discovered that the entire top and upper part of the left side of Mr. Wither's head had been torn off by a rifle blast and in my option, such a wound was as if a load of buckshot was fired at close range." Mr. McCarthy concluded as he turned to face the five members of the Civilian Board.

"So you feel that Mr. Wither's was killed with a direct shot to the head?" Chairman J. Johnson asked the Coroner, as whispers began to take over the courtroom.

"Possibly, yes." Coroner McCarthy replied

"Do you have any other evidence to share with the panel?" Chairman J. Johnson asked as he tried to quiet the room once more.

"Yes Sir." Coroner McCarthy responded as he turned to the next page of his tablet. "At 8 am on June 7th, the morning after the incident, both I and many of the people who are sitting in this courtroom today gathered at the scene and conducted a Coroner's Jury, which allows all investigating parties to explore the crime scene together so that they can collectively assist in the investigation."

"As I assessed the crime scene, I noticed that in regards to the victim's vehicle that its retractable canvas top was up, and that it contained a group of perforations right over where Mr. Withers was seated at the wheel. The holes, about a half dozen in number, were either jagged, L-shaped, or round, but all were splashed with blood."

"The bullet was located inside the vehicle and showed evidence that its speed was nearly exhausted when Mr. Wither's was struck, which helps confirm that it was shot into the vehicle, otherwise the bullet would have certainly been carried farther than the point in which it was found."

As the coroner sat down, Colonel Patrick J. Hamrock walked up to give his account of the incident, which simply continued where Coroner McCarthy had left off. "After the Coroner's Jury completed its investigation, we began to question if the shot had possibly been fired from the street and entered the front of the vehicle, instead of ricocheting off the pavement, as the shooter had claimed."

"With no bullet hole in the windshield itself, we wondered if perhaps the bullet traveled through the space between the left front section of the canvas top and the upper rod of the windshield. This space between the rod and the canvas was to the front and left of where Mr. Withers's head may have been when he was driving." The Colonel added before he sat back down.

After each of the remaining witnesses were given their chance to speak, including 16-year-old Grant Withers, the Civilian Board retired to the judge's chambers to discuss the evidence presented to them and their findings caused quite an uproar, especially in the bench that held the victim's family.

"After listening to the accounts from all present, the Civilian board, as well as myself have concluded that the bullet which killed Mr. Ernst Wither's ricocheted after striking the stone pavement and struck him in the head. The guard is found not guilty." Chairman J. Will Johnson announced as he watched the faces of the family go from one of hope, to one of shock and disbelief.

"Court is adjourned."

As the family of Ernst Withers quickly emptied into the marble-lined halls of the Courthouse and headed outside for some much needed fresh air, they were immediately reminded that Ernst wasn't the only victim of the flood. Covering the sidewalks and lavish lawns of the Courthouse the family noticed freshly washed clothing items, shoes, and linens laid out to dry in the sun, as store owners attempted to salvage what they could from their own personal misery.

Arriving by the truckload, piles of mud-encrusted merchandise had been delivered to wash women who sat on the shores of the Arkansas River and attempted to scrub off the filth using washboards laid across rocks and gravel, in what felt like a never-ending quest.

After a good scrubbing, the goods were then collected and laid out across any available lawn, or downtown sidewalk to dry, with some items even being draped across the remains of flood-ravaged wooden furniture or hung from trees. The river washed items were then offered at discounted prices so that the stores could reap at least a little profit, as the downtown areas continued their attempts to return to normal.

But why were all of the flood-damaged shoes full of oat and barley sprouts?

A well-known trick that helped waterlogged shoes retain their shape while they dried, was to fill them with oats, barley, or a similar type of grain before setting them out in the sun. This would allow the grain to absorb the water from the shoe leather, but with so many shoes sitting out in the sun, a lot of them now included unintentional plants for their new owners.

Flood washed clothing drying outside the Rosenblum clothing store at 121 South
Union Avenue- Courtesy of The Pueblo County Historical Society

Selling flood ravaged clothing outside The Mineral Palace-
Courtesy of The Pueblo County Historical Society

Newspaper Ad for river washed clothes-Authors personal collection

A different collection of freshly washed fabric could also be seen hanging out of the upper windows of the Nuckolls packing plant, but at first glance, many people questioned if the building was trying to dry out fire hoses instead. The packing plant used burlap to wrap up their meats and hams, and with the fabric purchased in huge bales, it caused quite a stir when it was hung out of the windows to dry.

With the cleanup continuing throughout the rest of the day and on through the weekend, June 13th brought a bit of good news to Pueblo in the form of Sprinkling Wagons.

After the flood had decimated the downtown area, the City Council had sent out requests for aide across the state, with Denver's 37-year-old Mayor Dewey Crossman Bailey offering to not only send Pueblo anything that they needed in the way of machinery, tools, or equipment but as many extra men that they needed to assist them in the rehabilitation of their city.

When Pueblo's City Council' requested Electrician's, Mayor Bailey responded by sending Denver's Chief Electrician Harry Reid and his assistants to help re-wire the flood-ravaged City. On Friday, June 10th, the Pueblo City Council had asked the Mayor for Sprinkling Wagons, and the Denver Mayor quickly arranged for six of his finest wagons to be loaded onto a train car and sent immediately to Pueblo.

Due to arrive on the 3 pm train, the wagons would be used to carry water to the areas of Pueblo where the water mains had not yet been repaired and their arrival would also help stop the spread of water-borne diseases like Typhoid.

But the City Council wasn't the only one getting things done.

Since arriving in Pueblo on the afternoon of June 7th, Lieutenant Colonel William Goff Caples had been sending Telegrams and making phone calls to every contact he had, in order to help the flood-ravaged city and when a Telegram came across the wire from the United States Secretary of War during the afternoon of June 13th, the Lieutenant Colonel just smiled.

"The City of Pueblo, Colorado will be issued an Allotment of $100,000 or as much as thereof as deemed necessary to be used for Sanitation purposes."

Newspaper cartoon showing that help was headed to Pueblo - Courtesy of The Pueblo County Historical Society

The money had been approved by not only the 61-year-old Secretary of War John Wingate Weeks, who had just taken office on March 5, 1921, but 59-year-old Colorado Senator Lawrence Cowle Phipps, 62-year-old Colorado Senator Samuel Danford Nicholson, and 49-year-old Colorado Representative Guy Urban Hardy as well.

Not to be outdone, the Pueblo Chapter of the Red Cross also announced that they had just tallied up all their donations and discovered that, as of June 13th, they had raised $35,746.95.

But Lieutenant Colonel Caples still had another trick up his sleeve.

On Wednesday, June 15th, the Lieutenant Colonel received word that the Tanks he had requested from Fort Mead, Maryland would be arriving by train the following morning. The machines went by the name M1917 and were the first mass-produced Tanks in the United States.

Using the specifications of France's Renault FT or the FT17, the United States had begun building these mini tanks to use them in the War, but of the 4,440 ordered only 950 were produced, with none completed in time to see the battle. One of the problems with the production was that the French specifications were in Metric, which was not compatible with American machinery which used the Standard system.

With almost 1,000 tanks now sitting on Military bases around the country, but with no War to fight, the tanks were used for more domestic purposes, such as handling mobs during the 1919 Washington Race Riot, as well as the 1920 Lexington Riot, and now in 1921, they were heading to Colorado to help the citizens of Pueblo pull trolley cars out of the mud.

As the sunrise greeted the residents of Pueblo on the morning of June 16th, Army Captain Bennent, Colonel Patrick J. Hamrock, and 34-year-old Lieutenant Colonel Clem Arthur Newton, who was in charge of Pueblo's Military District were busy supervising the unloading of eight M1917 mini tanks which would be handled by the numerous soldiers who accompanied them on their journey from Fort Mead, Maryland to Colorado.

Once unloaded, the little two-person tanks went right to work pushing mud and moving sections of collapsed buildings out of the street, which unfortunately resulted in the discovery of more bodies.

While pushing over a large, brick wall, the body of a man was discovered underneath, while another tank battered down the remains of a wood-framed house and found the bodies of two women inside. Unfortunately, the bodies had been decaying for around 12 days, which made identifying them rather difficult, but the man was recognized by his boss and his death truly broke his heart.

A Tank knocking down a framed house, in which two bodies were discovered - Courtesy of The Pueblo County Historical Society

The Tanks pulling a train car out of the street- Courtesy of The Pueblo County Historical Society

The deceased man was identified as 45-year-old Daniel Glover and he had been such a devoted employee at the Pryor Furniture store that his boss had ordered him a gift to show his gratitude, but unfortunately, Daniel had died before he could receive it. For the three months preceding his unexpected death, Daniel Glover had been begging his employer to purchase him a bright blue Uniform cap that was embroidered with the word Pryor's in gold letters, but his boss just kept pushing the subject aside.

In reality, the cap had already been ordered for him as a surprise, but it arrived on the afternoon of June 3rd after Daniel had already headed home from his shift at the furniture store. To add to his employer's grief, Daniel's body had been found only one block from the Pryor's furniture building, which meant that he had ventured the five blocks from his home to fight rain, hail, and rising floodwaters to check on the store that had held his heart.

CHAPTER 16

A chorus of frogs and the basket maker

Everyone loves a parade, but unfortunately, most of the residents of Pueblo were not asked to put down their shovels, or even wash the mud off their faces to attend the Governor's military parade on the morning of June 16th.

Because they were not invited.

Wait…

Why was Pueblo putting on a military parade?

Flood cleanup crew consisting of men and young boys- Courtesy of The Pueblo County Historical Society

Governor Shoup of Colorado, like all Governor's, not only commanded the National Guard in his State but also inspected them from time to time, and since most of them, as well as the Army Rangers, were already in Pueblo helping with the cleanup, he decided to inspect them while he was there.

But he wanted to do it in style.

The mess hall at Camp Shoup-Courtesy of The PCCLD Special Collections

The Army Rangers during the Governors Military Parade- Courtesy of The Pueblo County Historical Society

Flood refugee tents at Camp Shoup- Courtesy of The Pueblo County Historical Society

Arriving at the newly constructed Red Cross Refugee camp around lunchtime, 52-year-old Governor Oliver Henry Nelson Shoup and his entourage were greeted by Colonel Hamrock and Captain Orville Dennis of the Colorado Rangers, who led them over to the tent that contained the officer's Mess Hall. Once there, they were introduced to the top members of the Red Cross, who took them on a tour of the camp.

After viewing the tents, wash stations, and kitchens, the Governor and his men were led back over to the Officers Mess Hall for a special luncheon, where the group learned that the tent they were sitting in had just been completed as their vehicles arrived.

"I do marvel at the speed that has been evidenced in completing the Officers tent as well as the quality of the food. I don't think I've ever had a meal taste so good." The Governor announced with a flirtatious smile. "Simply wonderful."

When the luncheon was complete, Governor Shoup and his men were then led over to the camps bulletin board, where he was handed a bottle of Manitou Springs, Colorado Mineral water and as a collection of Motion Picture Machines began to whirl, the Governor smashed the bottle against the board while declaring "As of today, this camp should be named Camp Shoup!"

While the excitement was at its peak, the Governor and his men were then led over to a review stand where they could sit and watch the military parade that the Governor himself had requested.

With Line Officers commanding them, a squadron of Cavalry led the parade followed by six companies of Infantry, the National Guard, a Howitzer Company, and a battery of artillery. This was immediately followed by the Military personnel from the Fitzsimmons Hospital, located in Aurora, Colorado, who never even hesitated to help when they were asked to staff Pueblo's refugee camps with their own Doctors and nurses. Following behind them was an Army Mule train and the mini Tanks, which had arrived in Pueblo just hours before.

Standing up at his podium, and looking down at the 500 Soldiers that had just completed their inspection, Governor Shoup grabbed his notes and began to address the crowd.

"As I stand here today, I first want to compliment the men on their unusual good spiritedness and proficiency during this crisis, under adverse conditions." He announced as the hot summer sun began to beat down on his audience. "The new Pueblo will cost $50,000,000, but Pueblo must not be satisfied with anything else. She has bravely gone through her ordeal by water and from that ordeal, she must emerge a better commonwealth."

"To be satisfied with the mere replacement of losses sustained would be unworthy of the Pueblo spirit. I, here and now, solemnly pledge myself to leave untouched more of the resources open to the Governor of this great state, in helping in the rehabilitation of Pueblo. Every means at my command will be used to help resume her proud place among the great productive cities of the west."

As cheers of agreement and a round of applause began to fill the air, the Governor stepped away from the podium to allow 41-year-old Major Arthur Moorehead to speak.

"The state troops that have been assisting in the cleanup will be held in Pueblo until enough debris has been removed from the streets that traffic will not be hindered, or so that traffic Policemen can take over. Heretofore, it has been said that there are no funds available for the payment of State Troops until some months after being mustered out of active service, however, Governor Shoup requested a special appropriation for paying the troops."

"A precedent is being established in the history of Colorado State Troops, in that we are paying off all men in full before their departure. This means that all will leave Pueblo with sufficient funds to carry them thru until they are back in civilian pursuits."

Dismissed

Just as Major Moorehead turned back around to face Governor Shoup, he heard the crowd behind him begin to cheer once again, not only for the Governor's willingness to pay the Troops but for the aerial tricks that an airplane was doing as it buzzed the crowd.

Flown by 40-year-old Lieutenant Myron Edron Wagner, who was stationed at Fort Sill, Oklahoma, the two-seater biplane once again climbed up to an altitude of 6,000 feet before doing spinning nose dives, loops, and stall turns until he was so close to the ground that he could be seen waving at the Governor.

The plane he was flying was a De Haviland 4, also called a DH -4, and had been dubbed "The Liberty Plane" during the War. When the United States entered the War in 1917, they did not possess combat-worthy aircraft, so the British DH-4 was chosen because of its simple construction and its ability to be mass-produced.

It was also chosen because it could hold the new American 400-horsepower Liberty V-12 engine, which is how the plane earned the name "The Liberty Plane".

After the War, the planes were modified by moving the pilot's seat back and a new, unpressurized gas tank forward, which allowed the Air Service to use the planes around the United States for transport, air ambulances, air Photography, forest fire patrol, and even allowed the creation of the United States Army Border Air Patrol in 1919 to end the attacks on American Homesteads by Mexican bandits.

The Liberty planes also performed as Air Racers, which was why Lieutenant Myron Wagner was able to perform his amazing stunts at Governor Shoup's Military Parade in Pueblo, Colorado.

After entertaining the crowd for a bit longer, Lieutenant Wagner flew off from the Governors Military parade and headed over to Pueblo's flooded downtown area. Flying at an altitude of 10,000 feet, he pulled out his camera and snapped a series of pictures of the flood damage, which would allow the city to use them for making maps and survey reports, as well as aiding the city engineers in Pueblo's reconstruction.

Flood photo taken by Lieutenant Myron Wagner showing the downtown area- Courtesy of The Pueblo County Historical Society

Flood photo taken by Lieutenant Myron Wagner showing the Santa Fe bridge and damaged tracks. The Nuckolls Packing plant can be seen on the right- Courtesy of The Pueblo County Historical Society

As the crowd dispersed and things quieted back down, Governor Shoup and his men headed back up to his temporary Mansion in Colorado Springs, while the tanks, National Guardsmen, and the Army Rangers headed back downtown to not only continue moving debris but burning the bloated bodies of horses on oil-laden stacks outside of town.

But tonight, instead of listening to frogs sing after the sun went down, the people of Pueblo were instead invited to listen to a male quartet sing along to the flowing ivory keys of a piano.

Under the direction of Lieutenant Colonel Newlon F. Shroeder, the Scott School of Music and Expression was treating both the Military and refugee camps to Musical Concerts, which would now continue every evening, after a Military order was put in place to bring a little joy to such a dark time.

Performing on alternate nights the Boy Scout band, the Steel Workers Chorus, and numerous acts from the Scott's School would be driven around to the camps so that each one could receive a wonderful night of entertainment. Starting promptly at 7 pm each night and ending at 10 pm, the music and singing lit up the night and gave people something else to think about after a long day.

And the excitement just kept coming

On the morning of June 17th, the people of Pueblo learned that they would once again be able to attend the Theater, but not to watch a Vaudeville performance, but to watch a newly released movie about the Pueblo flood. Despite appearing a tad bit premature since Pueblo was still in the process of

Flood debris being cleaned up at second and Main. Pryors Furniture store can be seen in the back ground. The building was repaired within the month and still stands today- Courtesy of The Pueblo County Historical Society

Gold Dust building at 130 South Union Avenue where Raymond Davis sought refuge
- Courtesy of The Pueblo County Historical Society

Two Boy Scouts posing with the Army Rangers. One is on the truck fender, while the other is standing
on the far right of the picture- Courtesy of The Pueblo County Historical Society

removing debris and mud from their downtown areas, The Floyd Fairyland Film Company was anxious to premiere their film as they had already made arrangements to show it around the country.

"In and around Pueblo after the flood" which would be shown at The Palm Theater, located at 106 West 4th Street, had been filmed by 68-year-old John Wilbur Clarence Floyd and edited by his partner 36-year-old Claude Cleveland Corrigan. The film was produced from five reels of film taken by Floyd between June 3rd thru June 9th and was not only meant to memorialize the flood but to capture something he himself had experienced back in 1889, before motion picture cameras were widely available.

A catastrophic flood.

While living in Pennsylvania with his first wife Erma, disaster had struck the region on May 31 when the South Fork Dam burst, sending 20 million tons of water barreling through the town killing 2,209 people. Both Floyd and his wife survived the onslaught of water, but she contracted Typhoid fever soon after and died at the age of 25.

Heartbroken, Wilbur Floyd focused on his Photography business and prided himself with not only being one of the first Photographers to capture a nighttime outdoor image, with the aid of camera lights but for receiving a patent for his newly invented Photographic-print washer with its built-in rocking tray.

He was also able to find love once again when he married his second wife Jessie in 1892, but then helplessly watched her die in 1896 when she was 24.

Luckily for Wilbur, his third wife Blanche was of hardier stock and after a few years of running their Photographer business, they moved to Pueblo, Colorado, where they set up The Floyd Fairyland Film Company in 1915.

But being a silent film cinematographer was not as easy as it sounded.

"To take a motion picture and get it correctly on the film, one must be able to make the mind and hands perform two things at the same time. One hand must wind the film and the other adjusts the machine and both hands must work constantly at their separate task. I have had my machine for a long enough now to manage it, but at first, it seemed to me the work was about the most difficult I have ever taken."

As a bonus, to anyone who wanted to not only view the film but take home a special souvenir of the flood, 36-year-old Swedish Photographer Theodore Anderson was offering photos of the flood at his downtown studio, located at store number 110 in the McCarthy Building. For 25 cents each, his customers could choose from over 200 different 5 x 7 photos which were taken when the floodwaters were around six feet deep.

With the film beginning to play and display the horrors of the flood across the screen, the audience was unaware that this magical night also marked another milestone, as it was also the last day that any bodies were discovered, which brought an end to one of the worse aspects of the storm's destruction.

Throughout the day and into the night of June 18th not a single body was discovered in Pueblo, which was celebrated on June 19th with a final body count of 104, but everyone knew that more had perished. The list of the missing was still at over 300, but it only contained the names of people reported by others, and with the squatter towns stripped bare of entire families, the Red Cross felt that the real number was probably closer to 600.

The Red Cross also released a statement that 5,965 people had been affected by the flood which badly damaging 57 houses while washing away 602, which, it was explained, could have easily taken their occupants with them to a watery grave.

The flood picture book-Authors personal collection

As the cleanup continued around Pueblo, a usual corpse was discovered on June 20th in the alley behind C.S. Gallup Saddlery Company at 112 West 4th Street and it caused quite a stir, as it appeared to of been dead for quite a while.

The body was discovered by a group of children who were searching through the alley for discarded goodies to take home, but when they pulled back the fabric that was covering a wooden box, they found themselves face to face with the ghastly scowl of a dead woman instead.

Terrified, the children ran screaming down the alley and into the arms of the nearest adults, who just so happened to be 82-year old Michael Studzinski and 38-year-old John O. Jackson from the County Commissioners office.

After calming the children down, they were led over to the mysterious box which indeed held a body, but not one that was fresh enough to of died in the flood. As Mike remained with the children's unexpected find, John flagged down a group of Army Rangers who immediately delivered the body to the McCarthy and Brown Mortuary, where Coroner Ray McCarthy got straight to work.

"Well, the deceased appears to be a woman around 40 years of age, and looking at her rate of decomposition, I would say she died about nine or ten months ago. Now, I am curious why the body is wrapped in what appears to be some type of old, thick burlap, but not the kind I've ever encountered before." Coroner McCarthy explained to the Rangers, as he continued to examine the body. "Now I need you to get the word out so we can find her slayer, as it appears that she was brought up out of some dark cellar."

As the word of the unusual body began spreading around town, it caught the ear of 24-year-old James Arthur Wimmer, who walked into the Mortuary and asked Coroner Ray McCarthy an unexpected question.

"Are you the ones who have our mummy?"

After realizing Arthur's question was sincere, the Coroner asked him to explain his odd request, and the answer was just as unexpected.

"Well, that thing has been in our saddle shop for about 20 years, but it was discovered a score of years back up at Mesa Verde Park and has been stored in our place ever since," James explained, as he was led back to see his father's odd collectible.

"From all the rain it became very damp in the cellar of the store, so we took it out and left it in the alley to dry last night, but when we came back to the store yesterday it was gone. I read the story of the murder mystery in the Chieftain and I came right over to get our mummy back."

"Where did your father get it?" Coroner McCarthy asked as he helped James put the body back into its box. "It seems like an odd collectible."

"Well, we have had it in storage along with a lot of other curios from a fellow who left Pueblo about 15 years ago. He said that these cliff dwellers lived about 500 years ago." James explained as he carried his father's oddity back to his truck.

But this mummy was a lot older than that.

The mummy that C.S. Gallup Saddlery Company had been storing in their cellar came from Mesa Verde National Park, which is near Cortez, Colorado. Mesa Verde translates to Green Plateau in Spanish and was named for the forest of trees that topped the Cliff dwellings that were built into the canyons.

Archeologists who studied the dwellings believed that the Native Americans who built their villages into the cliffs did so around 450-750 A.D. and due to the excessive amount of baskets found at the site, referred to them as the basket makers. Neighboring Tribes called the Cliff Dwellers the Anasazi, which means "The Ancient ones" or "The Enemy Ancestors".

In 1874, a 31-year-old photographer named William Henry Jackson was led through Mancos Canyon, at the base of Mesa Verde and photographed it, which publicized the sacred site for all to see. Unfortunately, this caused a swarm of Curio hunters, which pounced upon the site, destroyed the stone dwellings, and carried away hundreds of artifacts and mummies which they sold as novelties.

Which is how this mummy ended up in the C.S. Gallup Saddlery Company's basement.

With the mummified basket weaver now returned to her cellar and the children who found it busy rummaging through more alleys, the people of Pueblo were discovering that their city was unexpectedly springing to life.

Located at the corner of Victoria Avenue and South Grand Avenue sat The Pierce Seed Company and their motto of "Our seeds will grow" was very evident, as flowers and vegetable plants were springing up all over town. With the flood washing in rich, fertile soil, the city had turned into a self-pick community vegetable garden, which proved that Pierce's seeds could truly grow anywhere.

Even on the keys of a flood-ravaged piano.

A farmer, who saw his home and outbuildings submerged in six feet of water, witnessed the marvel of the Pierce seed packets when he discovered a layer of green leaves growing on his piano. Wiping the mud and the small plants off its ivory keys, he discovered a radish packet from the local seed company nestled underneath the tiny plants, with the store's motto printed right across the front.

As June ended and July faced its own enviable demise, the city found that it was able to rebuild enough businesses and homes to empty Camp Shoup, but what should the Red Cross do with all the tents and supplies?

What about using them to build a Children's summer camp?

On July 24th it was decided that the Red Cross tents, as well as all of their kitchen and dining room supplies, would be given to the Pueblo's Child Welfare Bureau, so they could be used in the construction of a children's summer camp high up in the mountains above Rye, Colorado, which was a little over 32 miles south of Pueblo.

Receiving an outpouring of support, 45-year-old Child Welfare Director Miriam Muir Darley received a very generous donation from the nearby town of Canon City, which allowed the Director to hire carpenters and build six cottages, a bunkhouse, a dining room, and a kitchen. The donation totaled $5,778.76, as an anonymous donor had matched Canon Cities donation of $2,889.38, which left enough money left over to purchase the food and supplies the children would need.

For freshwater, the use of a local spring was donated by 53-year-old Austrian native Paul Madnock, while The Colorado Fuel and Iron Company donated and installed a 1,800-foot water line to connect the spring to the camp.

Not to be left out, the Pueblo County Commissioners donated 25 acres of Pueblo Park ground in the foothills of the Green Horn Range, just above Rye for the Camp, so that the Pueblo Child Welfare Department wouldn't have to contend with a mortgage.

The Children's Welfare Camp was officially dedicated on Sunday, August 14th, with the first group of children totaling 130, mostly boys, between the ages of 4-16 years of age. Most of the children chosen to attend had spent time in the refugee centers, but the group did include a few special cases involving frail children from the local Pueblo Orphanages, as their doctors hoped that a healthy dose of "Air Tonic" in the mountains would help them regain their strength.

Loaded into the back of three large Army trucks, the children were driven up to the camp for their 10-day visit, where they would be urged to eat amazing quantities of rich milk, bread & butter, meat, rice, sugar, and other bodybuilding foods.

As the children mostly arrived with only the clothes on their backs, clothing had been donated by The Red Cross, The Christian Science Relief, The Parent Teacher Association, The Ladies of the Christian Church, The Pikes Peak region of The Eastern Star in Colorado Springs, the Eastern Star Chapter of Pueblo No. 7 & No. 13, P.E.O Sisterhood of the Methodist Church and numerous donations from people who simply labeled their items "From a friend".

Each boy received two suites of underwear, two pairs of stockings, two pairs of shoes, two pairs of overalls, three shirts, one hat or cap, ten handkerchiefs or clean cloths, a comb, a toothbrush, toothpaste, a heavy sweater or heavy woolen poncho, pajamas, two towels, and two washcloths. At night the boys would sleep between woolen blankets, while during the day they would eat and play in the fresh mountain air.

After 10 days, the Army trucks returned with a group of girls, who had been counting the days until their time at camp, while the boys piled back into the trucks for their return trip home. Each girl received two suits of underwear, two pairs of stockings, two pairs of shoes, three dark dresses or loose blouses with a Sailor collar, one pair of bloomers, two towels, two washcloths, one warm sweater or coat, one hat, a comb, a toothbrush, toothpaste, nightdress, and an apron.

Like the boys before them, the girls gathered around the flag pole and watched as a large American flag was raised, followed by a proper salute and the singing of the American creed of loyalty to the stars and stripes. After 10 days of fresh mountain air and rich, wholesome food, the Army trucks returned once more, and by the evening they would bring back the third and last group of children, which was a mixture of both boys and girls, who danced beneath the stars before the camp closed for the summer.

As September arrived and the nights began to cool, the people of Pueblo found that the June flood had been memorialized in a fictional short story called "Once a crook." Written by former Pueblo Chieftain Reporter Meredith M. Davis, who now resided in Denver, the story depicted a crime that happened during a terrible flood in the imaginary town of Preston, caused by the raging Ardmore River.

When asked why he didn't just write a factual story about the flood, Meredith responded, "The flood trials of my characters are based on what actually happened to two Pueblo men, but naturally the crook part is fiction. In reality, the two men were washed down the Arkansas River for four miles and lived to tell the story, but I felt that I had to shorten the distance that the two men were carried by the roaring river, for fear that it would not be thought possible."

But it was.

Wait, whatever happened to…

Did The Mountain States Telephone and Telegraph Company ever show their appreciation to the employees who worked during the flood?

After the flood water's settled and the Telephone Company was back in working order, Mr. Ben S. Read, the President of the Mountain States Telephone and Telegraph Company, arrived in Pueblo and personally handed each of the 41 employees, who had worked during the flood, a bronze plaque.

The Plaque was the size of a credit card and was engraved with each employee's name and read "For invaluable service during the June 3, 1921 flood, and who bravely stood the test, which none but strong hearts could have endured."

On December 29, 1922, Byron Thady (The 20-year-old Night Wire Chief who almost drown trying to save the cable records) and Mrs. Josephine Pryor (The Day Chief Operator), as well as thirteen of the telephone girls attended the Mountain States Telephone Companies annual recognition banquet in Denver, Colorado, where two more medals were awarded.

Byron Thady received the Gold Theodore N. Vail Metal and a check for $500, while Mrs. Josephine Pryor was awarded the silver Theodore N. Vail Metal and a check for $250.

Did Charles Raymond Lewis, who stayed to watch the levee's break and floated around the lobby on a couch, ever find his cousin Bert?

On the night of June 3rd, the two men were separated when Bert took the last trolley to their rooming house, while Raymond stayed downtown to watch the Main street levees break. On the afternoon of June 4th, both men had headed down to the local morgues to see if the other had died during the flood and while watching the bodies being unloaded from the trucks, spotted each other standing on the opposite side of the street.

After being reunited, both men offered to help bring in bodies, but with enough men helping already, their offer was refused, so they instead helped clean up debris until they could take the train back to Montrose, Colorado.

Did Inez Edmondson, the colored Vaudeville singer
from Chicago, survive her near-drowning?

After the mortician discovered that Inez had a pulse, as he tried to embalm her, she was taken to the hospital where she went on to make a full recovery. Her mother Mary McAllister had noticed that her own name was listed in the newspaper under the dead, but when she visited the Mortuary to view the body, she discovered that the woman listed as Mary had been transferred to a hospital.

Curious if the woman could be her daughter Inez, Mary visited the hospital and was relieved to find that her daughter had survived the flood. Mary McAllister had also been feared dead by her daughter Inez, as Mary had been washed downstream after her excessive weight had flipped over the rowboat that was being used to rescue her and her daughter.

Did Scout Master Doctor Edwin Cary survive being tossed off
his rowboat, after saving his son Robert from drowning?

During the night of June 3, 1921, Scout Master Cary and his son Robert attempted to use a rowboat to reach the King Lumberyard, which was on fire, but their rowboat flipped over in the strong current. The Scout Master managed to rescue his son and put him back into the boat before he himself was washed downstream.

Scout Master Cary's body was found on June 10th, near a town called Boone, Colorado which is 20 miles east of Pueblo. After his burial in Pueblo, Colorado, his wife Marie and their two sons, Robert aged 11 and Wesley aged 6 moved to Omaha, Nebraska.

Whatever happened to Denver & Rio Grande Train No.
3 passengers Daniel and Charles Creedon?

During the first flood on the night of June 3, 1921, both 24-year-old Daniel Edward Creedon and his 22-year-old brother Charles Leo Creedon tragically died. Witness accounts state that one brother was reportedly washed out of a Pullman car's shattered window, while the other was crushed between the Denver Rio Grande No. 3 and the Missouri Pacific No. 14 when the Pullman cars rocked into each other during the flood.

Daniel's body was found on June 4th, but Charles's body wasn't found until June 12th, as it had washed several miles downriver. Due to the condition of his body, he was identified only by the signet ring he wore on his finger.

The two brothers had visited Colorado to pay respects to their mother, who died when they were very young, and on June 16th both Daniel and Charles were buried next to her in Buena Vista, Colorado.

What happened to car salesman Ross Edmondson, after he moved all the Buick's up to the Mineral Palace Park during the flood?

When 20-year-old car salesman Ross Harold Edmundson first heard the fire whistle sound on June 3, 1921, and discovered that a flood was coming, he took it upon himself to move as many of his employer's brand new Buick automobiles up to higher ground as he could, choosing Mineral Palace Park as their haven from the water.

His action's appeared to of paid off handsomely, as the 1930 census shows that he still was employed at the same Colorado Motor Car Company, as does his February 16, 1942, World War 2 draft card.

At the time of this writing, Ancestory.com only showed Census records up to 1940, but I have a feeling that his employment with the Colorado Motor Car Company continued until his death in 1953.

Did Bernard Kelly ever get his new suit for his freshman year at Central High School?

After the flood, Bernard Kelly got a job at a warehouse washing mud off of tin cans, which were then sold at bargain prices, and the money he earned allowed him to buy a new suit with long pants for school. The Taub Brothers clothing store was selling washed, cleaned, and pressed Hart, Schaffner & Marx suits for only $10 at their Great flood sale, and Bernard couldn't have been happier.

What happened to Stephanie Blatnick and her chickens?

During the night of June 3, 1921, 15-year-old Stephanie, her mother Mary, and her sisters Anna and Kerstina were led out of the family's home at 903 East B Street by her older brother and eventually spent the night inside of a train caboose, which kept them and Stephanie's chickens out of the driving rain.

Around 10 am the following morning, the family headed back towards their house and discovered that it had been pushed off its foundation, causing it to lean onto a nearby building. Part of the living and dining room walls had been ripped off and there was no furniture left on the first floor, but the second floor was intact.

The family moved into a house on Routt Avenue but walked down to the old house every day to dig for their belongings in the mud, which quickly took on a terrible odor. About a week after the flood, Stephanie developed a sore throat and was taken to the Army Hospital at Mineral Palace Park, where she was diagnosed with Scarlet Fever.

After Stephanie recovered, the family's house was put back onto its foundation, repaired, and still stands today. (I wonder if the homes current owners are aware of its history)

Did the Boy Scouts ever get rewarded for all the work they did during the flood?

In honor of all the work the Pueblo Boy Scouts from Troops 6 and 14 did during the flood and all of the help they gave during the cleanup efforts, the Scouts were each presented with the Heroism Award.

This metal is earned by a Scout who has saved or attempted to save a life at minimal personal risk. The Scouts also earned patches for Civics, life-saving, and signaling, which they proudly wore on their sashes.

The Pueblo Office of The Western Union Telegraph Company also presented Troops 6 and 14 with a $100 check, as a thank you for delivering over 10,000 telegrams around the Pueblo area before the phone lines were restored. As an additional thank you, the General Office of The Western Union Telegraph Company donated $5,000 to the National Boy Scout Council.

The $100 check was used towards the construction of a Boy Scout Camp, which was built at South Creek, three miles above the town of Beulah, which is about 30 miles southwest of Pueblo. Camp Burch opened on August 17, 1921, and was attended by over 125 Scouts that first week. The Scouts also enjoyed the luxury of a phone line, which was donated and installed at no cost by the Mountain States Telephone and Telegraph Company.

Camp Burch remained in use until the San Isabel Scout Ranch was constructed in the 1960s.

What happened to the rescued Newfoundland dog that was pulled up onto the train engine?

During the height of the flood, Engineer Madison Champness Coffey and his crew pulled a large Newfoundland dog out of the water and onto the coal car of their train's engine but were forced to leave the animal behind when the men swam for the safety of a nearby building. The following morning Engineer Coffey and his crew waded through shoulder-deep water to bring food for the dog and check on his condition, but unfortunately still had to leave the terrified animal on the train's engine.

When the floodwaters finally subsided, Engineer Coffey and his crew retrieved the dog, but it is unknown which man adopted their new mascot.

Where was the last flood victim found?

The last flood victim was found in the 1950s, east of Pueblo, when a farmer found an odd-looking pile of driftwood at the edge of his property. Pulling at the strange collection of broken furniture, old store signs, and loose boards, he discovered a skeleton and called the police.

After removing the body, and judging from its clothing, as well as the articles found around it, it was determined to be a victim of the 1921 flood. The farmer's property was off the Arkansas River and the area in question was a side stream that appeared to of caught the body and debris as it flowed down from Pueblo.

Did Pueblo ever UN-straighten their "straightened" Arkansas River?

After the Arkansas River was curved up at an unnatural angle in 1874 to "straighten it", the city admitted its deadly mistake after the 1921 flood and took steps to fix what they had done.

In 1922 a group called the Pueblo Conservancy District was formed by the state of Colorado as a flood control authority and by May 1923 they had not only laid out plans to move the Arkansas River back to its natural channel but to build dikes.

"We propose to provide protection by the combination of a large channel through Pueblo and a retarding barrier across the valley about six miles above the city, for partly regulating great floods before they reach the channel at Pueblo. The improvement, including the retarding barrier, will protect Pueblo from a flood two to three times as great as that of 1921, depending upon the relative duration and intensity of the rainfall causing the flood, and the construction will be of a permanent character."

The realigning of the river was completed in 1925, which now placed it alongside Union Depot and its rail beds, but the "straightened" 1874 section of the river was left open and continued to be filled with water from a newly constructed channel that branched off from the newly aligned Arkansas River.

But why?

The first reason was that during the 51 years that the "straightened" section of the river was operational, The Southern Colorado Power plant was constructed and the water from the 1874 channel was used to maintain the supply of water that they used for condensing purposes. The second reason was that the city did not have enough excess dirt available to fill in the entire channel and even if they did, the expense would be extreme.

On August 21, 1991, a newly formed group called the Historic Arkansas River Taskforce decided that they wanted to beautify the 1874 section of the river, as well as the power plants cooling ponds, and turn the area into a multi-use river park. Finally, at the cost of 12.5 million dollars, the city held the official grand opening of the Historic Riverwalk of Pueblo on October 6, 2000.

Did anyone ever find Elijah Alvert Bruner, the Conductor of the Manifest freight train No. 62?

Despite a $250 reward and numerous searches, Conductor Bruner's body was never recovered.

What happened to 16-year-old Grant Wither's, after he watched his father Ernest Withers get murdered by a night security guard?

After Ernest Withers's death on June 6, 1921, Ernest's widow Noma moved her three sons Newton, Granville (Grant), and Ernest Jr. to Los Angeles, California in 1927, where Grant began showing an interest in being a movie actor. During an audition, Grant's physical appearance caught the attention of Hollywood, as he was not only tall, and handsome with rugged good looks, but he possessed a hairy chest, which was very sought after in regards to male actors.

Appearing in over 200 movies and 30 Television shows, Grant lived the high life and mingled with the top celebrities of the time such as his drinking buddy John Wayne who was his best man when he married his 4th wife. Unfortunately, Grant fell into a terrible depression following the death of his mother Noma on March 28, 1958, at the age of 74, of which he never recovered. One day short of the one-year anniversary of his mother's death, propped up in bed with the book "Home before dark" and a suicide note in his lap, 54-year-old Grant Withers committed suicide by overdosing on sleeping pills.

"Please forgive me, my family. I was so unhappy. It's better this way".

Was the new mother who was found buried up to her armpits in the mud, while holding her newborn infant above her head, ever identified?

Possibly.

When I first discovered the story of Frank Spicer and Edward Harrison's rescue from an island of debris in the middle of the Arkansas River, and how they had found a trunk containing a life insurance policy belonging to a woman named Mary Fueda, I decided to research if Mary had survived the flood.

I soon discovered that an Austrian native named Mary Fueda was found alive following the flood, but was soon admitted into the Colorado State Hospital for the insane, as she was unable to process the experience. The Ancestory.com records for the hospital show that she was still listed as an inmate in both the 1930 and 1940 Census, before dying in 1969 at the age of 86. (As of this writing, Ancestory.com's records only go to 1940, but Findagrave.com gave me the information on her death)

After combining Mary's diagnoses and her families Ancestory.com census records for 1930, which listed a son named William who was born in 1921, I began to strongly believe that Mary was the woman who had been trapped in the mud. Also, the 1920 census records for her family, which included her husband George and seven children, lists their address as 259 Alek Street, which is located in the Grove, which was one of the two squatter towns destroyed during the 1921 flood.

Unfortunately, little William is only mentioned in the 1930 census and then vanishes. His father George and older brother John both died a month apart in 1934, so I fear he may have followed suit.

Can you tell me more about R.T Frazier's Paper Mache horse that was returned to them after being found stuck in a tree after the flood? Where is it now? Can I go see it?

The horse, which has been named Lucky, now lives at the Pueblo, Colorado Heritage Museum, located at 201 West B. Street. The building that contains the museum is also the original Denver & Rio Grande Freight Depot building, which if you recall is the same building that the Telegraph operators had to row their boats to , in order to retrieve the rolls of Telegraph wire they needed to re-wire the flood-damaged Telegraph poles.

When the horse's original owner's Robert and Kittie Frazier, who owned the saddle shop, were reunited with their horse, Kittie fixed his ears and re-painted him before placing him inside their store's front window and sliding a saddle onto his back.

Following Robert Frazier's death in 1931, a former employee of Frazier's named Fred McConnell, who went by the name Mack, had just opened up his own saddle shop at 116 South Union Ave in Pueblo and asked if he could have the horse for his store window, which Kittie agreed to.

When Fred retired in 1961, his son Frank took over, but on October 27, 1989 Anderson's Carpets, which was located right next door to the saddle shop, caught on fire. As the fireman fought the blaze, a few bystanders pointed out the famous 1921 flood horse in the front window and asked them to save it, which turned out to be the only thing they could save. With his business gone, Frank McConnell retired and gave the horse to the Pueblo Museum, where it sits on display near some of R.T. Frazier saddles.

Does the Bruin Inn at Helen Hunt Falls still exist and if so, how can I visit it?

The original Bruin Inn burned down in the 1950s, with only the horse barn called "The Cub" surviving until it was torn down in 2012. A replica of the Bruin Inn was built on its original foundation and turned into a visitor's center and museum.

You can still visit the falls, which are located at 3440 North Cheyenne Canyon Road, Colorado Springs, Colorado and it's free for the viewing, but get there early, as parking spots are limited.

Does the children's summer camp in Rye, Colorado still exist?

Unfortunately, no.

After being used for only a month in the fall of 1921, the camp was sold and became a Tuberculosis Camp for a few years before being dismantled and the land sold once again, this time as farmland. The farms and homes that currently occupy the land still access their water from the original steel pipes that were installed by the Colorado Fuel and Iron Company to provide the natural spring water to the camp.

You mentioned that a few babies were born during the flood, were you able to discover their names?

Yes, I was able to discover nine babies born during the flood.

Lupe F. Lazo- born inside the courthouse on June 4, 1921. He died in action during WW2, in Italy.
Edward Marvin Miklich- born June 5, 1921
Harold Ray Henry- born June 3, 1921
Stephanie Ann Kocman- born June 3, 1921
Jose Jesus Perez- born June 3, 1921
Marie F. O'Connor- born June 5, 1921
Navo Soledad Navarro- June 5, 1921
Frederick Henry Herring-born June 3, 1921. He went on to become a Captain during WW2.
William Fueda- born June 3, 1921

Where are the flood victims buried? Were their graves respected?

Most of the Pueblo, Colorado cemeteries contain at least a few graves of flood victims, but one cemetery, which will remain anonymous for obvious reasons, left the graves to be defiled in the worst possible way.

While visiting this particular cemetery, and unable to locate a few graves I was interested in visiting, I met a grave keeper who took me to the historic section and told me a grisly story. As we walked, he explained that years back the owners of the cemetery had informed him and his co-workers that they wished for the historic section to be fixed up with a sprinkler system, sod, and landscaping, as they needed to expand and make more lots available for purchase.

As we arrived at the restored historic section, which looked just as pristine as the rest of the cemetery, he pointed to one of the tombstones and revealed a secret.

"There is nobody buried underneath this stone or any of the others." The grave keeper explained as he pointed across the beautiful lawn. "When we first began working in this section, a lot of the stones had fallen over and the ground was nothing but dirt, cactus, overgrown weeds, and these weird, large holes. But as we dug up the first grave to find out what made the holes, we discovered empty, disintegrating coffins."

"Wait, why were the coffins empty?" I asked, with a curious expression.

"The foxes ate the dead." He explained as he motioned for me to follow him towards the back of the cemetery, in order to view what remained of the untouched historic section. Only a few rows away from the lush lawns and manicured graves, I found myself faced with acres of dirt, cactus, weeds, and knocked over or tilted tombstones that resembled what the grave keeper had described to me earlier.

At the base of one of the flipped over tombstones, he pointed out a large hole. "These are fox dens and they go all the way down to the coffins. They not only ate the remains, but made nests out of the bones and clothing."

"Now, come to think of it, there might be a few dead foxes buried in the newly restored historic section. See, after we discovered what happened to the first few graves, we just filled in the rest of the holes with dirt, set the stones upright, and laid down sod."

Did the Coroner from Chapter nine, named Abraham Lincoln, have any brothers? If so, were any of their names Presidential?

In Chapter nine I wrote about a 59-year-old Pueblo Coroner named Abraham Lincoln Fugard and out of curiosity, I looked him up on Ancestory.com to see if any of his siblings had Presidential names, and I wasn't disappointed.

When I pulled up his family tree I discovered that he had an older brother, born two years before him, named George Washington Fugard, which made me very happy. Unfortunately, their parents lost their patriotism when it came to naming their sisters, who were named Zada, Eleanor, Dora, and Abba.

What happened to Dallas Cuenin and his wife Lydia? Did her unborn baby survive?

When the flood stuck the Denver & Rio Grande train No. 3, Lydia was 7 ½ months pregnant with the couple's first child and despite being rolled, tumbled and tossed around a flood stricken Pullman car, and then faced with hyperthermia, little Frederick Murrell was born on August 19, 1921. Sporting blonde hair and hazel eyes, he was joined by Sister Retta Marie in 1923 and Brother Melvin Lee in 1925.

Did Nettie Darr ever find the bodies of her children, after they slid off the roof of the house they rode on when the flood hit the town of Rocky Ford?

After Nettie was rescued, she waited three weeks for the bodies of her loved ones to be located, with her eight-year-old Step-son Richard being the first to be found. His little body was discovered tangled in a barbed-wire fence close to where he had slid off their roof raft, while her husband Arthur's body was found buried in the sand three miles east of where their house had been.

Arthur Darr's body was only discovered after a search party noticed a single foot sticking out of the sand along the river. His body was so battered and decomposed that he was identified only by the tattoo on his arm. A man who had been trapped in a tree near Arthur Darr, during the flood, was interviewed by the Ordway New Era newspaper concerning Arthur's final moments.

"Arthur and his father were hanging onto a tree when he watched his family being swept away, which is when he lost his mind from the strain. He became frantic and tore his hair from his head in handfuls. A little later he jumped to his death in the flood, unable to stand the strain any longer."

In regards to Nettie's 10-month-old son Charles, his body was found 11 miles east of Rocky Ford, but was so battered and decomposed that he was only identified by his little dress, but Nettie still smiled at the discovery of her infant son. The other two boys, six-year old Delbert and five-year-old Leedew were never found.

One large tombstone contains the names of Arthur and all four of his sons, with Richard and Charles sharing the same coffin with him.

It is unknown if 14-year-old Vera's body was ever located.

"Those of us who are inclined to grumble at our slight misfortune should remember the story of Mrs. Darr and instead of complaining, feel thankful that our lot lies along pleasant lines."

- The Ordway New Era News- June 24, 1921

Endnotes

A strip of beaded leather and the prophecy

Colorado Daily Chieftain August 3, 1921 "Indian predicted a flood for Pueblo"

The Arkansas River flood of June 3-5th 1921 by Robert Follansbee and Edward E. Jones- Washington Government printing office 1922

A torrent of water and the bags of wet cement

The Arkansas River flood of June 3-5th 1921 by Robert Follansbee and Edward E. Jones- Washington Government Printing office 1922

The Fort Collins Courier Colorado- June 3, 1921 "Farms damaged in Pueblo County by downpour"

The Fort Collins Courier- June 6, 1921 "Pueblo, CO Girls drown in cloud burst"

Ancestory.com- Robert Sylvester Gray

Ancestory.com- Mayme K. Gray

Ancestory.com-John F. Ferren

Book- "The case of train #3" by Arthur Osbourne Ridgway- Rocky Mountain Railroad Club, Denver, Colorado- 1956

Salida Mail Volume #40- June 10, 1921

Ancestory.Com- Daniel Edward Creedon

Ancestory.Com- Charles Leo Creedon

Chaffee County Democrat July 18, 1921-Pueblo flood victims buried at this place

Chaffee County Democrat July 11, 1921-Victims of Pueblo flood

Ancestory.com-Ester "Etta" Curtin Creedon

Book- "Centennial history of Illinois college-1829-1929" by Charles Henry Rammelkamp

Pueblo Lore-June 2011. Historic Interview with Bernard Kelly

Ancestory.com- Bernard Kelly

Book "-Swallows-From the 1860s to the 1990s. A Glimpse of the past "- Swallows Cemetery Association 1997-Pride City Printing

Substreet.org-Solvay Coke

Ancestory.com-James Hezekiah Clagett

Book- "Swallows-From the 1860's to the 1990's-A glimpse of the past" by the Swallows Cemetery Association- 1997-Pride City Printing

Gold belt byways. Com

Florence Daily citizen June 6, 1921 "Flood reported coming down Arkansas River"

Florence Daily citizen June 6, 1921 "Twenty feet of water rushes down Phantom Canyon"

Book- "The case of train #3" by Arthur Osborne Ridgway-Rocky Mountain railway club- 1956

Florence Daily Citizen June 6, 1921 "Florence men are successful in getting to Portland with relief"

The Florence Citizen -The Pioneer edition 1971

Colorado Daily Citizen June 4, 1921-Flood extra

Book- "From trappers to tourists, Fremont County, Colo-from 1830-1950" by Rosemae Wells Campbell-Filter Press- 1972

Canon City record February 18, 1904 "The new Portland cement plant"

Canon City Record September 26, 1907 "Concrete". The new fireproof town in this county"

Montrose daily press volume 12, number 287 June 7, 1921 "Florence truck growers suffer"

Herald Democrat June 5, 1921 "Disaster is extensive"

Portland cement Association

Museum.canoncity.org "The little Train Company that could"

Pueblo Chieftain, May 30, 1993- "Flood!"

Geology and Thorium deposits of the Wet Mountains, Colorado A progress report-by R.A. Christman, United States Government Printing Office, Washington-1959

The double-edged knife and the flying trees

The Kiowa County Press- June 10, 1921

The great Pueblo flood of 1921-by Bernard Kelly

Ancestory.com- Bernard R. Kelly

Ancestry.com-Eileen P. Kelly

Book- "The case of train #3" by Arthur Osbourne

Interview with Jim Birrer-by Author

Ancestory.com- Joseph William Birrer

Florence Daily Citizen June 3, 1921

Colorado Daily Chieftain June 4, 1921

Ancestory.com -Harry K. Inman

Acmoc.org

Akron Weekly Pioneer Press August 12, 1904

U.S. World War 1 Draft Registration card- Thomas Jefferson Turner

Florence Daily Citizen June 6, 1921

Colorado's Daily Chieftain June 19, 1921

Ancestry.com-John Black Sinclair

Kancoll.org-The Dodge City Cowboy band

Geological Survey Bulletin 707, guide book to the western states-2007

The founding of Colorado City (1859) by Ladonna Gunn-Old Colorado City Historical Society

Significant flood events in the Pikes Peak Region throughout the Past Century-Old Colorado Historical Society

Protesting cattle and the bravest sister in the world

The great Pueblo flood of 1921-by Bernard Kelly

Montrose Daily Press June 17, 1921 "Raymond Lewis was the coolest man in Pueblo, on the night of the big flood".

Colorado Daily Chieftain- July 18, 1921

Ancestory.com- Bertie Monroe Lewis

Ancestory.com-Charles Raymond Lewis

Book-The case of Train No.3- by Arthur O. Ridgeway- the Rocky Mountain Railway Club 1956

Book- Colorado South of the Border-by Ralph C. Taylor-Sage books 1963

Book- Pueblo, a Pictorial History- by Joanne West Dodds-Donning Company Publishers 1982

Ancestory.com- David Moses Wilson

Salida Mail June 10, 1921 "H. J. Clagett-Salida, met a Jinx

Substreet.org-Solvay Coke

Ancestory.com- Madison Champness Cofffey

Ancestory.com-Ira Imri Hupp

Ancestory.com- Joseph Nathaniel Miller

Ancestory.com- Ernest Patterson Alexander

Ancestory.com- James Hezekiah Clagett

Book "Tragedy at Eden" by Dow Helmers- O'Brien printing company 1971

Waterlogged shoes and a box full of chickens

BPW League member relates the experience in 1921 flood-Stephanie Blatnick

Ancestory.com- Stephanie Blatnick

Book-The Case of train No. 3- by Arthur Osborne- the Rocky Mountain Railway club 1956

Ancestory.com- Madison Champness Cofffey

Ancestory.com-Ira Imri Hupp

Ancestory.com- Joseph Nathaniel Miller

Ancestory.com- Ernest Patterson Alexander

Colorado Daily Chieftain July 4, 1921 "Labor Temple undergoing renovation: damaged $6,000"

Colorado Daily Chieftain July 19, 1921 "Cleaning out Colonial"

Ancestory.com- Helen Welch

Ancestory.com- William Henry Foster

Ancestory.com- Ira Clyde Foster

The Mountain States Monitor-The Pueblo Flood – Colorado Telephone Company February 1, 1959

Ancestory.com- Edna May McCumber

Ancestory.com-Byron Ernest Samuel Thady

Ancestory.com-Josephine D. Pryor

Ancestory.com-Margaret Williams

Preparednessadvice.com/lighting/homemade-oil-lamps

The Pueblo Chieftain June 6, 1992 "Telephone workers stuck with tasks during flood"

Man's best friend and a frantic game of fire hockey

Book-The Case of train No. 3- by Arthur Osborne- the Rocky Mountain Railway club 1956

The Mountain States Monitor-The Pueblo Flood – Colorado Telephone Company February 1, 1959

The Pueblo Chieftain- June 6, 1992 "Telephone workers stuck with tasks during flood"

Pueblo Star-Journal and Chieftain -June 3, 1971- Souvenir edition

Ancestory.com-Francis E. King

Ancestory.com-George E. King

Ancestory.com-William K. Tappen

Ancestory.com - Harvey Granville Burtis

Ancestory.com-George W. White

Ancestory.com -Charles Hopkins

Sciencestruck.com

Colorado Daily Chieftain- June 19, 1921 "Boy Scouts render great aid during Pueblo's flood period"

Ancestory.com-Doctor Edwin Rucaldo Cary

Pueblo.us/history of mineral place park

Colorado Daily Chieftain- June 22, 1921 "Pueblo operator gets world scoop-sent out first distress call."

Ancestory.com - Howard Coriour Hayden

Ancestory.com-Emory Albert Mitchell

Fort Collins Courier- June 4, 1921 "Thousands drowned in Pueblo and loss of property estimated over $10,000,000"

Colorado Daily Chieftain-May 14, 1921 "57 floats in industrial parade"

Colorado Daily Chieftain- September 17, 1921 "Pueblo Gas Company seeks permanent rate increase"

Pueblo Star-Journal and Chieftain-June 3, 1971- Souvenir edition

Ancestory.com - Walter White Munn

Ancestory.com-George John Henry Schnarre

The Pueblo Star Journal-June 3, 1981 "Schnarre, flood survivor, recalls pain of the great disaster of 1921"

The Canon City Daily Record- June 7. 1921 "Record reporter sees ghastly sights"

Pueblo Lore-June, 2011 "The flood from top of the Opera house" by John A. Martin

Ancestory.com -John Andrew Martin

Colorado daily chieftain-April 28, 1921 "Majestic Vaudeville"

Ancestory.com-Robert John Lewis

Ancestory.com-Maxwell Hughlett

Ancestory.com -Earl David Houston

Pueblo Star-Journal- March 13, 1950 "Hero of 1921 flood remembers the lives he could not save"

Ancestory.com -Frank Dillon Spicer

Book "Colorado- South of the Border" by Ralph C. Taylor-Sage books 1963

Ancestory.com-Theodore James Kramer

Salida Mail Volume 40, No. 102- June 7, 1921 "T.J. Kramer refugee relates story of night of horror"

Ancestory.com-Margaret Fitzpatrick

Ancestory.com-Frederick Dallas Cuenin

Salida Mail Volume 40, No. 103 -June 10, 1921 "H.J. Clagett-Salida, met a Jinx"

A storm drenched kitten and the well-built couch

BPW League Member relates experience in 1921 flood- Stephanie Blatnick

Ancestory.com-Joseph B. Roberts

Ancestory.com-Charles E. Wayland

Ancestory.com-Mary McAllister

Ancestory.com-Inez McAllister

Herald Democrat- June 8, 1921 "Danger of pestilence passed Pueblo begins to clean up"

Book "South of the Border" by Ralph C. Taylor-Sage Books 1963

Herald Democrat-June 8, 1921 "Danger of pestilence passed Pueblo begins to clean up"

Montrose Daily Press Vol XII No. 296- June 17, 1921 "Raymond Lewis was the coolest man in Pueblo on night of big flood"

Ancestory.com-Charles Raymond Lewis

Ancestory.com-Bert Lewis

Ancestory.com-Otto Wilfred Snapp

Ancestory.com-William Riggs Bratton

Creede Candle- July 9, 1921 "O.W. Snap and family and Mrs. Black have arrived in Creede"

The Pueblo Chieftain-August 27, 2019 "In the details: The rich history of Temple Emanuel"

templeemanuelpueblo.net

Ancestory.com-Michael Lawrence Valley

Herald Democrat- June 6, 1921 "Man marooned in garage 12 hours death all around him"

The Mountain States Monitor- February 1, 1959

Ancestory.com-Albert E. Schaubel

Colorado Daily Chieftain- June 26, 1921 "Garage owner saves life of a small Kitten"

Carsguide.com-dort-sports-tourer

Ancestory.com-Fred Oral Clasby

Ancestory.com-George Montgomery Knebel

Canon City Daily Record- June 7, 1921

Pueblo Chieftain- May 29, 2011 "A flood of memories"

The blood-soaked hero and a Warehouse full of lanterns

Colorado Daily Chieftain- June 10, 1921 "Train load of cattle caught and left"

Ancestory.com-Frederick Dallas Cuenin

Salida Mail Volume No. 40, #103-June 10, 1921 "H.J. Clagett-Salida, met a Jinx"

Salida Mail Volume 40 # 102- June 7, 1921 "D.J. Kramer, refugee, relates story of night of horror"

Book "The case of Train No. 3" by Arthur Osbourne Ridgway - published by the Rocky Mountain Railway Club, 1956

Ancestory.com- Rosie B. Farrar

Ancestory.com-Frank Nicholas DuCray

Ancestory.com- Sarah J. Wellwood

Canon city daily Record-June 7, 1921 "Mrs. Wellwood, mother of R.S. Beall is about 70 years old"

Colorado Daily Chieftain-June 14, 1921 "Miss Farrar's body recovered"

Plateau voice-June 10, 1921 "Sheriff DuCray gives graphic story of flood wrecked trains"

Ancestory.com-Daniel Edward Creedon

Ancestory.com-Charles Leo Creedon

Pueblo Star-Journal- March 13, 1950 "Hero of flood remembers the lives he could not save"

Colorado Daily Chieftain-June 17, 1921 "Escape was opened for passengers"

Ancestory.com-Henry C. Borndruck

Ancestory.com-Dayton J. Kramer

Book- "Colorado-South of the Border" by Ralph C. Taylor- Sage Books, Denver 1963

Ancestory.com-Ruby Ellis

Ancestory.com-Eleanor Demfer

Ancestory.com-Dorothy Lustkandl

Colorado Daily Chieftain-June 19, 1921 "Survivor on Rio Grande No. 3 tells graphically of experience"

The butcher knife and a man named Abraham Lincoln

Book- "The case of train No. 3" by Arthur Osborne-published by the Rocky Mountain Railroad club-1956

"The great Pueblo flood of 1921" by Bernard Kelly-Pueblo Lore, June 2011

Colorado Daily Chieftain- June 20, 1921 "City officials busily engaged in work at Mineral Palace"

Colorado Daily Chieftain- June 19, 1921 "Where is the 8th street Bridge?"

"Out of the Attic" Article 3 by Robert F. Blazich June 1985- Pueblo Lodge No. 90

Ancestory.com- Elza Alexander Cress

Ancestory.com-William H. Cale

Colorado Daily Chieftain- April 6, 1901 "Dropped dead"

Ancestory.com-George Frank Phythian

Ancestory.com-Harry Mitchell Wilcox

The Western Star- June, 24. 1921 "Tells of the Pueblo Flood"

The Department of the Interior-"The Arkansas River Flood of June 3-5, 1921"-Washington 1922

Out of the Attic: "Article 3"-written by Robert F. Blazich-Pueblo Lodge No.90

Book-"Pueblo-a pictorial history" by Joanne West Dodds- Donning Company Publisher-1982

Salida Mail- June 7, 1921 "D.J. Kramer, refugee, relates story of night of horror"

Plateau voice-June 10, 1921 "Sheriff DuCray gives graphic story of flood wrecked trains"

Colorado Daily Chieftain- October 20, 1921

Pueblo Lore- June 2011 "The Great Pueblo flood of 1921"-by Bernard Kelly

Ancestory.com-Joseph Hubert Abell

Ancestory.com-George Thomas Morrissey Jr.

Ancestory.com-George Thomas Morrissey Sr.

Book-"South of the Border" by Ralph C. Taylor-Sage Books-1963

A screaming Hog and the waterlogged bananas

The Western Star, June 24, 1921 "Tells of the Pueblo flood"-by Mrs. Vella Rockefeller

Plateau Voice, June 10, 1921 "Sheriff DuCray gives graphic story of flood wrecked trains"

Salida Mail June 7, 1921 "D.J. Kramer, refugee, relates story of night of horror"

Canon City Daily Record, June 7, 1921 "Memorial Hall"

Pueblo Lore, June 2011 "My Grandfather, unsung Hero" by Fran Reed

The New York Times, June 5, 1921 "City a Panorama of Ruin"

Colorado Daily Chieftain, June 22, 1921

Colorado Daily Chieftain, June 17, 1921 "Quick wit"

Ancestory.com- Ross Harold Edmundson

Ancestory.com- Blanch Edmondson

Colorado Daily Chieftain, June 20, 1921 "City official busily engaged in work at Mineral Palace"

Ancestory.com-Everett Edson Colby

Colorado Daily Chieftain, June 2, 1921 "Police to patrol park beats"

Fort Collins Courier, June 4, 1921 "Thousands drowned in Pueblo and loss to property estimated over $10,000,000"

Colorado Daily Chieftain, June 22, 1921 "Pueblo operator gets world scoop-sent out first distress call"

Ancestory.com-Howard Coriour Hayden

Ancestory.com-Emory Albert Mitchell

Ancestory.com-Ellsworth Logan Stapp

Ancestory.com-Edwin Booth Clements

Ancestory.com-William John Berns

Ancestory.com- Joseph Henry Hoskins

Denver Post, June 15, 1921 "Heroic wire men face death to put Pueblo in connection with Denver by Telegraph"

News from Ninety, June 1985 "Out of the attic: "Article 3"- by Robert E. Blazich

The Mountain States Monitor, Feburary 1, 1953 "The Pueblo flood develops an artist"

Ancestory.com-Elwyn Halford Davis

Ancestory.com- Wilma A. Cary

Nardini Block/ Arcade Building- Architectural report

Sunbathing rattlesnakes and the bestial monster

Pikespeak.us.com

The Schaeffer Dam Project 1907-1909

The Beaver land and Irrigation Company-Schaeffer Dam reports 1908

Book-"Zebulon Pike, Thomas Jefferson and the opening of the American West" by Jay H. Buckley- University of Oklahoma Press 2012

"The miracle of the Skaguay Power Plant" by Winfred Ward Clark

Book-"Swallows: from the 1860s to the 1990's" by the Swallows cemetery Association- 1997

Empire magazine May 28, 1967 "The last of Swallows Valley"- by Glenn Richmond

Ancestory.com-Robt Eugene Spaulding

Ancestory.com –Robt Eugene Spaulding US Civil war prisoner of war records 1861-1865

Ancestory.com- Ella Wilder

Ancestory.com-Saraphine Omeara

Ancestory.com-Reverend Benjamin Dunlop Dagwell

Ancestory.com-Rosetta Booth

Ancestory.com-Oscar Charles Alverson

Ancestory.com-Florence Mishou

Colorado Daily Chieftain June 19, 1921 "Organization of the baby tents"

Colorado daily chieftain June 17, 1921 "How Pueblo chapter Red Cross came to a big emergency"

Ancestory.com-Frank Allman

Colorado Daily Chieftain June 19, 1921 "Boy Scouts render great aid during Pueblo's flood period"

Fort Collins Courier June 10, 1921 "5 babies born to women rescued from Pueblo flood"

Ancestory.com-Bruce Albert Gustin

Ancestory.com-Charles Leaming Tutt

Ancestory.com Wilbur F. Cannon

The vintage news.com

Colorado Daily Chieftain, June 5, 1921 "How pictures of the flood were secured by the Chieftain"

Colorado Daily Chieftain, June 10, 1921 "Sheriffs forces on river bank"

Fort Collins Courier, June 6, 1921 "Gambling raid nets 3 men, two dice and a pot of $10"

Colorado Daily Chieftain. June 8, 1921 "Paper publishing during flood time"

Colorado Daily Chieftain. June 8, 1921 "Pueblo Elks # 90 tends thousands"

Herald Democrat, June 6, 1921 "Farmers are fleeing"

Great Divide, June 12, 1921 "Souvenir of the great Pueblo flood"

Herald Democrat, June 6, 1921 "Farmers are fleeing"

The aerodynamic speeder and a lake full of bodies

Democrat, June 6, 1921 "Farmers are fleeing"

The Arkansas River Flood of June 3-5, 1921. United States Geological survey, Department of the Interior

Denver Post June 8, 1921 "Rich farm area devastated as the Beaver dam goes out"

Ancestory.com-George E. Reigel

Florence Daily Citizen June 6, 1921 "The Schaeffer Dam with 92 feet of water breaks"

Canon City Record, June 5, 1921 "Schaeffer Dam- Water was reported to be 75 feet height and 300 yards wide when the whole Dam gave way"

Penrose Schaeffer Dam Project-Penrose Library 1907-09

Canon City Record June 6, 1921

Book- "Down Memory Lane" by Della Goode Lancaster-Sherry Johns Publishing 2012

Book- "Swallows: from the 1860s to the 1990's" by the Swallows Cemetery Association 1997

Colorado Daily Chieftain June 5, 1921 "How pictures of the flood were secured by the Chieftain"

The vintage news .com

Ancestory.com-James Thurman Kinch

Ancestory.com-Floyd Arthur Banning

Ancestory.com-Anton Christie Washington Wiegel

Ancestory.com-Louis Justus Hausman

Ancestory.com-Henry M. Clifford

Ancestory.com-James Austin

Great Divide June 12, 1921 "Souvenir of the great Pueblo flood"

Ancestory.com-Rowland Griffiths Edwards

Colorado Daily Chieftain June 11, 1921 "Towards the Southeast stretches Death Lake"

Colorado Daily Chieftain August 11, 1889 "A great flood"

Colorado Daily Chieftain April 16, 1874 "City Council"

Ancestory.com-Albert Marksheffel

Herald Democrat June 13, 1921 "Eliminate bread line/ use church as exchange"

Herald Democrat August 10, 1921 "Tales of heroism from Pueblo flood"

Colorado Daily Chieftain July 31, 1921 "Preacher did heroic deed during flood"

The glass-filled china hutch and a box of oranges

Ancestory.com-Michael Clera Studzinski

Ancestory.com- Durbin Vanlaw

Ancestory.com- George A. Lotts,

Book "They all came to Pueblo-A social history" by Joanne West Dodds- Donning Company Publishers 1994

Colorado Daily Chieftain June 15, 1921 "City Commissioner has strenuous work"

Colorado Daily Chieftain June 8, 1921 "Paper Publishing during flood time"

Colorado Daily Chieftain June 15, 1921 "One store robber trapped by flood"

Colorado Daily Chieftain June 12, 1921 "Freaks of the flood"

Colorado Daily Chieftain June 19, 1921 "One man's benefit from flood water"

Ancestory.com-George Nicodemus

Creede Candle August 6, 1921 "Curious ways of a flood"

Ancestory.com-John Lee Dennis

Fort Collins Courier June 16, 1921 "Sow washed into car sets up housekeeping with big new family"

Herald Democrat June 6, 1921

Cheyenne Record June 9, 1921 "Pueblo battles back to life 30 dead in Arkansas Valley"

Fort Collins Courier June 6, 1921 "Hundreds dead and thousands suffering from flood and fire in Pueblo"

Herald Democrat June 5, 1921

Pueblo Chieftain June 8, 1921 "Woman carries body of man in lap ten miles to reach Pueblo morgue"

Ancestory.com-Ernst Edmund Withers

Ancestory.com-James Lee Lovern

Ancestory.com-Frank Stephen Hoag

Ancestory.com- Charles King McHarg

Pueblo Chieftain June 8, 1921 "Woman carries body of man in lap ten miles to reach Pueblo Morgue."

Ancestory.com-Edwin Pomeroy Kendall

Colorado Daily Chieftain June 11, 1921 "Fountain Principals son funeral held"

Booklet-The Arkansas River flood of June 3-5, 1921-by the Department of the Interior 1922

Ancestory.com-Ralph Leonard Hufford

Ancestory.com-Francis Thomas Lewis

Ancestory.com-Gertrude White

Ancestory.com-Bert Waters

Ancestory.com- Elijah Alvert Bruner

Los Animas Leader Volume 49, No. 3 June 9, 1921 "Arkansas valley is swept by flood"

Fort Collins Courier June 20, 1921 "Local man gets a letter about a flood victim"

Colorado Daily Chieftain June 26, 1921 "reward offered for body of Rail man"

Book-"South of the Border" by Ralph C. Taylor-Sage Books 1963

Ancestory.com-Frank Dillon Spicer

Ancestory.com-Edward McMahon Harrison

Colorado Daily Chieftain June 23, 1921 "Champion Inland boatman"

Herald Democrat June 6, 1921 "Fresh floods impede work and add to suffering"

Denver Post June 7, 1921 "Ernest E. Withers killed as he drives auto thru city streets at midnight"

Colorado Daily Chieftain June 9, 1921 "Among the missing"

Ancestory.com-Lester Swink

Ancestory.com-Grace Swink

Ancestory.com-Nettie Darr

Ancestory.com-Vera Platt

Ancestory.com-Arthur William Darr

Ancestory.com-Jacob Franklyn Darr

Ancestory.com-Margaret Catherine Platz

Ancestory.com-Mendhous Platz

"The day I'll never forget" written by Nettie Fern Moore

The Sunday Chieftain, June 3, 1962 "Mrs. Moore, Las Animas, lost family in 1921 flood and barely survived."

A blood-covered teenager and the hand of God

Pueblo Lore April 2013 "Grant Withers: Pueblo's own movie star"-by Robert W. Ogburn

Denver Post June 7, 1921 "Ernest E. Withers killed as he drives auto thru city streets at midnight"

Herald Democrat June 7, 1921

Colorado Daily Chieftain June 8, 1921

Fort Collins Courier June 7, 1921 "Business man killed by guard"

Pueblo star journal June 11, 1921

Ancestory.com-J.E. Creel

Ancestory.com- George Francis McCarthy

Ancestory.com –Newton Wayne Withers

Great Divide June 12, 1921 "Souvenir of the great pueblo flood"

Herald Democrat June 6, 1921

Fort Collins Courier June 7, 1921 "Relief work is now systematized and is making fast headway"

The Mountain States Monitor February 1, 1959 "The Pueblo flood"

Ancestory.com-Frank Eugene Eden

Book- "They all came to Pueblo- a social story" by Joanne West Dodds-Donning Company Publishers 1994

Colorado Daily Chieftain June 11, 1921 "Phone situation"

Salida Mail Volume #40. # 104 June 17, 1921 "Salida girl relates experience in flood"

Colorado Daily Chieftain June 19, 1921 "Boy Scouts responded early to call from flood-stricken"

Colorado Daily Chieftain June 19, 1921 "Boy Scouts render great aid during Pueblo's flood"

Book- "The magnificent Century 1882-1982"-a pictorial history of Central High school, Pueblo, Colorado

Classic auto trader.com-1915 Ford

Historynet.com-light conversion-Heliograph

Ancestory.com-John Donald Price

Ancestory.com-Frank Jackson Allman

Ancestory.com-Hallie August Sorenson

Ancestory.com-Paul Pedrick McCord

Ancestory.com-John Howard McGill

Ancestory.com-John Creader Risher Jr.

Ancestory.com-Walter Wilson Munn

Ancestory.com-William Edward Gammon

Ancestory.com-Thomas Bearden O'Kelly

Colorado Daily Chieftain June 8, 1921

Ancestory.com-Frank Joseph Medina

Herald Democrat June 8, 1921 "Danger of pestilence passed Pueblo begins to clean up"

The Pueblo Chieftain June 11, 1921 "Centennial picnic party marooned in mountain inn"

Colorado Daily Chieftain June 18, 1921 "Two bodies found deep in Death Lake"

Colorado Daily Chieftain June 25, 1921 "Disease fight winning its way"

Ancestory.com-Doctor William Elhanan Buck

Colorado Daily Chieftain June 19, 1921 "Swat the pesky house fly and swat him early with Hofstra"

Colorado Daily Chieftain July 9, 1921 "Swat the fly campaign getting great results"

Calender-12.com "Moon Phases 1921"

An angry waterfall and shoes filled with barley sprouts

Cheyennecanon.org

Libraryweb.coloradocollege.edu

Colorado Daily Chieftain June 11, 1921 "Centennial picnic party marooned in mountain Inn"

Colorado daily Chieftain June 23, 1921 "Difficult removal"

Colorado Daily Chieftain June 10, 1921 "Cleaning up of Pueblo is well underway"

Colorado Daily Chieftain June 15, 1921 "City Commissioner has strenuous work"

Kiowa County Press June 10, 1921 "Epidemic of typhoid threatens to trail in wake of disaster"

Colorado Daily Chieftain June 11, 1921 "E.E. Withers funeral was held Thursday"

Ancestory.com-Hubert M. Walters

Colorado Daily Chieftain June 13, 1921"Military finding in Withers case"

Colorado Daily Chieftain June 11, 1921 "Coroner's verdict in Withers case"

Headquarters Chief Sanitary Officer food restrictions Memo-June 9, 1921

Herald Democrat June 11, 1921 "Guard fired fatal shot"

Pueblo Lore April 2013 "Gran Withers "Pueblo's own Movie star" by Robert W. Ogburn

The Montrose daily Press June 6, 1921

The Denver Post June 7, 1921 "Pueblo business man killed"

Colorado Daily Chieftain June 18, 1921 "Denver Officially organizes for Pueblo"

Fort Collins Courier June 16, 1921 "Denver Sprinklers sent to aide Pueblo"

Ancestory.com Dewey Crossman Bailey

Ancestory.com-John Wingate Weeks

Ancestory.com -Lawrence Cowle Phipps

Ancestory.com- Samuel Danford Nicholson

Ancestory.com- Guy Urban Hardy

Fort Collins Courier June 14, 1921 "Army is given $100,000 to use in Public work"

Book -"The Encyclopedia of Tanks and Armored fighting vehicles" by Christopher F. Foss, Amber books 2007

Colorado Daily Chieftain June 17, 1921 "Dan Glover died in path of duty"

Colorado Daily Chieftain June 22, 1921 "Military force is reduced as conditions improve"

Palisade Tribune Volume July 29, 1921" In Appreciation"

Colorado Daily Chieftain June 16, 1921 "Giant tanks to do battle in Pueblo sector shortly"

Colorado Daily Chieftain June 19, 1921 "Whippet Tanks pulling trolleys out of traffic"

Colorado Daily Chieftain June 22, 1921 "Where the mud goes"

A chorus of frogs and the basket weaver

Ancestory.com- Arthur Moorehead

Ancestory.com- Myron Edron Wagner

The Smithsonian National Air and Space Museum

Colorado Daily Chieftain June 17, 1921 "Camp Shoup is christened with suitable ceremony"

Colorado Daily Chieftain June 16, 1921 "Evening concerts provided for camps"

Colorado Daily Chieftain July 17, 1921 "Private showing of flood movies"

Ancestory.com- John Wilbur Clarence Floyd

Ancestory.com- Claude Cleveland Corrigan

The Daily Patriot June 1, 1889 "Great Calamity, several hundred lives lost"

Historiccamera.com J.W.C. Floyd, Photographer

Colorado Daily Chieftain June 21, 1921 "Body of woman in box claimed by local business man as mummy"

Colorado Daily Chieftain June 15, 1921 "City Briefs"

Ancestory.com-Theodore Anderson

Ancestory.com- Michael Studinski

Ancestory.com- John O. Jackson

Colorado Daily Chieftain May 26, 1921 "Death claims James Wimmer as result of auto accident"

Colorado Daily Chieftain June 21, 1921 "Body of woman in box claimed by local businessman as mummy"

Book "Mummies and their mysteries" by C. Wilcox-Millbrook Press 2017

Book "Mesa Verde National Park: Life Earth Sky" by Susan Lamb 2001- published by Sierra Press

Colorado Daily Chieftain June 26, 1921 "Still in the ring"

Loveland Reporter July 22, 1921 "Flood planted seeds in streets in Pueblo"

Colorado Daily Chieftain June 18, 1921 "Driftwood"

Montrose Daily Press June 23, 1921 "602 houses are a total loss in Pueblo, reported"

Colorado Daily Chieftain June 19, 1921 "Yesterday was the first say since the flood, no bodies"

Colorado Daily Chieftain June 17, 1921 "Persons sought by Rangers"

Colorado Daily Chieftain July 17, 1921 "Children's summer camp to be at Rye"

Ancestory.com-Paul Madnock

Ancestory.com- Miriam Muir Darley

Colorado Daily Chieftain July 24, 1921 "To abandon refugee camp"

Colorado Daily Chieftain July 24, 1921 "Big heart of Canon City responds to child welfare needs"

Colorado Daily Chieftain August 15, 1921 "Child welfare camp at Rye formally dedicated Sunday

Colorado Daily Chieftain July 28, 1921 "Red Cross to give clothing to kids at summer camp"

Herald Democrat August 26, 1921 "Pueblo kids are given chance"

Colorado Daily Chieftain September 14, 1921 "Flood fictionalized by ex-pueblo newsman"

National Museum of the United States Air Force

Wait, whatever happened to...

The Mountain States Monitor, December 29, 1922 "Four Thousand Telephone people gather in Denver"

Montrose daily press Vol XII, #296, June 17, 1921 "Raymond Lewis was the coolest man in Pueblo on the night of the big flood"

Book- "South of the Border" by Ralph C. Taylor-Sage books- 1962

Ancestory.com-Doctor Edwin Rucaldo Cary

Colorado Daily Chieftain, June 19, 1921 "Boy Scouts responded early to call from flood-stricken"

Chaffee County Democrat, July 18, 1921 "Pueblo flood victims buried at this place"

Salida Mail Vol. 40 #105, June 21, 1921 "Son's buried near grave they came to decorate"

Ancestory.com-Ross Harold Edmundson

Ancestory.com-Ross Harold Edmundson WW2 draft card

Colorado Daily Chieftain June 17, 1921

Pueblo Lore, June 2011 "The great Pueblo flood of 1921" by Bernard Kelly

BPW League member relates the experience in 1921 flood- by Stephanie Blatnick

Ancestory.com- Pueblo, Colorado June 1921 birthdays

Annual report of the Boy Scouts of America 1924

Colorado Daily Chieftain August 1, 1921 "Western Union gives Scouts $100 check"

Colorado Daily Chieftain, June 27, 1921 "Boy Scout Camp opens in August"

Book- "Colorado south of the border" by Ralph C. Taylor-Sage books 1963

Pueblo Star-Journal and Chieftain, June 3, 1971 "Souvenir edition"

Book- "A Pueblo Story- the Historic Arkansas Riverwalk of Pueblo" by Judy Kochevar-published by The Pueblo Conservancy District- 2002

Pueblo Riverwalk.org

Pueblo Lore April 2013 "Grant Withers: Pueblo's own movie star" by Robert W. Ogburn

Ancestory.com-Mary Fuyda

The Heritage center.us

The Puebloan-"Lucky the horse", November 22, 2018

Ancestory.com- Frederick Henry Herring

Ancestory.com-Lupe F. Lazo

Ancestory.com-Edward Marvin Miklich

Ancestory.com-Harold Ray Henry

Ancestory.com-Stephanie Ann Kocman

Ancestory.com-Jose Jesus Perez

Ancestory.com-Marie F. O'Connor

Ancestory.com-Navo Soledad Navarro

Ancestory.com- Abraham Lincoln Fugard

"The day I'll never forget" written by Nettie Fern Moore

Ordway New Era newspaper- June 24, 1921 "Bodies are still being recovered"

Ancestory.com-Frederick Murrell Cuenin

Ancestory.com-Retta Marie Cuenin

Ancestory.com-Melvin Lee Cuenin

CPSIA information can be obtained
at www.ICGtesting.com
Printed in the USA
FSHW020952170421
80492FS